Jan Scott is Emeritus ~~P~~ ━━━━━ ~~cine~~
at the University of New ━━━━ the
Brain and Mind Research ~~Institute at the University of Sydney~~
and at NTNU, Trondheim in Norway. She is an internationally
renowned expert in the use of cognitive behavioural therapy
in the treatment of depression and bipolar disorder. She is a
Fellow of the Royal College of Psychiatrists, the International
Association of Cognitive Psychotherapists, and a trustee of the
International Society for Affective Disorders.

The aim of the **Overcoming** series is to enable people with a range of common problems and disorders to take control of their own recovery programme.

Each title, with its specially tailored programme, is devised by a practising clinician using the latest techniques of cognitive behavioural therapy – techniques that have been shown to be highly effective in changing the way patients think about themselves and their problems.

Many books in the Overcoming series are recommended under the Reading Well scheme.

Titles in the series include:

OVERCOMING ALCOHOL MISUSE, 2ND EDITION
OVERCOMING ANGER AND IRRITABILITY, 2ND EDITION
OVERCOMING ANOREXIA NERVOSA, 2ND EDITION
OVERCOMING ANXIETY, 2ND EDITION
OVERCOMING BODY IMAGE PROBLEMS INCLUDING
BODY DYSMORPHIC DISORDER
OVERCOMING BULIMIA NERVOSA AND BINGE-EATING, 3RD EDITION
OVERCOMING CHILDHOOD TRAUMA
OVERCOMING CHRONIC FATIGUE, 2ND EDITION
OVERCOMING DEPERSONALISATION AND FEELINGS
OF UNREALITY, 2ND EDITION
OVERCOMING CHRONIC PAIN, 2ND EDITION
OVERCOMING DEPRESSION, 3RD EDITION
OVERCOMING DISTRESSING VOICES, 2ND EDITION
OVERCOMING GAMBLING ADDICTION, 2ND EDITION
OVERCOMING GRIEF, 2ND EDITION
OVERCOMING HEALTH ANXIETY
OVERCOMING HOARDING
OVERCOMING INSOMNIA, 2ND EDITION
OVERCOMING LOW SELF-ESTEEM, 2ND EDITION
OVERCOMING MILD TRAUMATIC BRAIN INJURY AND POST-
CONCUSSION SYMPTOMS
OVERCOMING OBSESSIVE COMPULSIVE DISORDER, 2ND EDITION
OVERCOMING PANIC, 2ND EDITION
OVERCOMING PARANOID AND SUSPICIOUS THOUGHTS,
2ND EDITION
OVERCOMING PERFECTIONISM, 2ND EDITION
OVERCOMING RELATIONSHIP PROBLEMS, 2ND EDITION
OVERCOMING SEXUAL PROBLEMS, 2ND EDITION
OVERCOMING SOCIAL ANXIETY AND SHYNESS, 2ND EDITION
OVERCOMING STRESS
OVERCOMING TRAUMATIC STRESS, 2ND EDITION
OVERCOMING WEIGHT PROBLEMS, 2ND EDITION
OVERCOMING WORRY AND GENERALISED ANXIETY DISORDER,
2ND EDITION
OVERCOMING YOUR CHILD'S SHYNESS AND SOCIAL ANXIETY
STOP SMOKING NOW, 2ND EDITION
THE OVERCOMING LOW SELF-ESTEEM HANDBOOK

OVERCOMING MOOD SWINGS

2nd Edition

A CBT self-help guide for depression and hypomania

OVERCOMING

JAN SCOTT

ROBINSON

ROBINSON

First published in Great Britain in 2001 by Robinson,
This edition published in 2022 by Robinson

1 3 5 7 9 10 8 6 4 2

Copyright © Jan Scott, 2001, 2010, 2022
Illustrations by Liane Payne

The moral rights of the author have been asserted.

IMPORTANT NOTE
This book is not intended as a substitute for medical advice or treatment.
Any person with a condition requiring medical attention should consult a
qualified medical practitioner or suitable therapist.

A CIP catalogue record for this book
is available from the British Library.

ISBN: 978-1-47214-676-2

Typeset in Bembo by Initial Typesetting Services, Edinburgh
Printed and bound in Great Britain by Clays Ltd, Elcograf S.p.A.

Papers used by Robinson are from well-managed forests
and other responsible sources.

Robinson
An imprint of
Little, Brown Book Group
Carmelite House
50 Victoria Embankment
London EC4Y 0DZ

An Hachette UK Company
www.hachette.co.uk

www.littlebrown.co.uk

Contents

Part One:
Understanding Mood Swings

Part Two:
Learning How to Cope: Understanding Mood Disorders and Implementing Basic Self-Management

Part Three:
Self-Management of
Depression and Mania

Part Four:
Putting It All Together

Acknowledgments

I am grateful to the many people who have enlightened my thinking, supported my clinical and research work or offered words of encouragement at different points in my career. First and foremost, I was extremely fortunate at a very early stage in my psychiatric training to meet with Professor Aaron T. Beck. More than anyone, he has changed the face of psychotherapy practice and research. The fact that we are even considering the use of cognitive therapy for individuals with bipolar disorder is down to his continued commitment to identifying the benefits of psychological therapies across the spectrum of mental disorders. His leadership and generosity have done much to unite cognitive therapists around the world and enabled them to collaborate and support each other's endeavours. Second, I am grateful to my patients and clients who have helped me to understand better the problems of and potential ways to cope with bipolar disorder. I am grateful also for the funding made available to me for my research, from large-scale grants from national and international sources through to smaller donations from philanthropists and even individual families who donate to research charities. All of this support is appreciated. Last, but not least, several individuals have encouraged, cajoled and supported me whilst I changed jobs, moved house, worked abroad, came back to England and then accepted several international visiting professorships and (somewhere along the line) wrote the second edition of this book. I have decided not to name (or shame!) them publicly. They know who they are, and I hope they know how important they are to me and of course, I thank them for their kindness and their patience.

Jan Scott

Preface

This book is aimed primarily at individuals who experience significant swings in their mood from the depths of depression to the highs of mania. As well as individuals with bipolar disorder (which is sometimes referred to as manic depression), this book may prove useful to those who experience less severe, but nevertheless disruptive ups and downs in how they feel.

Since the first edition of this book appeared, we have seen a range of new ideas and developments in the field of bipolar disorders. For example, the diagnostic criteria for mania and hypomania have been modified, cognitive theories of mood dysregulation pay more attention to the role of sleep–activity rhythms, and there have been further advances in the treatment of bipolar disorders. Also, nearly everyone has access to or uses electronic and digital devices and most engage with social or news media. So, this second edition of the book has tried to take all these developments into account.

Greater awareness of the role of activity and energy as well as different mood states in mania has led to some revision of the symptoms used to make a diagnosis of bipolar disorder. These changes are reviewed to make sure readers are provided with up-to-date information. Likewise, research work on rest–activity patterns has helped improve our knowledge about the key elements of healthy sleep routines. So, the advice on self-monitoring of sleep patterns has been updated to reflect these new ideas. In addition, scientific studies on sleep–wake cycles have led to the development of a specific therapy model called CBT-I (cognitive behavioural therapy for insomnia) that can be used to address sleep problems. This new edition of the book also reviews new information about the role of exposure to natural and artificial light in affecting moods and behaviours. Given these developments in chronobiology and chrono-therapeutics (i.e., sleep and circadian rhythm research, CBT-I and light therapies), several sections of the book include additional information about self-help techniques that have been taken from CBT-I. Some ideas are presented on how some of the interventions that modify exposure to different forms of light can be included in self-help. Also, light and dark therapies are briefly discussed, especially if there is some evidence to suggest these approaches can help people with bipolar disorder.

In other chapters, I briefly discuss some of the new medications that are now available for bipolar disorder. Given the pace of drug developments, I try not to get caught up in detailed discussion of each new medication (there is a danger those discussions would be out of date before this new edition is published!). Instead, I focus more attention on the issue of how groups of medications are classified and how some have been re-targeted for use in bipolar disorder. This is deliberate, as it is increasingly clear that this classification of medications can confuse or worry individuals when they receive a prescription.

Regarding cognitive theories, there is new evidence about the role of thinking processes as well as the content of automatic thoughts in triggering or maintaining anxiety and depression. The issue of so-called *repetitive negative thinking* and cognitive processing are mainly included in the chapters about depression. Furthermore, the book highlights that several scientific studies demonstrate that two new models of CBT called mindfulness-based CBT (MBCBT) and rumination-focused CBT (RFCBT) can be very useful in clinical settings to help individuals overcome anxiety and depression. So, I explore which mindfulness and rumination-focused techniques can be instituted as self-help approaches. I am sure that some of you, but not all of you, will find techniques taken from these new approaches useful for managing or preventing depression and anxiety. However, there is only limited research on using RFCBT or MBCBT for individuals with bipolar disorder. As such, I cannot recommend any of the mindfulness or rumination-focused techniques in a self-help programme for reducing symptoms in acute hypomanic or manic episodes nor for severe mood swings. This advice may change in the future if we have more information and research available. But for now, if you do want to explore if these new approaches can be used for all phases of your mood swings or bipolar disorder, it is recommended that you consult a specialist who is trained in MBCBT or RFCBT.

Electronic and digital media are now part of the day-to-day life of most individuals. Individuals with mood swings have also found several online groups that offer valuable support and advice. Furthermore, access to digital or electronic devices can assist you in undertaking more accurate self-monitoring of sleep duration and daily activity levels. Using these devices won't change what information you are encouraged to record, but it may be that you prefer to use these devices rather than a notebook. The good news for readers of this book is that many of the self-monitoring assessments and templates are now available for you on a dedicated website (https://overcoming.co.uk/715/resources-to-download). However, it is true to say that the online world may be a blessing, but it can also be a curse for individuals with mood swings. So, this edition of the book looks at some forms of social media use that may be less helpful when you are experiencing mood swings and examines some of the risks, such as problems associated with online shopping and gambling. Ideas about how to manage these issues are now included in the discussion of self-control and communication techniques.

Access to so many different social and news media websites means that an individual with bipolar disorder can quickly find out about new treatment developments, but the media sources may also increase personal exposure to fake news about health problems. As such, I've rewritten and extended the section that discusses 'becoming an expert on your mood swings'. This now examines how you might assess the quality and reliability of health-related items available through social and new media and gives some hints about how you might identify fake news, by which I mean misinformation and disinformation about your general health and about mood swings.

Lastly, in thinking about your own self-management strategies, I've added some information about 'advanced treatment directives'. These may become important if your mood swings ever become so severe that you need inpatient treatment. Being admitted to hospital can be incredibly stressful for anyone but, for individuals with bipolar disorder, it often feels like they have lost any control over what happens next to them. So, this new edition includes brief notes on how to plan ahead, so that if the worst should happen, your preferences are known in advance about the types of care and treatment that you are most comfortable with, and those that you do not want to receive.

Overall, there are several additions to this second edition, but some things remain the same as before, most notably the structure and layout of the book. It is still divided into four parts, each of which starts with a set of aims. I would encourage you to check these lists first, to be sure you understand the overall aims of the section. You can then decide if all or some of each part of the book is of interest to you. However, before you get underway, there are four topics that I'd like to highlight:

1. Didn't I read that somewhere before?

I have *not* assumed that you will all start at page 1 and read the whole book in sequence. So, to make things easier for those who zoom in on certain sections, some parts of the book will overlap with earlier chapters. This makes it easier for those who jump between sections to follow the basic ideas being presented. Whilst this strategy may feel unnecessary to those who systematically work their way through the text from start to finish, it's worth remembering that a little repetition is often useful, as it will help information to stick in your mind.

The techniques I describe in this book to try to help you deal with your mood swings are drawn from cognitive behavioural therapy (CBT). (More information about this approach is given in Chapter 5.) I have tried to describe each technique in sufficient detail for you to try it out on your own. However, this is not always simple, and you may not always understand what I am saying at first glance. If this happens, don't give up on the book straight away; it will help if you read through the description of the techniques a couple of times. Putting any new idea or activity into practice is bound to be easier if you are clear about what you are trying to do and why.

2. Why all the notes and records?
Throughout this book I encourage you to write things down. Please be aware, that whilst some of you will assume this means using a paper notebook, I also mean these statements to imply digital recordings and any other use of electronic or online media that you use routinely. It seemed unhelpful to state this every time I mention self-monitoring or recording observations, etc., so please bear in mind that every time I suggest making notes this refers to any format you chose for self-monitoring or other exercises.

The important thing to be aware of is that you will gain more in the long term if you do make a record whenever I suggest creating lists, recording thoughts, collecting information about what you did, evaluating your own activities and your responses to them, monitoring your moods, etc. Many individuals are reluctant to put things down on paper or digitally, and believe they can do most of these exercises in their head. I want to discourage you from this approach. I am not disputing your ability to remember information, but there are two important reasons for keeping detailed records. The first is that you are often asked to do something with the information; for example, to change an activity or challenge an unhelpful thought, and to see what happens next. In these situations, it is useful to have a record of how the techniques applied to you and personal information on how you did things, so that if you need to return to using this book in the future you are not simply reliant on my descriptions; you can draw on your own experience. Secondly and very importantly, writing it down makes it real. If you write down what you think and you can re-read it, this is very powerful. Also, you gain a little distance from it and will find working on it a lot easier. Many obstacles or barriers to achieving your goals are far more apparent when you make notes than if you just work through things in your mind. I really recommend you buy yourself a notebook to keep all the information together or set up electronic files that you save securely. Being able to return to and review this personal information will be just as important to your skills development and progress as anything I say or suggest.

3. Aren't there more questions than answers here?

Two individuals using this book, even if they both have similar experiences of mood swings or bipolar disorder, will differ in many other ways and may have quite different needs. The starting point for this book is that I acknowledge that no two individuals are the same. To help understand your needs, we must apply an approach called 'guided discovery'. This means helping individuals discover things for themselves. This book sets out to guide you toward identifying the problems that concern you most and then to describe the techniques that other people have found useful in overcoming similar (but not necessarily the same) difficulties. This book is not about me trying to persuade you to accept my view, nor about offering information that is available in lots of other self-help books or textbooks on mood disorders. The key aim is to engage you in self-discovery, so you can then work out how to cope more effectively with your day-to-day problems.

To guide you toward understanding your mood swings and identifying problems to work on, I will ask you hundreds of questions. Try not to be irritated by this; it is the only way to work out what the particular issues are for you. Most importantly, try not to turn the page if you see a list of questions on the horizon. The answers you give represent the critical first step in the process of overcoming your mood swings. You will also begin to learn the right questions to ask yourself to get to the root of any other problems you encounter in the future. Being clearer about problems puts you in a much better position to develop effective solutions.

4. How long does this go on for?

Working through the book from start to finish, repeating exercises and becoming confident in using the techniques described will probably take three to six months. However, if some of the approaches benefit you, you are looking at a lifelong commitment! At this stage, the most important thing is to take your time and go at a pace that suits you.

Part One of the book begins with important information about the nature of mood swings, the causes of bipolar disorder, and the types of treatment available. It ends with a description of the cognitive behavioural model of mood disorders. The second part focuses on self-monitoring and self-regulation, including managing problems in accepting medication. The third part deals with the self-management of depression and hypomania. The fourth part looks at how you can monitor your mood swings in the future and how to apply your new skills to other aspects of your life.

Learning the techniques described in Part Two will help you in working on the issues described in Part Three. Likewise, the skills you have gained from Parts Two and Three can then be applied to the problems discussed in Part Four.

Try to be kind to yourself. Think of other occasions where you have mastered new skills. For example, driving a car feels very unnatural when you are first learning but becomes second nature over time. In the same way, learning this new set of cognitive and behavioural techniques will not happen overnight, and there may be a few minor setbacks along the way. With practice, though, you will become increasingly confident that you can use the approaches described in this book and evaluate which work best for you. Furthermore, practice makes these skills permanent. I hope that, over time, you will develop a set of skills that help you feel that you have as much control over your mood swings as possible, rather than feeling that they are in control of you.

PART ONE

UNDERSTANDING MOOD SWINGS

Aims of Part One

At the end of reading Part One of this book, I hope you will have:

- gained a greater understanding of mood swings and the different types of mood disorders;
- learned about the links between events, thoughts, feelings and activities;
- developed an understanding of the vulnerability and stress factors that may increase the likelihood of experiencing an episode of a mood disorder;
- reviewed the types of treatment and interventions available to individuals with mood disorders and know basic facts about the most common acute and longer-term medications prescribed;
- learnt about the characteristics of effective psychological therapies offered to individuals with mood disorders;
- developed an understanding of the cognitive behavioural model of mood disorders, including the key role of underlying beliefs and automatic thoughts;

- noted the types of problems that may be targeted with techniques drawn from cognitive behavioural therapy.

1

What are mood swings?

We all experience different, sometimes intense, moods in reaction to day-to-day life events. However, some people experience extreme ups and downs that make it difficult for them to sustain a good quality of life. This book aims to help people identify and manage such mood swings and the problems associated with them. To achieve this goal, we need first to develop a shared understanding of moods, mood swings and mood disorders.

Defining mood states

Most dictionaries define 'mood' as a 'state of mind' or a 'prevailing feeling or emotion'. Mood states are like the colours of the rainbow: each shade is distinct, but they blend into one another at the edges. Moving through the different shades of emotions is often a normal and appropriate response to the situations in which you find yourself. Although people are not always aware of their mood state, or sometimes struggle to find the word that best captures how they feel at any one moment, it is very rare to be devoid of any emotion.

Not only does your mood change in response to circumstances, but your mood in turn also influences the way you think and the way you behave. The phrase 'seeing the world through rose-tinted glasses' clearly refers to the notion that when we are happy, we see the positives and ignore the negatives in our environment. Likewise, many individuals who feel sad are totally focused on what is wrong with their world, finding it impossible to recall the good things in their life or shift their attention away from the negative things in their environment. This often leads them to avoid the very people or activities that may help change their mood. In ways such as these, moods play a significant role in how we live our lives. The important factors that influence mood and the way mood influences our actions can be demonstrated through imagining yourself in the following two situations.

Who goes there?

You are lying in bed at night and you hear a noise downstairs.

Try to identify how you might feel if this situation arose, in a single word if you can (this is the best way to try to describe a mood). Now try to answer the following questions:

- What's going through your mind?
- How would you react in this situation?

Many of you may have felt *anxious,* thinking that there

was an intruder in the house. Individuals often notice that anxiety can be associated with physical changes, such as a faster heart rate or trembling hands. Depending on the circumstances (e.g., whether you are alone in the house or sharing it with others) and the degree of your anxiety, you will have reacted in any of a variety of ways (e.g., hidden under the blankets or woken a flatmate and jointly gone to explore the situation). Now, let us assume that you went to explore the cause of the noise and found that it was your cat. How would you feel then? Rather less anxious, I hope; but this change in mood might be accompanied by amusement in some, or by feelings of irritation in others.

This example has demonstrated that mood states may be determined in part by life events. The next scenario tries to explore the sequence of events and emotional and behavioural responses to them, in more detail.

Things can only get better!

You wake up one morning having slept badly and are immediately aware of a pain in your neck. You feel irritable. You spill coffee on your clean shirt and end up being late leaving the house for your appointment. You are too far behind schedule to use public transport, so you invest what seems like a small fortune in a taxi cab. You are feeling 'out of sorts' but manage to arrive on time at a meeting where you are meant to be presenting a brief but important talk to a large gathering of people. Some of these people you know well and some you have never met before.

This scenario conjures up a lot of questions, so you may find it easier to scribble your responses on a sheet of paper. Try to answer as many of the following questions as you can:

- When you spilt the coffee, what went through your mind? Were the comments you made inside your head forgiving and supportive or punitive and self-blaming?
- If you were kind to yourself, did your upset mood stay the same or did it improve?
- If you were being self-critical, did your mood change? If so, how did it change?
- Likewise, did you chastise yourself for taking a taxi or congratulate yourself for your problem-solving skills?
- What does the term 'out of sorts' mean to you? Were you sad, depressed, irritable, angry, etc.?
- Can you rate the intensity of this emotion (where 0 = minimum possible and 100 = maximum intensity of feeling)?
- When you got to the meeting, were the people who know you aware that you were 'out of sorts'? If so, what was it they noticed about you that was different? Were you doing anything that gave these individuals a clue as to your mood?
- Did your emotional state catch the attention of people who didn't know you? If so, what is it that they may have noticed?
- Did you write these answers down or did you just answer the questions in your head?

Different people will answer these questions in different ways. The clearest point of individual variation is when you identify what the phrase 'out of sorts' means to you. For some, spilling the coffee will have led to a barrage of self-criticism ('I'm so clumsy') and feelings of sadness ('I can't do the simplest thing'). For others, the same event may have led to thoughts like 'The world is conspiring against me', or 'It's not fair'. Such thoughts are more often associated with feeling irritable or angry. At this stage, the most useful learning point is that it is helpful to *be as specific as you can be in describing your own emotions.* The reasons for this are simple but important: the more aware you are of how you feel, the easier it will be to understand how each mood state arises. Also, knowing what mood you are experiencing will largely dictate which strategies may be most helpful in changing uncomfortable or unhelpful feelings.

Did you think my last question about whether you wrote down your responses was unfair? (Be honest!) It was not meant to catch you out. The reason for including this question was to gauge how confident you feel about your ability to remember specific information and how comfortable you feel with writing things down. Making notes was not vital to the success of that exercise. However, as we explore more complex issues in greater detail, it may become harder to retain all the relevant facts in your head as well as working out how to use the techniques that I will describe to help you change things. This is particularly true if you are trying to look at changes in your moods, thoughts and behaviour over several days. For this reason, you may wish to think about getting a notebook where you can record important information for your own use or setting up some digital files. We will come back to this issue later in the book, but we now need to explore the '*things can only get better*' scenario a little more.

The first thing to note is that, unlike the first example (a noise in the night), here it is not so clear what event has led to the sad or irritable mood state. A poor night's sleep and a pain in the neck may have played a role; feeling anxious about giving a presentation may have been a factor. The pain and irritability or anxiety may have contributed to spilling the coffee. However, the most important aspect of that event is the thoughts you had about yourself in response to what happened and how those thoughts influenced how you felt and how you behaved afterwards. It is important to note that whilst many of the behaviours will be easily observed by people who know you well, sometimes the behaviour is characterised by procrastination or avoidance. In these circumstances, the behaviour you need to become aware of is the 'absence' of a positive action, e.g., the failure to complete a task or the lack of engagement in an activity that may get you out of the vicious cycle.

The next issue to consider is whether you were able to control your feelings and your behaviour. For some of you, the intensity of the emotional reaction and the associated changes you experienced may have been too difficult to cope with, and your upset may have been obvious to others. Whatever pattern developed, we can use the information you gathered to establish a crucial sequence in the origins of mood swings, namely the *event–thought–feeling–behaviour* link. Furthermore, as shown in Figure 1, the way you act in response to each mood will generate new thoughts that in turn will further affect your mood and behaviour. In this way it is possible to enter a vicious cycle where moods, thoughts and behaviour become more and more negative. Or it is possible to enter a positive cycle, sometimes spiralling up and up to a point where you feel 'high' and out of control.

Figure 1: The event–thought–feeling–behaviour cycle

Defining your own moods

You may have found the examples described rather difficult to relate to; so, before exploring mood swings in detail, it is important to apply the general model to your own real-life experiences. To do this, try to pinpoint the last time you were 'in a good mood' and the last time you were 'in a bad mood'. Take each of these mood states separately and for each one see if you can answer the following questions:

1. Can you describe the exact nature of the mood you experienced? (Try to find one word that captures how you felt, but also try to be more specific than just 'good' or 'bad'.)

2. Can you rate the intensity of each emotion (0 = lowest intensity possible, 100 = highest possible)?

3. Can you remember any events or situations associated with the onset of this mood (where you were, whether you were alone or with others, what you were doing at the time you became aware of the particular feeling)?

4. Can you identify any specific thoughts that you had at that time or any themes that were going through your mind relating to how you viewed yourself, your world or your future?

5. Were there any other experiences (such as physical symptoms or biological changes) linked with this mood state?

6. What impact did the mood have on you and how you functioned?

7. Did anyone else notice or comment on any changes in you or your functioning?

8. How long did that mood state last overall (hours, days, weeks)?

9. Did anything particular occur that led to a change in your mood (making it either better or worse)?
10. Are the answers you have given typical or untypical of how things are when you are in this mood state?

The answers to questions 1–5 will demonstrate some elements in the 'event–thought–feeling–behaviour' chain. Don't worry if there are gaps in your answers. Some people find it difficult at first to identify specific events or situations that precipitate mood shifts. Developing your awareness of these processes and being able to record them will take time and practice. Sometimes it still seems impossible to establish the links. This may be because in certain mood disorders (such as bipolar disorder), mood changes may also result from internal changes in the body's chemistry. Yet even where mood shifts are caused by chemical changes, some of the techniques described in this book to manage the symptoms of mood swings can still be very effective.

The answers to questions 6–10 give some indication as to whether your mood swings are so serious that they meet the profile of a 'mood disorder'. The next chapter explores these issues in more detail.

CHAPTER SUMMARY

- *Mood* is the term we use to describe feelings or emotions.
- There are links between what happens to us, how we view what happens to us, how we feel and how we behave:

    event–thought–feeling–behaviour

- How you behave or react to a situation will influence further your thoughts and feelings.
- Behavioural responses may include avoidance or procrastination, i.e., the absence of an adaptive reaction.
- Sometimes this process leads a person into a downward spiral, where they become more and more depressed.
- Alternatively, this may lead into an upward spiral, with a person becoming more and more elated.
- Mood, thoughts and behaviour can affect physical or biological processes in the body.
- Mood swings can have a negative impact on a person's quality of life.

2

When do mood swings become a problem?

Mood swings that are particularly problematic usually share all or some of a range of characteristics. They are often:

- *unpredictable,* frequently fluctuating but without obvious precipitants;
- *uncontrollable,* emotional responses that seem inappropriate reactions to events and are beyond your control;
- *extreme,* with moods always experienced as intense highs or lows;
- *excessive,* with very frequent ups and downs occurring over many years;
- *extensive,* marked changes of mood that last a long time;
- *accompanied by associated changes,* in your thoughts, your activity and energy levels, the way you behave and possibly in the biological systems that impact on day-to-day functioning;

- *disruptive to lives,* causing significant problems for the individual experiencing them and/or for others.

Different types of mood disorder

If your mood swings have most of these characteristics, it is possible that you have a *mood disorder.* The major difference between mood disorders and other forms of mood swings is that mood disorders tend to show a consistent pattern of symptoms that occur together whenever a significant mood disturbance occurs (this collection of symptoms is referred to as a *syndrome*). Also, the changes persist for prolonged periods of time. The most common mood disorders are:

- dysthymia (chronic minor depression);
- major depressive disorder (unipolar disorder);
- bipolar disorder (also called manic–depressive disorder).

To understand the main differences between these disorders, we need to look at the nature and degree of the mood changes and the associated features of each problem. As shown in Figure 2, *dysthymia* and *major depressive* (or *unipolar*) disorder are characterised by a depressed mood with no 'highs'. The typical pattern in major depressive disorder is periods of depression interspersed with periods of normal mood. Dysthymia has less severe symptoms than major depression, but there are relatively few periods of normal mood. Furthermore, feelings of sadness are very persistent, occurring virtually every day for two or more years. Not surprisingly, individuals with dysthymia frequently report a lack of self-confidence and low self-esteem.

The term *bipolar disorder* (or *manic depression*) encompasses several syndromes characterised by both downswings and upswings. Individuals with *bipolar I disorder* experience episodes of major depression and mania. Recently, the diagnostic criteria have been revised, to reflect the fact that mood change is accompanied by changes in activity. As such, the essential criterion for the diagnosis of mania is that the individual experiences an abnormal period of persistently elevated mood and persistently increased activity or energy. The time period for this continuous change is at least one week; also, it is acknowledged that the dominant mood state might be irritability (rather than elation).

So, this essential criterion highlights that someone who is manic can show different mood states. For example, some individuals can present with *euphoric mania* (where the person is elated and full of optimism) but others may present with *dysphoric mania* (where the person is high but also irritable, impatient and agitated). Less common forms of bipolar I disorder also exist, such as *rapid cycling* (where a person experiences four or more episodes of mania or depression within 12 months) or *mixed episodes* (where a person manifests features of mania and depression simultaneously).

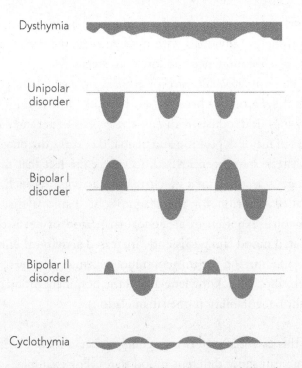

Figure 2: Patterns of mood change in mood disorders

Bipolar II disorder (characterised by episodes of major depression and less intense 'highs' called *hypomania*) and *cyclothymia* (an unstable mood state, with milder ups and downs than those of bipolar I or II disorder) are together known as the *bipolar spectrum disorders*. Although these are less severe than bipolar I disorder, individuals with bipolar spectrum disorders still have to cope with significant difficulties in their daily lives.

The criteria for making a diagnosis of hypomania are similar to those for mania, but, for example, the essential criterion requires a shorter duration for mood and energy changes (of four days). Typically, hypomania tends to have more of the positive and few of the negative features of mania. However, individuals with bipolar II disorder still experience severe and debilitating depressive episodes, and these are often more frequent than those experienced by individuals with bipolar I disorder. Cyclothymia is characterised by less intense emotional shifts, but mood changes occur in an unpredictable way over many years, disrupting the lives of individuals and their families.

Table 1 identifies some of the typical features of the depressive and manic phases of bipolar I disorder. You may find it useful to compare the descriptions of these states with the list you made relating to your own 'good' and 'bad' moods in Chapter 1. This will give you some indication as to whether your symptoms are the same as those seen in the most common mood disorders. However, it is important to note that the list you have drawn up is unlikely to be identical to the information provided as I have outlined in the table only the commonest features of mania and depression. To be classified as bipolar I disorder, the symptoms have to be present for at least seven days for mania and at least fourteen days for major depression. In reality, the symptoms usually persist for considerably longer. In bipolar spectrum disorders, many of these symptoms occur in a less severe form and for shorter periods of time.

Table 1: Characteristic symptoms of depression and mania

	Depression	Mania
To diagnose, must have:	Depressed mood or loss of interest or pleasure in things you used to enjoy. This must last at least 14 days. This change should be accompanied by 5 of the following symptoms:	A distinct period of abnormally and persistently elevated, expansive or irritable mood and abnormally and persistently increased goal-directed activity or energy. These features should last at least one week and present most of the day, nearly every day (or any duration if hospitalisation is necessary). These changes should be accompanied by 3 (or more) of the following symptoms (4 if the mood is only irritable):
Accompanied by:	✓ Reduced interest, fatigue or agitation	✓ Excessive investment in pleasurable activities (that have a high potential for painful

- ✓ Insomnia or increased sleep (hypersomnia)
- ✓ Significant weight loss or gain
- ✓ Reduced or increased appetite
- ✓ Reduced ability to think or concentrate; or increase in procrastination and indecisiveness
- ✓ Feelings of worthlessness
- ✓ Recurrent thoughts of death

These symptoms cause significant distress and/or impair social, occupational or other important areas of functioning

Also:

consequences e.g. spending money beyond your means)
- ✓ Reduced need for sleep
- ✓ More talkative than usual with a pressure to keep talking
- ✓ Subjective experience of thoughts racing
- ✓ Increased self-esteem
- ✓ Grandiose ideas
- ✓ Distractibility (i.e., attention too easily drawn to unimportant or irrelevant external things)
- ✓ Increased restlessness or agitation

These symptoms cause significant impairment in social or occupational functioning, or to necessitate hospitalisation to prevent harm to self or others, or there are psychotic features.

If you are not sure about the nature of your problems, or wish to explore these issues in more detail, it may be useful to look at some of the references provided at the end of this book (p.355). Alternatively, you may wish to seek advice from other relevant organisations or professionals. Some contact points are suggested in the section of 'Useful addresses' (p.359).

Psychosis: The most severe episodes

In very severe episodes of depression or mania, a person may lose touch with reality and develop psychotic symptoms. These may include experiencing unusual sensations (called hallucinations) such as hearing voices when no one is around or seeing things that no one else can see. Alternatively, the individual may develop abnormal beliefs about themselves or their world (termed delusions). The content of the delusions is usually influenced by the individual's mood state. In mania, people frequently believe that they are special and have the power to change the world (e.g., believing that they have special skills as a negotiator and should fly to New York to negotiate world peace). In depression, people have a very negative outlook, often holding the conviction that they are evil and responsible for many of the injustices in society. Psychotic symptoms usually subside as the individual's mood returns to normal. Although relatively rare, these symptoms can cause great concern, especially if the person is unable to recognise or accept that their abnormal beliefs are a product of their mental state and not a reflection of

22

reality. In such extreme situations, treatment in an inpatient setting is frequently recommended.

Treating bipolar disorder

The next two chapters explore the causes of bipolar disorder and current approaches to treatment. Some of the information in these chapters may be of interest to people with unipolar disorders, but other texts published in this series, such as *Overcoming Depression* by Paul Gilbert and *Overcoming Low Self-Esteem* by Melanie Fennell may be more useful. Details of these books are given in 'Useful references'.

CHAPTER SUMMARY

- Mood disorders are characterised by
  - persistent mood disturbance, accompanied by a consistent pattern of change in a person's thinking, behaviour and physical functioning.

- The most common disorders associated with mood swings are:
  - recurrent unipolar depression;
    bipolar I disorder;
    bipolar II disorder;
    cyclothymia.

- Bipolar disorder is also referred to as *manic depression*.
- All types of mood disorder can cause severe disruption to a person's day-to-day life.

3

Who is at risk of bipolar disorder?

This chapter first looks at who is at risk of developing the most common forms of bipolar disorder. It then explores the factors that may cause the onset of bipolar disorder or that increase the likelihood of relapse.

The who and when of bipolar disorder

If we combine all the different subtypes of bipolar disorder together, then it is estimated that they affect about 1–4 per cent of the general population. About 0.5–1 per cent have bipolar I disorder. The exact number of individuals with bipolar spectrum disorders (bipolar II disorder and cyclothymia) is more difficult to determine as these problems may go unrecognised for many years. Unlike unipolar disorders, which affect more women than men, bipolar I disorder affects men and women approximately equally. The other bipolar spectrum disorders tend to be more common in females. However, mood swings of any type do not respect status: individuals from all walks of life and social backgrounds are equally likely to be affected.

Recent research suggests that mood swings often begin in adolescence and that the average age of onset of bipolar disorder is the early twenties. Most people who develop a bipolar disorder experience at least one episode of depression during their early adolescence and their first episode of hypomania or mania between the ages of fifteen and twenty-five. Earlier age of onset is more common in individuals with a family history of bipolar disorder. Also, there appear to be some geographical differences, with earlier age of first episodes of mania and hypomania in the USA compared with Europe. The exact reasons for these differences are uncertain, but research groups around the world are examining this finding, as it may give important insights into the causes and diagnosis of bipolar disorder. Onset of bipolar disorder after the age of forty does occur, but is less common, and it is always important to ensure that later development of symptoms is not associated with an underlying medical condition.

Duration and recurrence

By definition, mood disorders are recurrent disorders. Most individuals experience an episode of depression before they experience their first episode of mania or hypomania. Indeed, vulnerability to the latter may come to light because the medication used to treat depression sometimes sparks off an episode of hypomania. Recovery from the acute symptoms of mania usually takes one to three months, while full recovery from the acute symptoms of depression may take about six months. These estimates are very approximate; individuals vary enormously in how soon the most intense symptoms begin to settle and how long it takes for them to become symptom-free.

Nineteen out of twenty individuals who experience an episode of mania will experience at least one further episode of mood disorder at some point in their life. This often occurs sooner rather than later; there is a 50–50 risk of a further episode of mood disorder in the year after recovery from the last episode. On average, people with bipolar disorder experience about four episodes during the ten years following the onset of the disorder. A past history of frequent episodes tends to predict a similar pattern for the future.

The why of bipolar disorder: The causes

For many years, researchers emphasised the role of biological factors such as genes and brain biochemistry in causing bipolar disorder. With the passage of time, it has become apparent that no single theory effectively explains why some individuals develop bipolar disorder and others do not. Increasingly, researchers have emphasised how several interconnected biological, psychological and social factors may play a role in the onset of bipolar disorder.

The most coherent explanation of the development of bipolar disorder is the *stress vulnerability model*. This suggests, first, that some people have a particular vulnerability to developing a mood disorder; and second, that the onset of the disorder in an 'at risk' individual is likely to occur when they are faced by increased environmental, emotional or physical stress factors – what we call 'stressors'. This section will describe the most well-recognised vulnerability factors and then explore some of the factors that may trigger the onset or recurrence of intense mood swings.

Vulnerability factors

Vulnerability to develop bipolar disorder is probably inborn or laid down at a very early stage in an individual's life. The most important elements in vulnerability all relate to biological factors: genetics, disturbances in brain biochemistry and disrupted circadian rhythms. Future research (such as that undertaken by the Human Genome Project) may eventually show links between these three areas. For example, genes are likely to influence brain biochemistry and selected genes seem to be associated with certain sleep–wake patterns or circadian rhythm profiles. At the other end of the spectrum, the role of psychological factors is considered. Personality characteristics are probably *not* a risk factor for developing bipolar disorder in their own right, but they may influence the age at which the first episode occurs or the frequency of relapse.

GENETIC FACTORS

It has long been suspected that genes play a part in vulnerability to bipolar disorder. The increased likelihood that the children, sisters and brothers of a person with bipolar disorder will also develop a unipolar or bipolar disorder clearly indicates that mood disorders may be inherited. If one parent has bipolar disorder, there is a one in seven chance that their child will develop bipolar disorder. If both parents have a bipolar disorder, the risk increases to somewhere between one in two and one in three. This suggests that the more genes a person shares in common with an individual or individuals with bipolar disorder, the more likely it is that they too will develop the disorder. This has been confirmed by research on twins who have a family history of bipolar disorder. If one member of a pair of twins has a bipolar disorder, the likelihood that the other twin will develop bipolar disorder is much greater in identical twins (who share all their genes in common) than in non-identical twins (who have half their genes in common).

Research to date suggests that several different genes, rather than one single gene, may be important in increasing the likelihood that an individual may develop a mood disorder. However, not everyone with a family history of bipolar disorder goes on to develop that disorder (indeed most people do not). This suggests that people inherit only the *risk* of developing a mood disorder; they do not inherit the disorder itself. This may sound unnecessarily complicated, but a simple analogy may help to make the difference clear. Consider what happens if you dissolve some salt in a pan of water. If you then put the pan over a source of heat, the salt (vulnerability factor) lowers the temperature at which the water boils (disorder develops). However, the possibility (risk) that the water will boil at a lower temperature is not apparent simply from looking at the water in the pan. It is only obvious when heat (a stress factor) is applied.

BRAIN CHEMISTRY

The brain comprises many millions of nerve cells with a vast number of interconnections. Information is carried between these cells by chemicals called neurotransmitters. The chemicals pass from one nerve cell to receptors (a kind of docking station) on adjacent nerve cells. There are many different neurotransmitters in the brain, but three of them – noradrenalin (also known as norepinephrine), serotonin and dopamine – have repeatedly been shown to be abnormal in individuals with mood disorders. These three neurotransmitters are collectively known as monoamines. Some studies have reported abnormalities in the levels of monoamines in the brain; other research has suggested that there are changes in how the nerve cell receptors respond to these neurotransmitters.

The monoamines are known to be active in those parts of the brain that influence our emotions, thinking and the way we behave, but it is difficult to establish the exact role in mood disorders played by imbalances in neurotransmitters. Brain chemistry certainly affects behaviour; but we also know that behaviour (which can in turn be affected by thinking and emotions) may affect brain chemistry. So, it is not clear whether the observed abnormalities in monoamines cause an episode of mood disorder or arise as a consequence of an episode.

To be certain that imbalances in neurotransmitter levels

play a role in mood disorder, we need to know how this effect is produced. Current theories suggest that monoamine abnormalities increase the likelihood of a more extreme reaction to physical or emotional stressors and that the imbalance also delays the return of the nervous system (and therefore the individual) to the previous state of equilibrium.

CIRCADIAN RHYTHMS

The term 'circadian' derives from Latin and means about (*circa*) one day (*diem*). Many processes in the body are carefully regulated by the rhythmic release of certain chemicals and hormones. The most obvious example of this is the sleep–wake cycle, although blood pressure, body temperature and many other biological functions also change in a precise and regular pattern over the course of a day. Genetic factors may play a role in setting each individual's internal biological clock. However, environmental factors, particularly the number of daylight hours and social factors, such as a regular lifestyle (e.g., regular mealtimes, social activities, etc.), also significantly influence an individual's circadian rhythms.

Disruptions in circadian rhythms can be associated with mood disorders. For example, mania is more common in the summer months in the northern hemisphere (when exposure to daylight is longer). Episodes of mood disorders may also occur following long-haul airline flights that can disrupt the sleep–wake cycle. These findings have led many researchers to propose that abnormalities in an individual's 'biological clock' may play a role in the development of mood disorders. It has also led to speculation about the types of stressors that are most likely to disrupt circadian rhythms and may precipitate episodes of mood disorder. Recent scientific studies have confirmed that people who develop more severe mood swings are likely to show some abnormalities in their sleep–wake patterns (also referred to as rest–activity rhythms). This research, alongside the increased emphasis on activity and energy disturbances in bipolar disorders, means that clearer proposals can be put forward about how to monitor the 24-hours of circadian rhythm patterns. Also, more detailed understanding of these issues has helped in the development of additional techniques for managing sleep routines and of developing more stable patterns of daily living (see 'Self-regulation' p.166).

PSYCHOLOGICAL VULNERABILITY FACTORS

This term encompasses many aspects of personality, including the different ways we think, feel, behave and cope. I use this concept, rather than just referring to an individual's 'personality', as the use of blanket terms such as 'neurotic' or 'personality disorder' has done little to help us unravel the role of individual psychology in the development of mood disorders. Also, few people fit neatly into the rather arbitrary personality categories described in textbooks.

Personality can be thought of as the sum total of an individual's actions and reactions. Some aspects of personality may be inherited, but much of who we become is shaped by our early environment and childhood learning experiences. There is evidence linking the development of unipolar disorders with adverse early circumstances, but it is not yet clear if this applies equally to bipolar disorder. Nor is a person with a particular personality 'type' any more likely to develop bipolar disorder than any other individual. Research in this area is complicated by the fact that typical features of some personality profiles (e.g., so-called 'larger than life' characters or people who show marked changes in mood over a few hours) overlap with those of bipolar spectrum disorders such as cyclothymia. However, the most important message is that there is no evidence of any personal inadequacies in individuals who develop mood disorders.

If no overall personality profile makes individuals vulnerable to bipolar disorder, do any individual characteristics specifically increase the risk of developing it? Again, the answer is probably no. There is a small body of evidence suggesting that how people respond to stressors, and what coping strategies they employ, may have a bearing on the age at which at risk individuals experience their first episode of mood disorder.

How a person acts and reacts, and what coping style they adopt, also plays a role in increasing or decreasing the likelihood of relapses. For example, it seems that relationship problems cause more stress to a person who has a strong belief that he will not be able to cope unless he has someone he can rely on. This stress may lead him into a downward spiral. Similarly, an individual with bipolar disorder who believes that she should control her own destiny finds situations that undermine her prospects for self-determination particularly stressful. These examples suggest that the importance of a particular life event differs between individuals depending on the underlying beliefs they have about themselves, their world and their future. These beliefs in turn will influence how individuals think and feel about a situation, how they respond and what coping strategies they employ. Also, people who brood about negative experiences and aren't able to shift their mindset and move on (a characteristic called ruminative response style) are more prone to experience a range of different mental health problems. Rumination becomes more frequent in everyone from adolescence onwards, but it is especially common in females, and is associated with problems such as anxiety and depression. Whilst not proven beyond doubt, this thinking pattern is probably more common in people who develop bipolar disorder. It may not be a cause of the disorder, but it may increase the risk of depressive episodes and may worsen the episodes that do occur.

On a positive note, it is true that certain coping styles can protect a person against a further episode of mood disorder. For example, a person with well-developed problem-solving skills may be able to take the sting out of many potentially stressful experiences and prevent a vicious downward spiral into depression. Most importantly, as discussed later in this book, it is possible for you to modify how you act and react in situations that are particularly stressful to you.

Stress factors

Stress–vulnerability models emphasise that biological factors such as genes may play a part in increasing an individual's risk of developing a bipolar disorder, but that events or experiences will affect whether that vulnerability becomes apparent. The factors described below may be associated with either the onset or the recurrence of bipolar disorder.

PHYSICAL FACTORS

In individuals with a vulnerability to developing bipolar disorder, there are many physical stressors that may precipitate an episode of mood disorder. Disorders of the endocrine glands, such as an overactive thyroid, may disrupt circadian rhythms and lead to depression or to mania. Alcohol may act as a physical stressor, disrupting sleep and other circadian rhythms, and possibly causing monoamine imbalances. Similar reactions occur in response to excessive use of stimulants, such as illicit drugs, nicotine or caffeine. Other medical disorders and some of the medications used in treatment (e.g., steroids), can also precipitate mood changes and the associated symptoms of bipolar disorder.

LIFE EVENTS

There is a well-documented association between the occurrence of life events such as the loss of a significant person and the onset of depression. Research also shows that individuals who experience other types of interpersonal life events, such as the break-up of a relationship or other types of loss events, such as being made redundant, may also develop depression. In contrast, people who are perfectionists may not be affected so obviously by one major life event but may find more minor but frequent life events ('hassles') particularly stressful.

As noted in the discussion of psychological vulnerability factors, life events associated with the onset of a mood disorder often have a special meaning for that individual. This more intense response may be associated with changes in brain chemistry or circadian rhythms. These changes in turn disrupt the physical state of that individual more than someone who is not at risk of developing a mood disorder. These disruptions may also be more prolonged, further affecting the individual's cognitions (beliefs, thoughts and images), feelings and behaviours. This interaction between the four aspects of the individual (biology, behaviour, emotion, cognition) and their environment was first described by Christine Padesky and Kathleen Mooney in the USA. It is illustrated in Figure 3.

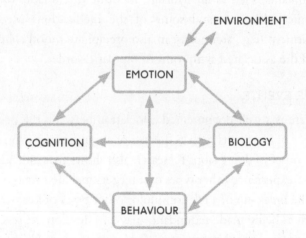

Figure 3: The five-system model, showing the links between an individual's cognitive, biological, emotional and behavioural functioning and the environment

It is often easier to explain the links between negative life events and depression than to understand how life events are associated with an episode of mania. Research from Pittsburgh in the USA suggests that events that particularly disrupt a person's day-to-day patterns of activity and their sleep–wake cycle may trigger the onset of mania. Examples are acute sleep disruption brought about by having to go out of the house unexpectedly in the middle of the night, or the substantial disruptions of daily routine caused by starting a full-time college course. The researchers found that these 'social rhythm disrupting' (SRD) events occurred more frequently in the eight weeks prior to the onset of a manic episode than in the eight weeks prior to the onset of a depressive episode. It is suggested that SRD events lead to changes in the individuals' circadian rhythms, in turn causing the observed disturbances in physical, cognitive, emotional and behavioural functioning.

SOCIAL FACTORS

No one lives in a vacuum; everyone's environment and quality of life will influence their state of well-being. An individual's social circumstances may increase or reduce the risk of experiencing more extreme mood swings. A key constituent of a person's environment is their relationships with other people. As noted earlier, interpersonal problems may be associated with the onset of an episode of mood disorder in a vulnerable individual. There is evidence that living in an environment where people have a negative style of interacting and are overly critical of each other may increase the risk of a vulnerable individual experiencing a mood swing. Conversely, the positive support and encouragement received from family or friends can buffer a person against the vicissitudes of daily life. A close, confiding relationship may actually help prevent a person at risk of mood disorder from experiencing more extreme mood swings. Such support also seems to reduce the risk of depressive episodes becoming persistent.

Sometimes the same vicious 'event–thought–feeling–behaviour' cycles that may tip one individual into a mood disorder can influence interactions between individuals. The reactions of other individuals to the way someone with a mood disorder acts will be determined by their interpretations of that person's behaviours. These interpretations in turn influence the observers' own emotional and behavioural responses. In this way the symptoms of mood disorder can be a source of stress and distress for all individuals in the immediate environment.

Interestingly, many relatives of people with mood disorders comment that hypomania or less intense 'highs' can be more distressing to cope with than mania. This may be because it is easier to accept that someone who is manic is out of control and unable to stop themselves from behaving inappropriately, whereas family members are often unsure that an individual with hypomania is unwell and may interpret that person's actions or behaviours as selfish or unkind. This highlights how important it is for everyone involved in a social network to understand the nature of mood disorders and the typical symptoms that a person may experience.

Such an understanding can go some way to reducing misunderstandings and tensions.

Living with someone who has a history of intense mood swings may bring long-term problems in relationships, ranging from repeated struggles to forgive indiscreet or ill-judged actions during manic episodes, to being overprotective and trying to wrap a person in cotton wool in the hope that this will prevent them from ever experiencing another mood swing. Again, strains of these kinds in a relationship may have an adverse effect on both parties, and it is important to try to identify and change negative patterns of interaction to improve each person's sense of well-being.

CHAPTER SUMMARY

- Bipolar and bipolar spectrum disorders affect about 1–4 per cent of the population.
- Men and women are equally likely to be diagnosed with bipolar I disorder.
- The first episode of mania or hypomania usually occurs between the ages of fifteen and twenty-five years. Earlier age of onset is more common in people with a family history of bipolar disorder.
- On average, a person with bipolar disorder will experience at least four episodes of disorder over the first ten years.
- The stress–vulnerability model offers the best explanation of how bipolar disorder develops.

- Vulnerability factors increase the risk that someone may develop episodes of bipolar disorder, but current research indicates that they do not *cause* the disorder.
- Vulnerability factors can be classified as biological and psychological.
  - Key biological factors include genetic inheritance, neurotransmitter abnormalities and circadian rhythm disruption.
  - Psychological factors affect the likelihood of having further episodes of bipolar disorder. An individual's underlying beliefs and their coping style will affect what events they find stressful and how they act and react.

- Stress factors may expose an individual's underlying vulnerability to developing an episode of mood disorder.
- Stress factors can be classified as physical factors, life events and social factors.
  - Physical factors include medical disorders but also the excessive use of alcohol or stimulants.
  - Life events include experiences with a specific personal meaning for the individual and SRD (social rhythm disrupting) events and/or other events that disrupt sleep–wake (circadian rhythm) patterns.
  - Social factors include the individual's social situation and interpersonal relationships.

4

Current approaches to treatment and management

For many decades, research on bipolar disorder focused on biological factors that might cause the disorder and on physical interventions – particularly medications – that might reduce the severity of symptoms. Little attention was paid to the role of psychosocial therapies in modifying factors that might precipitate an episode of bipolar disorder, or in helping individuals to overcome the adverse psychological or social consequences of such an episode. The efforts of individuals with mood disorders and their families and of patient advocacy groups means that this situation has changed. For example, in the UK, clinical services are increasingly required to offer access to social support and psychological therapies as well as medication to individuals with bipolar disorder.

This chapter offers an overview of the aims of care and treatment and the potential roles of physical and psychological therapies. The role of admissions, 'advanced treatment directives', the 'no treatment' option and complementary ('alternative') therapies are briefly discussed. Also, the section highlights some clinical interventions that are linked to 'healthy living' as these are increasingly offered to individuals with a range of mood and mental health problems. Lastly, I provide a concise update on new research about other types of treatment for depression and mania, such as the use of light therapies.

The aims of treatment

The primary aims of treatment for an individual with a bipolar disorder are to:

- reduce the acute symptoms and problems associated with depression or mania;
- restore an individual to their prior level of functioning;
- prevent any recurrence of mania and depression, or reduce the severity of episodes that do occur.

Individuals with a bipolar disorder will know only too well that these aims look very obvious when stated so briefly, but even these three main goals are sometimes very difficult to achieve in the real world. Also, these objectives represent the bare minimum individuals will want from any care and treatment package. There are many other potential issues to address. For example, many individuals will not simply wish to return to their previous level of functioning, they may want to extend further their day-to-day living and coping skills so that they function at a higher level than before the onset of mood swings. Others wish not only to overcome the difficulties associated with mood disorders, but also to improve their overall sense of health and well-being. In addition, individuals with severe, chronic or difficult-to-treat symptoms may identify other more individually relevant goals. For example, they may not be focused just on how to manage or live with a certain subset of symptoms, but they may want to explore interventions that help them attain a broader-based idea of personal recovery, including social networks and other lifestyle issues, etc.

Medication can help to achieve some of the aims of treatment, but it cannot resolve all the issues identified. Likewise, reliance on psychological therapy alone is rarely advisable. It seems that no single treatment can help an individual overcome all the symptoms and problems experienced, and that a combined approach offers the best management strategy. The degree of emphasis on medication or psychosocial approaches will differ from person to person and may vary according to the severity or phase of the mood disorder. Most individuals with bipolar disorder benefit from taking medication at some stage, if only because it stabilises some of the most distressing or disruptive symptoms. This is important for several reasons, not least because taking medication may help them become sufficiently settled to allow them to engage with and concentrate their attention on any psychological interventions being offered.

The degree of psychological support required by individuals varies enormously. Some find that informal support from people in their social network or membership of a voluntary organisation enables them to cope with their problems. Others benefit from a more intensive approach, such as an individual course of CBT, a framework that is explored in more detail in the next chapter.

A brief review of physical treatments

The term 'physical treatments' is used mainly to refer to medication, although it also includes other approaches, of which one of the most notorious is electro-convulsive therapy (ECT). Many individuals regard these as dubious options. However, to enable you to make an informed judgement about whether you will accept medication or other interventions, it is important to describe the rationale for these treatments, to establish the facts and try to dispel the less helpful myths. If nothing else, you can then make some personal decisions about your care and treatment preference after weighing up the pros and cons of the evidence.

Physical treatments are usually considered in two stages: the acute treatment phase, when the aim is to reduce the intensity of current symptoms; and the longer-term phase, when the aim is to prevent recurrent episodes of mood swings (so called prophylaxis or mood stabilisation). As well as briefly discussing common treatments for each phase of bipolar disorder, I will highlight some of the new treatments that are 'in the pipeline' or beginning to be prescribed. Also, I will comment on the problem of how different types of medications are classified (grouped together). I mention this topic as people often feel confused when they collect a prescription and read the name of medication on the prescription bottle and then go and look up information about it. People read the 'group name' for a medication and begin to worry that they have been offered the wrong treatment or a drug that is for a different problem rather than for bipolar disorder. So, I think it is helpful to acknowledge this and try to offer an explanation in the hope that it offers some reassurance.

Acute treatments

MEDICATION FOR HYPOMANIA AND MANIA

The treatment of hypomania and mania is similar. The main differences are that individuals with hypomania rather than mania may respond to lower doses of medication and are less likely to need to be admitted into hospital.

Mood-stabilising drugs are a key component of the treatment of mania or hypomania. As well as having longer-term benefits, many mood stabilisers have anti-manic properties, and some may even be recommended for the treatment of acute depression. There are some international variations in medication usage, but lithium is the most prescribed anti-manic medication worldwide. Some individuals decline the option of taking lithium, often due to concerns about side-effects, and so medications such as carbamazepine, lamotrigine and sodium valproate may be offered as mood stabilisers. Interestingly, medications such as carbamazepine and valproate were first developed as treatments for individuals with epilepsy, so they are technically classified as anticonvulsant medications. Likewise, more recent research has shown that some medications that are classified as anti-psychotics (so-called 'second-generation antipsychotics'), such as aripiprazole, quetiapine and others, can be effective mood stabilisers.

As noted above, the term mood stabiliser now extends beyond lithium to include medications that are technically classified as anticonvulsants and antipsychotics. The first thing to be clear about is that if you are offered an anti-convulsant as a mood stabiliser then this does not indicate that the prescriber thinks your manic symptoms are caused by epilepsy. It is far more likely that you have a certain pat-tern of symptoms, such as rapid cycling disorder (noted in Chapter 2), that appear to respond better to carbamazepine or valproate rather than lithium alone. Similarly, although antipsychotic medications such as olanzapine may be used in the treatment of hallucinations and delusions, clinical research has shown it may be immensely helpful for reducing agitation during an acute manic episode and for preventing future relapses. Other studies indicate that quetiapine may be a good choice for those with bipolar II disorder.

Psychiatrists and other medical and health professionals are aware that what is described as the 'nomenclature' (nam-ing and classification) of medications is no longer fit for pur-pose in the modern world of diagnostics and therapeutics. Several senior researchers, pharmacists and patient advocates are trying to develop new ways to label medications but, in the interim, the advice would be not to be afraid to ask what class of medications (as well as the name of the specific drug) you are being offered. Next, ask the prescriber to clarify which subset of your symptoms the medication will help, i.e., do not panic if you are told it is an antipsychotic. It is the labelling of the medication that is inaccurate as many medications have a diverse range of important and beneficial effects even though the original discovery and development was targeted at only a select set of symptoms.

The main problem encountered in treating mania with traditional mood stabilisers such as lithium and anticonvulsants is that the drugs can take seven to ten days to begin to have a significant effect. Given that mania is an emotionally distressing and potentially physically exhausting state, it is usual to offer additional medications. For example, benzodiazepines, such as clonazepam or lorazepam, are often prescribed in addition to a mood stabiliser during the first week or so of a manic episode in an attempt to reduce physical and mental agitation and to improve sleep. (Again, do not think your diagnosis has been changed because benzodiazepines are usually regarded as anti-anxiety drugs or anxiolytics.) The advantage of these medications is that they work very rapidly (within two to four days). As many individuals will be aware, longer-term use of benzodiazepines carries significant risks of dependence. However, short-term use during the early stages of mania can be justified, especially if an individual cannot tolerate antipsychotic medications or is experiencing high levels of anxiety.

Antipsychotic drugs may be particularly useful when a person's thinking is very disorganised, or they report delusions. Having very disrupted thinking or very rapidly changing sequences of ideas is a common feature of mania that can be helped by these medications. However, as noted above, antipsychotics can help with several other symptoms, such as reduced sleep and restlessness. The second-generation antipsychotics are now the most frequently prescribed of these types of medication, although some individuals are offered or may prefer to get older, first generation antipsychotics such as haloperidol. The latter are used less frequently because the side-effects can be troublesome and sometimes make a person feel more rather than less restless. However, the second-generation drugs may also cause such side-effects, although usually to a lesser extent.

These additional drugs can usually be withdrawn once the mood stabiliser has begun to have a clear effect. In some circumstances, a decision may be made to continue with the antipsychotic with the goal being to then prescribe it as a long-term mood stabiliser. A summary of side-effects of mood stabilisers is included in the Appendix (p.377).

Medication for depression

Antidepressant medication may be used if an individual experiences an acute depressive episode. These medications have to be used with some caution, as antidepressants, particularly some of the older antidepressants such as tricyclics, may bring on an episode of hypomania. Although this is uncommon, it is advisable to monitor mood changes very carefully while antidepressants are being taken. Most individuals who are prescribed an antidepressant continue to take a mood stabiliser. For someone who is feeling agitated or reports psychotic symptoms, mood stabilisers may be prescribed along with antipsychotic medication.

As with mania and hypomania, there has been some evolution in the thinking about how best to treat bipolar depression. This has largely arisen because nearly all of the best-known antidepressants, such as those classified as selective serotonin reuptake inhibitors (SSRIs), have similar but rather limited benefits in acute bipolar depression. Arguments about the reasons for this apparent lack of efficacy include the notion that these medications, although quite good at treating some mood and depressive symptoms, are simply not so helpful when it comes to some of the activity-energy symptoms that can occur in bipolar depression (such as people needing to sleep for very prolonged periods, eating more and being very lethargic). Further, increasing the doses of antidepressants to try to increase their benefits may backfire as it may precipitate a switch into a hypomanic episode. Research indicates that other types of medications, such as lurasidone, may be useful treatments for depression, i.e., if an individual experiences acute bipolar depression they should not be surprised if they are offered a prescription for a second-generation antipsychotic (because it seems to be at least as good as other antidepressants!).

One further issue with antidepressant medications is that it takes about one to two weeks for the benefits of taking the medication to start to become apparent. Further, it may be six weeks before any judgement can be made about whether the antidepressant is truly effective for that individual. This is important to understand, as it means that clinicians will encourage continuation with the medication even if there are few immediate gains.

If all of the above options fail to help an individual with severe depression, then they may require referral to a specialist treatment service. Some of the options that are being studied by scientists include the use of intravenous treatments such as ketamine. This type of intervention is now beginning to be included in clinical practice guidelines, but at the time of publication of this text, the treatment was not available routinely in day-to-day clinical services.

Electro-convulsive therapy and transcranial magnetic stimulation

A small proportion of those individuals admitted to hospital may be so unwell that they also need treatment with ECT. Very rarely, an individual is offered ECT because their acute symptoms have previously responded especially well to this approach. In some circumstances, ECT may be offered to outpatients, but this approach requires careful management as there is a need to monitor a person's physical and mental well-being before and after receiving each ECT treatment. For many people, admission to hospital is recommended for the duration of the course of ECT (which usually comprises six to twelve treatments over a period of about three to four weeks).

Eight out of ten people who receive ECT appear to benefit. More importantly, improvement in very severe disorders may be more rapid than can be achieved with medication alone.

How ECT actually works is unclear. One theory is that it improves the sensitivity of nerve-cell receptors to neuro-transmitters, leading to stabilisation of the brain activities that regulate emotions.

Another treatment that has been offered for bipolar depression that involves stimulating the brain is called repetitive transcranial magnetic stimulation (rTMS). This is a non-invasive procedure that is technically easier to deliver to people compared with ECT. Basically, a magnetic coil is held over, but not in contact with, a person's head. This allows delivery of repetitive magnetic pulses to stimulate nerve cells in the brain to reduce symptoms of depression and improve concentration and attention. However, the main concern about using rTMS in bipolar depression is that there is a potential risk of triggering an episode of hypomania. Although this risk is no greater than that reported with antidepressant medications, it means that the intervention must be used with caution and the course of treatment must be carefully monitored. Currently, rTMS is offered at some but not all centres that treat individuals with bipolar disorders. One reason that some centres do not cur-rently offer rTMS is because it is unclear whether rTMS is associated with any additional benefits over and above those associated with using medications.

New treatments that target circadian rhythms

As well as new medications, intravenous ketamine and rTMS, there are several scientific publications demonstrating the benefits of a range of new interventions for bipolar disorders. Many of these are linked to stabilising circadian rhythms by changing the timing or amount of exposure to certain types of lighting or by increasing blood levels of the hormone melatonin which alters the time at which someone will fall asleep. These *chrono-therapies* are beginning to be used more widely for the treatment of bipolar disorders because of the links between sleep–wake cycles and the onset or persistence of mood episodes.

I will not give the full background to all the elements of the circadian system that are implicated in sleep–wake patterns and how these link to bipolar disorders. However, to understand the rationale for the new treatments, it is helpful to note three important facts. First, melatonin is a very important hormone that regulates the rhythmic activity of the circadian system. Disturbances in the amount of melatonin available and timing of changes in levels of melatonin may disrupt rest–activity patterns, particularly the timing of the onset of sleep. Second, when exposure to sunlight and daylight are reduced, such as during winter, some people experience depressive episodes (often referred to as seasonal affective disorder). Many of the symptoms can be reversed or prevented by exposure to bright light in the morning. Likewise, some evidence suggests manic episodes might be more common in summer months, leading to theories about the possible benefits of reducing light exposure (so-called dark therapies) to reduce the risk of manic recurrences. Third, daytime exposure to blue light (which is part of the normal spectrum of daylight) is important to maintaining healthy body chemistry and the functioning of body systems. However, evening exposure to blue light can have detrimental effects as it disrupts sleep patterns and can destabilise mood and cognition. Studies show that blue light is commonly present in artificial indoor lighting systems and in the screens of electronic and social media devices.

Using the information about factors that improve or worsen the regularity of circadian rhythms, researchers have demonstrated that giving melatonin tablets at specified times may help improve sleep patterns in bipolar disorders. Melatonin will not be of benefit to most people if given alone, but it can be useful when added to other ongoing treatments. Its use has been discussed more in recent years because it is a naturally occurring substance and, unlike many other sleep medications, it does not appear to be accompanied by any risks of dependence and has relatively few side-effects.

The use of morning bright light therapy for seasonal depression is well known. More recent scientific studies have demonstrated that this intervention may also be useful for some, but not all, individuals with bipolar depression. However, it is important to note that the bright light boxes used in clinical settings are very carefully calibrated. This is because it is important to calculate precisely the brightness of the light, the type of light and even the distance of the light source from the eye. As such, these light boxes are not usually the same as the commercially available lamps that can be purchased by members of the public. Also, it is recommended that individuals with mood swings do not experiment with these lamps without discussing the benefits and risks with a mental health professional.

Perhaps the most novel research that is currently ongoing involves the use of interventions that reduce an individual's exposure to blue light in the evenings and at night-time. These interventions should only be prescribed by clinicians with expertise in bipolar disorders and are currently only used in specialist centres. However, the basic principle is that either the lighting system in an inpatient unit is modified so that light exposure is reduced significantly for long periods (so-called 'darkness therapy') or the lighting is modified so that, from early evening onwards, the artificial lights in the environment have lightbulbs that are 'blue light depleted' (the light exposure is returned to normal in the morning). In addition, all televisions and electronic devices can be fitted with screens that are specially designed to block out blue light. This type of *blue-depleted light* intervention has been shown to improve sleep patterns in some hospital patients with severe physical illnesses as well as those with mental health problems. Whilst it does not work for everyone, it may reduce the symptoms of mania in some inpatients who are simultaneously receiving other medications and mood stabilisers. Furthermore, ongoing scientific studies suggest that, if the lighting system cannot be changed, it may be possible to wear specially designed glasses that block blue light. This approach is being explored at specialist research centres, and the findings so far are encouraging. However, it is noteworthy that individuals with mania may find it quite difficult to adhere closely to the schedule of wearing blue-blocking glasses at certain times of day or for a specified number of hours per day.

In summary, these interventions represent an interesting new angle on helping reduce the symptoms of mania and depression that appear to be linked more closely to disruptions in circadian rhythms and that may be triggered by the type or timing of a person's exposure to light. The hope is that these interventions will have a limited number of negative effects or side-effects, but we await more detailed large-scale studies to be sure that they can be used more widely for individuals with mood swings. The main reason these specific interventions have been highlighted is because, should they become more mainstream in the coming decade, they would link well with self-help techniques to manage sleep–wake patterns that are advocated in this book.

Admission to hospital

If a person experiences an episode of mania that is totally out of control and unresponsive to treatment, or a severe depression accompanied by psychotic symptoms or intense suicidal ideas, they will almost certainly need to be admitted to the hospital. Admission is sometimes helpful in other situations too, for example enabling careful observation of an individual's response to medication. It may also ensure a person avoids actions or behaviours that are dangerous or that they may regret later. Research suggests that, after they return to a normal mood state, most individuals hospitalised with a severe episode of bipolar disorder are grateful that they were admitted, even though they may have been ambivalent about this option or even actively opposed it at the time.

Longer-term treatment (prophylaxis)

Individuals with a bipolar disorder will nearly always be offered a prescription for longer-term treatment with a mood stabiliser to reduce the severity or frequency of mood swings. As noted earlier in this chapter, whilst everyone agrees that a mood stabiliser is a medication that reduces the risk of or prevents the occurrence of depressive, hypomanic or manic episodes, there are now many medications can that be included in this category. A key issue for future research is to decide which individuals will benefit from which specific mood stabiliser. This would be very helpful as it might stop people having to try one prophylactic medication for an extended period of time to see if it prevents relapses and then having to try a different one for an extended period of time.

At present, it is estimated that about six out of ten individuals who take lithium for prophylaxis report improvement and about half of all these individuals respond very well indeed. For those who do not respond to lithium or do not like taking it, there is a good chance that one of the other mood stabilisers will help. Some people benefit from a combination of two mood stabilisers prescribed together. Individuals with a bipolar disorder who also have drug- or alcohol-related problems tend to respond less well to all of the mood stabilisers. Likewise, having multiple physical and mental health problems alongside bipolar disorder tends to be associated with a reduced benefit from a mood stabiliser. Alas, all mood stabilisers can cause side-effects and some, such as lithium, require regular blood tests to be taken to monitor whether the amount of medication being prescribed is likely to be effective. Other mood stabilisers are not advised for certain subgroups of individuals, e.g., medications such as lamotrigine should not be prescribed for some women (e.g., if they are of childbearing age) as the medication can be harmful to the development of a baby during pregnancy.

Most mood stabilisers need to be taken for about two years to determine if they have reduced the frequency or severity of mood swings. While research suggests that the benefits of mood stabilisers outweigh the disadvantages, many individuals struggle to keep taking them regularly as prescribed. Sometimes this is because of side-effects; other individuals simply fail to establish a regular routine for taking the tablets. However, it is equally common for individuals to report that they stop taking medication out of a desire to be in control of their own life, and because of the negative thoughts they have about prophylactic medication. This problem is discussed further in Chapter 8.

Advanced treatment directives

A major concern for individuals with bipolar disorder is how to strike a balance between being in control of your own life while also ensuring you receive timely treatment or hospital admission when you are unwell. The very nature of bipolar disorder or severe mood swings means that many individuals will have periods of time when they are fully in control of their daily life and function entirely independently. Alas, these periods may be interspersed with times when they are so unwell that they lose their ability even to recognise that they need treatment or hospital admission.

Collaborative projects between individuals with bipolar disorders, their families, advocacy groups, clinicians and researchers have examined how to use advanced treatment directives to address the issues outlined. The idea is that someone with bipolar disorders, in consultation with trusted friends, family and professionals, can write a self-binding agreement that explains what usually happens when they become unwell and what sort of treatment is usually helpful to them. This strategy fits well with the self-help and self-management approaches described in this text, e.g., the final section of this book describes developing personalised relapse prevention packages and thinking about what to do when symptoms get worse. So, extending your personal planning to include an advanced treatment directive means that you can record your preferences regarding treatments and give coherent reasons for these choices in advance of any difficult times. For example, you may explain that you find that you can tolerate certain medications well, and that you would prefer to be prescribed these named medications to other treatments, such as medications that have caused you distressing side-effects in the past. At the same time, if you use this approach, it means that people you trust can also know about your preferences and may help to ensure this information is given to the professionals involved in your care and treatment. Overall, thinking about such issues in advance (rather than assuming or hoping such things won't happen) may increase the chances that you will receive treatments you prefer or have confidence in, even if you are not able to recognise yourself that more intensive treatment is needed.

Currently, it should be noted that an advanced treatment directive is not an option for everyone and that these agreements are not accepted by clinical services worldwide. However, in my experience, few clinicians would dismiss such a document out of hand, and many more would endeavour to consider these preferences (unless there was a major reason or some clinical danger in following the expressed preferences). Some individuals with bipolar disorders feel that going through the process of writing an advanced treatment directive has helped them think through their choices of treatment (and reasons for these preferences), helped their communications with their family and improved their trust in clinicians and health services. Also, they say that it helped them come to terms with the notion that admissions or certain treatment interventions may sometimes be needed in the future, no matter how much they hope this won't happen. As such, planning and writing the agreement empowered them to feel they have some control on how their mood swings are managed, even if the time comes when they are so unwell that they lack the capability to explain their preferences and views. These self-help, self-management and empowerment themes will recur throughout this book.

The 'no treatment' option

As we have just noted, many individuals stop taking medication because of their personal attitudes and beliefs. A dislike of taking medication may be compounded by some less-than-ideal interactions with health-care professionals, as a consequence of which some individuals decide to vote with their feet and do not attend any appointments offered. These attitudes and actions are not peculiar to individuals with mood disorders and are just as likely to be seen in individuals receiving long-term treatment for medical disorders such as hypertension, asthma and diabetes.

If you do have a history of mood disorder and feel that you wish to take the 'no treatment' option, it is important to be sure that you are taking this decision in the cool light of day and not in the middle of an upswing or a depressive episode. Research suggests that individuals who stop taking mood stabilisers often make this choice when they have been symptom-free for some time and come to doubt that the benefits of persevering with medication exceed the negative aspects. Unfortunately, there is considerable evidence that mood disorders are more likely to recur than not, and that recurrence is more rather than less likely without treatment. Nevertheless, experience and research have taught me that at least 50 per cent of individuals to whom mood stabilisers are prescribed will stop taking them at some point. So, if you have stopped your medication or cannot be dissuaded from taking this course of action, the following ideas may be helpful to you.

The first and most important is to view this treatment-free period as an experiment. This has many advantages, not least that it keeps the door open for a return to treatment without such a decision being viewed by you or anyone else as a personal failure. Also, try to identify (and ideally record) how and when you will know whether this 'no treatment' experiment has been successful or not. How long will you try to go it alone? What are your criteria for success? Lastly, as this is an experiment, it will need to be evaluated; so, it is helpful to keep a record of your progress, so that you can make an accurate assessment of the outcome.

Below is a list of points that some individuals who stopped their treatment report that they have found helpful. The more of these you are able to include in your plan, the better:

- Review your decision by making a list of the advantages and disadvantages of this choice.
- Carefully consider if there is anything that someone might do, that would change your mind; if so, go to talk to them.
- Talk to people who know you and ask for their views on the advantages and disadvantages of what you propose.
- If you cannot talk to someone you know well, seek

advice or support from a self-help organisation for individuals with bipolar disorder.

- Read about bipolar disorder and try to assess how likely you are to experience a long symptom-free period, and what will protect you against relapse.

- If you are currently still taking medication but are definitely intending to stop, it is better to make this change very gradually. Research shows that suddenly stopping mood stabilisers increases the likelihood that you will have a relapse within a few months.

- Avoid non-prescription drugs, excess consumption of alcohol and caffeine or other stimulants.

- Try to regularise your day-to-day patterns of activity and keep a record of your mood and any other symptoms you experience so that you can assess your progress.

- Try to identify someone you trust, with whom you would be prepared to speak regularly to review your mood state and how you are coping.

- Agree on a plan with that person about what you will do if the experiment is unsuccessful, things are going badly, or you experience a recurrence of symptoms. Best of all, write down the plan in detail and both keep a copy.

Finally, it may be appropriate to consider the pros and cons of seeking a course of psychological therapy. However, you should be aware that most therapists would prefer you to be taking prophylactic medication, as well, and will almost certainly at some point want to discuss your rejection of the other treatments available.

Complementary therapies

Homoeopathic, herbal and other remedies

The appeal of complementary (alternative) therapies is easy to understand. These treatments are largely viewed as more natural and less noxious than the manufactured medications prescribed by doctors. However, it is not clear whether any homoeopathic or herbal remedies are of benefit in bipolar disorder. Treatment trials are currently under way to assess the antidepressant effects of St John's Wort (*hypericum perforatum*), but these studies seem to be the exception rather than the rule. Also, there is evidence that St John's Wort may reduce absorption of iron and other minerals into the body, which may make it a less attractive option than it first appeared. Some individuals might argue that melatonin supplements should be discussed here. It is fair to say that as well as being a prescribed drug, it is possible to buy over-the-counter preparations of melatonin. However, some caution may need to be exercised if you decide to try to buy this for yourself, as the best dose of melatonin to help people go to sleep may differ significantly from the dose available in over-the-counter tablets. Also, the latter often contain a small amount of melatonin and large amounts of other substances that will not help your sleep pattern and that may undermine your self-management of mood swings.

Overall, whilst many individuals report benefits from homoeopathic or health-store remedies, vitamin or dietary supplements, or other treatments, there is no simple way of assessing which, if any, of these may be of benefit to you. If you are tempted to try these substances, then it is probably helpful to consider the following precautions:

- Given the lack of evidence for their effectiveness, it is unwise to use these remedies *instead of* prescribed medications.
- If you are going to try any remedies, make sure you know exactly what is in the package and check the dosage instructions carefully. There is no standardisation across brands and the actual doses vary considerably between products.
- Before taking the remedy, seek reliable information and advice on any potential side-effects, adverse effects or potential interactions with the medications you are being prescribed.
- Always tell the person prescribing your medication what other remedies you are trying out.
- As the exact benefits or adverse effects of these substances may not be certain, it is better to avoid trying them out when you are experiencing acute symptoms or severe mood swings, or are under stress.

In summary, it is worth emphasising the need for caution. You may find a remedy that helps you relax or has other positive effects, but the fact that these remedies can be purchased over the counter does not guarantee either that they have benefits or that they are safe or free of side-effects.

Relaxation therapies

Relaxation therapy, aromatherapy, massage and meditation can all help people to relax. There is no evidence that these approaches are effective alternatives to standard treatments in individuals with bipolar disorder. However, given the importance in treating mood disorders of reducing stress and improving well-being, these may be helpful additional strategies, and many are discussed in the self-management section of this book.

Clinical interventions targeted at lifestyle factors

General issues related to healthy lifestyles are discussed in the chapters of this book that address self-monitoring and self-management. However, the boundaries are somewhat blurred between self-regulation of health behaviours that positively impact on well-being and clinical interventions, such as exercise therapy or help with alcohol misuse that may be recommended by a primary health care professional. So, it is worth briefly considering some of the clinical interventions and how they may apply to individuals with bipolar disorders.

Many health services now offer regular health checks to selected subgroups from the general population, such as older adults or those with long-term mental or physical health conditions. As well as monitoring heart and lung functioning (checking heart rate, blood pressure, breathing rates, etc.), they assess body weight (to identify individuals who are overweight or clinically obese) and screen people to assess their risk of developing diabetes, etc. The importance of early detection and treatment of these physical problems in individuals with major mental health conditions is increasingly recognised. So, it is possible that any health professionals you encounter will discuss your physical well-being as well as your mental health concerns. For some individuals who are overweight or those who have some unhealthy habits, these professionals may recommend additional interventions such as a diet plan, exercise therapy or even offer a 'prescription', e.g., for gym sessions.

There is no evidence that one specific diet or eating plan can prevent the onset of bipolar disorder or prevent episodes occurring. However, it is established that individuals with bipolar disorder are more likely than other members of the general population to be overweight or clinically obese and are at greater risk of developing a range of physical disorders such as diabetes and heart disease. These problems are not necessarily a consequence of taking medications for bipolar disorders, as scientific studies show that genetic factors that increase the risk for diabetes and other 'metabolic' problems are found more frequently in people who develop mood swings. As such, trying to develop healthy eating habits and aiming to maintain a healthy body weight are worthwhile and make it less likely that diabetes or other problems develop.

Research studies show that mild to moderately severe episodes of depression can be helped by exercise and that exercise interventions can speed up recovery from depression and anxiety. As with healthy diets, exercise alone is not an alternative to other treatments prescribed for bipolar depression, hypomania or mania. However, combining a new exercise regime with other clinically recommended interventions may be beneficial for some people with mood swings. Also, trying to be physically fit and healthy has many other positive effects. For example, it may help your sleep pattern.

There is a great deal of evidence that the intake of nicotine, alcohol, illicit drugs and even caffeine will worsen the course and outcome of mood swings. For some people, use of these substances becomes so problematic that a mental health professional advises them to join a treatment programme to help them stop these habits entirely. Other individuals prefer to use a 'harm reduction' approach, which entails minimising their exposure to all of these stimulants and keeping their intake to a minimum. This approach is used in clinical settings but can also be tried as a self-help technique. So, it is discussed in the next section of the book.

Psychological therapies

Most individuals with a bipolar disorder, and their families, need an opportunity to talk about the impact of the disorder on their lives and to get help in coming to terms with the problems it brings. These may include coping with stigma, low self-esteem, the loss of friends or employment, tensions within relationships, dealing with the symptoms of the disorder or with drug and alcohol misuse, or trying to make realistic plans for the future. Some individuals find that once their acute symptoms have settled, or medication has reduced the intensity of their mood swings, they are able to use their own problem-solving skills and start to cope on their own with the challenges ahead. Others are able to work through these issues by talking with people from their social network, or through contact with individuals involved in self-help or similar organisations. Mental health professionals can also offer education and support to help an individual to adjust to what has happened to them. However, many individuals welcome the opportunity to participate in a more formal course of psychological treatment.

From the late 1990s onwards, there has been a dramatic increase in scientific studies about the use of psychological therapies in bipolar disorder. As such, we now have evidence on their effectiveness for many different groups of individuals with bipolar disorder including those with different types of mood swings, younger people with their first clinical episode of mood swings (or those at very high risk of developing bipolar disorder) and older adults with long-term problems associated with bipolar disorder. All the research indicates that people who have a diagnosed bipolar disorder should use psychological interventions alongside medication rather than as an alternative to mood stabilisers or other drugs. For some individuals who do not have a bipolar disorder, it may be possible to use a psychological therapy for their mood swings without adding medication.

Overall, there is a growing consensus that the therapy models that are most likely to be helpful in treating bipolar disorder are: group psychoeducation, family focused treatment (FFT), interpersonal social rhythm therapy (IPSRT) and cognitive behavioural therapy (CBT). Both IPRST and CBT can be used with individuals or couples, or in group settings. Although the model (theory) behind each of these four therapies is slightly different, we now know that the approaches have important shared characteristics that go some way to explaining why they are well received by individuals who have mood swings:

- The model of the therapy is shared between the therapist and the individual, family or group.
- The model provides a framework for understanding the mood disorder and its impact on the individual.
- The model is used to develop a unique picture of each person's experiences and problems. It recognises that no two individuals have identical needs.
- The main aim of therapy is to develop an individual's self-management skills.
- The therapy is relatively brief and aims to enable the individual to deal effectively with their own problems.
- The interventions and techniques used to help a person change follow a logical sequence (work on the here and now, then plan for the future).
- The therapist and the individual work together to test out the ideas discussed in therapy by setting up real-world experiments.

- The therapist and individual work in partnership to discover what is helpful or unhelpful to the individual.
- The individual leaves therapy with a range of skills and knowledge that they can apply independently.
- Credit for change lies firmly with the individual, not the therapist.

You will notice that this list says more about the style of the therapy (a collaborative, problem-solving approach) than about the specific interventions that are employed. My experience of working with individuals with mood disorders suggests that *how* the therapy is conducted and delivered is as important as *what* techniques are tried. One of the appeals of CBT for many individuals is that it is low on advice and high on self-discovery and self-management. Interestingly, the fact that CBT focuses on helping people discover things for themselves is one of the reasons that it can be adapted for delivery via self-help manuals. Furthermore, these self-help or self-guided versions of CBT can be delivered via printed textbooks but also via digital or online programmes. These electronic versions are especially useful if people live in places where the clinical services have only limited access to trained CBT therapists.

Scientific studies have increasingly highlighted that the four key psychological therapy models share several strategies for managing key symptoms of bipolar disorder. For example, they all address sleep problems, and all examine how people can plan and self-manage their daily timetable and activities. I mention this simply because, if you are unsure whether CBT is the best approach for you, then it is worth considering other options, such as IPSRT (if you prefer individual therapy) or a psychoeducation group (if you prefer peer-group support). Alternatively, you may feel more comfortable if you were able to undertake a therapy that also involved other members of your immediate family. I cannot determine if these other options would work better for you, but I would encourage you to remain open to the possibilities. Nearly all individuals with bipolar disorder who engage with a psychological therapy develop a greater awareness of the nature of their problems. Furthermore, most of them gain useful ideas, self-help techniques and specific skills that change how they understand and manage their mood swings.

The rest of this book will draw on the techniques used in CBT to try to help you to overcome your mood swings. The approaches described in most detail are those that have been shown by scientific studies to be the *active ingredients* of therapy, i.e., the techniques that make CBT effective in reducing depressive or manic symptoms or the strategies that are reported by patients and clients as being most useful for preventing further episodes of mood disorder. To begin this process, we need to explore a CBT model of what happens to an individual at risk of a mood disorder and look at how to apply this model to your own situation. This is the subject of the next chapter.

CHAPTER SUMMARY

- The primary aims of treatment are to reduce symptoms, restore functioning and prevent relapse.
- A combination of medication and psychological support is likely to be more effective than either approach on its own.
- Medications used for acute mania typically include a *mood stabiliser* in combination with an *antipsychotic* medication or a *benzodiazepine*.
- Medications used for acute depression typically include a *mood stabiliser* in combination with an *antidepressant or antipsychotic*.
- Long-term treatment with a *mood stabiliser* such as lithium, an anticonvulsant or a second-generation antipsychotic is usually recommended to reduce the frequency or severity of recurrent episodes.
- Psychological inputs that may help include:
  - informal support from a social network;
  - regular contact with a self-help group;
  - long-term contact with a mental health professional.

- Psychological therapies shown by research to be effective are:
  - group psychoeducation;
  - family focused treatment (FFT);

- ° interpersonal social rhythm therapy (IPSRT);
- ° cognitive behavioural therapy (CBT).

5

Cognitive behavioural approaches to mood disorders

This chapter will take you through the key elements of the cognitive behavioural model and then highlight how this may be applied to your own situation. The chapter ends with a brief overview of the main issues that can be targeted with techniques derived from cognitive behavioural therapy (CBT).

A model of mood disorders

In the first chapter of Part One, we noted that the thoughts (or images) that go through an individual's mind largely determine their emotional response to an event. We also explored how events, thoughts, feelings and behaviour are linked together. When we went on to review the causes of bipolar disorder, we found that an individual's beliefs about themselves and their world influence which life events are stressful to them. Scientific studies also show that an individual's attitudes and beliefs about medication affect their adherence to treatment.

The term 'cognitive' is often used to describe these thoughts and beliefs. Both are key components of the model of mood disorders.

How do we develop beliefs?

Our beliefs usually develop during childhood. We start to develop a set of rules for living from how people act or react toward us, or from what we learn by observing other people's interactions. The attitudes and beliefs of family members, school friends, teachers and other people in our community also influence our early learning experiences and start to shape what we believe about ourselves and our world.

Even in infancy we start to notice repeated patterns in the responses and attitudes of others. These patterns influence the beliefs we develop. Most of the beliefs we hold are quite adaptive, that is, helpful in guiding our attempts to be considerate and well-balanced individuals. However, some individuals' experiences during this early stage of their cognitive and emotional development may lead them to evolve rules that are maladaptive (dysfunctional) and have an unhelpful influence on how they act and react. Here are some examples that illustrate this point.

PLEASE TRY HARDER

Brianna is ten years old. She lives at home with her parents but her father, a successful businessman, often has to travel away from home. Brianna has been doing very well at school, much to the delight of her father. At the end of the school term, Brianna returns home with a glowing school report. She has grade As for all subjects except mathematics, where she achieved a B grade. She is keen to show the report to her father. He eventually returns home – late, tired and somewhat preoccupied with a meeting he has to attend early the next day. He opens Brianna's report, glances through it and then says: 'Your grade for mathematics is a bit disappointing, what happened there? It's a shame it's your weakest subject, some people say that maths is the best measure of a person's intelligence. Oh well, you'll have to try harder next time . . .'

Over the next year Brianna works hard at mathematics. At times she feels rather anxious about her ability to do this subject, but her teacher is encouraging and seems pleased with her work. At the end of the year she returns with her school report. Brianna has a grade A for mathematics. Her physical education teacher (new to the school that term) has given her a grade B (the report does not show that this is the top mark this teacher gave; the rest of Brianna's classmates got a grade C). Brianna's father examines the report. He says nothing about her grade A in mathematics, but then says: 'Shame about your physical education mark. School isn't just about being a good academic, you know; a fit and healthy body is just as important as a sharp mind.'

This scenario is somewhat artificial, as it does not describe other aspects of the intervening period in Brianna's life. However, on the basis of the information given here, consider two issues. What beliefs do you think Brianna might have developed about herself through these experiences? What might she decide she has to do in future to be valued by other people?

The ideas that you might identify include 'I'm not good

enough,' and silent rules such as 'In order to be liked/loved, I have to be successful in everything I do.' If Brianna did grow up with these beliefs, how might she react as an adult if she failed to get an expected promotion at work?

UNHAPPY FAMILIES

Joshua is an only child of seven years of age who lives with his parents. For as long as Joshua can remember, home has not been a happy place: his parents are constantly shouting at each other and his father has left to live elsewhere for a while on two previous occasions. Each time his father has left, Joshua has had no idea why his father has gone or if he will return. Neither of his parents has discussed these departures or any other issues with him. However, at various times Joshua has been shouted at, ignored and/or neglected by his parents.

What beliefs might Joshua have about himself if he was shouted at, ignored and/or neglected? Given that his father left home twice without indicating when he might return, what beliefs might Joshua develop about other people?

Joshua's beliefs about himself could include: 'It's my fault', 'I'm not important', or 'I'm unlovable'. Regarding other people, Joshua may develop beliefs like: 'People will leave me', or even 'People cannot be trusted'. If these ideas are accurate reflections of Joshua's beliefs, how might he react in adulthood if his first serious girlfriend leaves him?

TAKING THE CHILD'S-EYE VIEW

It may take some time to grasp the ideas discussed in these examples, particularly as you need to remember to put yourself in a child's place and to understand what they would make of these situations. They do not have the wealth of experience and knowledge that you, as an adult, have accumulated. They are unlikely to make sophisticated judgements about the adults involved in the scenarios. Also, a child is rarely in a position to demand an explanation of what is happening; if no one tells them what is going on, they have to draw their own conclusions.

It is important to note that fixed, maladaptive beliefs do not tend to develop on the basis of a single incident, but most often evolve from repeated exposure to similar situations. In rare cases, however, a single event has such a powerful effect that it alone shapes a person's beliefs about themselves or other people. On a more positive note, the environment in which an individual grows up may also include protective factors (e.g., a parent, grandparent or teacher who is supportive). So, even if an individual is exposed to adversity, they do not always grow up with low self-esteem or unreasonable expectations of themselves.

How beliefs operate: Prejudices

As observers of the above scenarios, it is easy for us to pause and reflect on the interaction between individuals, to take a balanced view of the information (evidence) available and to view these incidents within a broader context of life experience. However, an observer has the advantage of being distant or detached from what is happening. If you are the person in the middle of a situation, it is not always easy to take a step back and look at it in a wider perspective: we often seem to react spontaneously or automatically. Our beliefs have influenced us for so many years that we are not usually aware that they drive our thinking (and thus our moods and actions). Not only do we fail to notice them operating, but we also never seem to question whether they are accurate or realistic.

The best explanation of how to understand the influence of maladaptive beliefs on a person's life was put forward by two cognitive therapists called Christine Padesky and Kathleen Mooney. They suggested that you should think of a mala-daptive belief as a prejudice you hold against yourself. People who hold prejudices are blind to how unrealistic or irrational their belief is, but it does influence their lives. For example, some common cultural stereotypes are that Americans are loud and that the English are 'cold fish' or 'rather aloof'. Comments along these lines may seem amusing, but suppos-ing an individual has grown up with a strong belief that the English are aloof and unfriendly and holds a prejudice against English people. If they meet some English people who are not very friendly toward them, what would they conclude? Most probably, that they were right all along. Furthermore, they now have evidence to reinforce their prejudice.

Now let us suppose the same individual meets a group of people at a party who are fun-loving and very friendly and welcoming – and they turn out to be English. How does the person with a prejudice against English people maintain their negative view in the face of this contrary evidence? The classic pattern is that they:

- fail to register that the people are English (*don't notice it*),
- make excuses such as suggesting the English people were behaving differently because they were on holiday (*discount it*),
- tell themselves that, as some members of the group had Scottish and American relatives, maybe they were not genuinely English (*distort it*),
- simply state that this group 'are the exception that proves the rule' (*make an exception*).

This example shows that if a person holds a prejudice (a rigid, maladaptive belief), they readily accept evidence that confirms their view. However, when they come across contrary information, they ignore it or, without realising, begin to adapt (distort) it so that it too fits with their belief system.

HOW PREJUDICED BELIEFS CAN WORK AGAINST YOU

Having explored the principles of how prejudices operate, let us apply these principles to the underlying beliefs that individuals hold about themselves.

Imagine a person's early childhood experiences led them to conclude that 'I am not likeable'. This belief (self-prejudice) may lead them to avoid social interactions, so that they are rarely exposed to evidence either to support or to refute their idea. If they are unfortunate enough to encounter someone who dislikes them, then their belief is reinforced, their mind is filled with negative thoughts and they may begin to feel sad. What if someone is nice to them and seems to like them? How do they react to this event? Sometimes they do not notice that the person is being kind. If they do notice, they may briefly feel happy, before doubts begin to enter their mind. Typical thoughts reported by such individuals include: 'They are only doing it because they feel sorry for me', or 'They probably won't like me when they get to know me'. The person once again begins to feel sad. For some, these doubts may also influence their behaviour, for example, preventing them engaging in social activities with a potential friend. Their self-prejudice has won again.

It is important to stress that only very rigid, unhelpful beliefs are likely to lead to problems. For example, a certain degree of perfectionism may help us to perform tasks to a desired standard. However, a fixed belief that, 'Unless I do everything absolutely perfectly, then I am a failure' can obviously put a person under a great deal of pressure. It may inhibit rather than encourage them to achieve what they set out to do and they may perceive evidence of having 'failed' across a variety of situations – at work, at home or in personal relationships. For a perfectionist, even relatively minor events that many other people would regard as unimportant irritations can be significant stressors. If the individual is also vulnerable to a mood disorder, these stressors may push them into a vicious downward or upward spiral.

Changes in mood may also change what aspects of ourselves or our environment we attend to, and this may activate an underlying belief. For example, if a person feels depressed, they will tend to notice how they keep failing to live up to their perfectionist standards. If a person is going high, they focus on their perceived achievements (e.g., producing a large number of business plans for schemes they wish to undertake), while at the same time, failing to attend to evidence that suggests they are not perfect (e.g., some documents are incomplete, or the schemes are unlikely to be financially viable).

As well as a degree of perfectionism, other common themes in the beliefs of individuals who experience mood swings are a desire to be approved of by other people and a wish to be in control of their lives and important situations. These beliefs are not unique to individuals at risk of mood disorders: similar ideas are common in the general population. However, knowing what types of beliefs you hold will give you clues as to how you may act or react during upswings or downswings. For example, if you like other people to approve of you, when you are depressed (mood) you may worry that you are not liked (thought) and avoid people (behaviour). When you are high (mood) you may seek out the company of important strangers (behaviour) because you think they will strongly admire you (thought). If you wish to be in control, depression may be associated with a sense of powerlessness as you constantly feel that you have no influence over events; when you are high you may become angry or irritable with those who try to prevent you pursuing risky ventures.

ARE YOU PREJUDICED AGAINST YOURSELF?

To begin to get a sense of your underlying beliefs, try to

CBT APPROACHES TO MOOD DISORDERS

complete the following three sentences (again, this idea comes from Padesky and Mooney):

I am . . .
People are . . .
The world is . . .

Try to use a single word or the minimum number of words you can, for each belief. Beliefs can usually be captured in one sentence rather than a paragraph.

Do not worry if this task seems difficult at this point. As mentioned previously, we are often not aware of our underlying beliefs, as they operate as 'silent rules' in adulthood. This is particularly true when in a normal mood state. If you did manage to complete the sentences, you may wish to pause and consider whether you have noticed the influence of any of these underlying beliefs on your recent actions or reactions.

It's the thought that counts

THE RELATIONSHIP BETWEEN AUTOMATIC THOUGHTS AND UNDERLYING BELIEFS

Underlying beliefs are present throughout our lives and operate across a variety of situations. A particular maladaptive belief will be activated by events that have some connection with the belief. For example, a silent rule that 'I am not likeable' may become activated by the break-up of a personal relationship or by receiving negative feedback from a work colleague. The immediate (or automatic) thoughts that we have about each event or experience apply to what is happening there and then, and help dictate our emotional response at that moment.

A key characteristic of automatic thoughts is that they are 'situation specific' – that is, the exact same thought does not usually recur again and again in different environments. However, there may be a common theme that links the thoughts together. Identifying this theme may provide important insights into an individual's underlying belief. For example, a person who is vulnerable to anxiety may find a number of situations difficult. They may find flying in an aeroplane is associated with anxiety, because of thoughts such as 'The plane may crash'. They may find walking a short distance on their own late at night equally anxiety-provoking, because of thoughts such as 'Somebody may attack me before I get indoors'. The thoughts are unique to the event; but the common underlying theme is that the person regards the world as a potentially dangerous place. Their reaction to perceived danger is anxiety. Furthermore, the level of anxiety that a person experiences in response to such thoughts may prevent them doing things, such as going out on their own.

TYPES OF AUTOMATIC THOUGHTS

Individuals who are depressed find that their automatic thoughts are dominated by themes of loss and failure. They view themselves as weak, they see their world as full of negative events, and they are drawn to information that they think demonstrates that their future is bleak. This negative style of thinking about themselves, their world and their future (called the *negative cognitive triad*) further increases feelings of depression and helplessness and will often lead them to avoid potentially uplifting situations. Thus, automatic thoughts powerfully affect the individual's quality of life; and yet, these negative thoughts are often inaccurate interpretations and represent a selective view of the available information.

It is important to emphasise that this 'tunnel vision' is not deliberate. All of us have automatic thoughts in response to the situations we encounter, and many of these thoughts are accurate interpretations, but some are not. We do not pick and choose when to distort our experiences. However, if our thinking *is* distorted it tends to promote more extreme emotional responses to events or situations. Automatic thoughts occur at a conscious level, but many individuals only become aware of their thoughts after they have learnt to focus on what goes through their mind if their mood changes. Once unhelpful automatic thoughts are identified, it is possible to modify them with resulting benefits for mood and behaviour.

Although there are differences in the automatic thoughts that individuals report, the types of thinking errors that occur (sometimes called cognitive distortions) are surprisingly consistent. Individuals may record that they have a set pattern of distorted information processing (e.g., always jumping to conclusions), while others find that their thinking shows many different errors. Some of the most commonly reported thinking errors are described below. You may like to assess whether you have ever thought in any of these ways:

- *All-or-nothing thinking (extremism)*: Do you ever look at things in black-and-white terms? Is there any room for doubt or do your self-statements demonstrate an extreme view of the world? Can you cope with the 'grey area' in the middle where things are neither brilliant nor dreadful? Examples of extremism include: 'It's absolutely awful,' 'It's totally perfect,' 'That should never happen,' 'You must always get it right.'

- *Overgeneralisation*: Do you ever come to sweeping conclusions based on one minor event or a small piece of a larger puzzle? Do you ever assume that if something happens once, it will always happen? If so, you may be engaging in overgeneralisation. Examples of such statements are: 'I'll fail the entire test,' 'I'm too quiet, people will never like me.'

- *Maximisation and minimisation*: Do you find yourself putting huge emphasis on either the strengths or the weaknesses of a person or the good or bad features of an idea? In depression, people exaggerate the importance of minor flaws, making statements such as 'I'm ignorant,' or underestimate their qualities: 'They're mistaken, I'm not really a generous person.' In contrast, when individuals are high or elated, they overestimate the gains and underestimate the losses associated with their ideas: 'I can't go wrong,' 'They'll love it.'

- *Mind-reading*: Are your moods or actions ever influenced by a belief that you know what other people are thinking about you? In reality, we may have a general idea about what a person might think, but we do not have any special powers that let us know exactly what is going through their mind. However, this thinking error is very common and can cause distress. Examples of mind-reading error are: 'She doesn't like me,' 'He only said that to make me feel better.'

- *Jumping to conclusions*: Do you ever try to guess how things will turn out in the future without weighing up the evidence? When individuals are depressed, they tend to predict negative consequences and assume catastrophic outcomes, making statements like: 'I know it's going to be awful,' 'Things are bound to go wrong.' Alternatively, when individuals are elated, they may predict everything will be wonderful: 'If I give up work and buy a boat, I'll be happy for ever.'

- *Personalisation*: Do you find yourself tending to take responsibility for everything, particularly blaming yourself for things that go wrong? Classic self-statements reflecting this cognitive distortion are: 'It's my fault,' 'I'm a bad father.'

Having noted the different thinking errors, it is worthwhile trying to recall any thoughts that went through your mind when you experienced a recent noticeable shift in your mood. Can you write down your mood state then, and any of your automatic thoughts? If you can recognise and record any of your automatic thoughts, is there any evidence of cognitive distortions? For example, personalisation may generate guilt; jumping to conclusions about the future may spark off anxiety; all-or-nothing thinking may be associated with depression; mind-reading that another person is not going to treat you fairly may give rise to anger.

Automatic thoughts and underlying beliefs are the key cognitive elements of the model of mood disorders. They are intimately linked with changes in mood and response, and also with an individual's physical functioning and quality of life. How all these aspects link together, and how cognitive behavioural therapy may be used to break into this cycle, are described below.

The cognitive behavioural cycle

Malik holds a belief that the world is a dangerous place. He also believes that, if his awful predictions come true, he will not be able to cope on his own. Malik constantly encounters events that generate unhelpful automatic thoughts about danger or not being able to cope. These lead to repeated experiences of intense anxiety. This begins to affect Malik's psychological and social functioning. He starts taking time off work, which leads to negative thoughts such as 'I'm a coward' and 'I'm useless'. This promotes feelings of sadness and depression. As well as being unable to get to his workplace, Malik is no longer able to attend social gatherings. Unfortunately, he eventually becomes unemployed and loses contact with friends. This has a number of associated problems, not least financial difficulties and social isolation. These conditions cause Malik even more stress (through exposure to additional negative experiences and situations) and distress (negative reactions to these difficulties), leading to loss of sleep, and other physical symptoms associated with low mood (e.g., not eating). These symptoms in turn lead to Malik feeling more depressed.

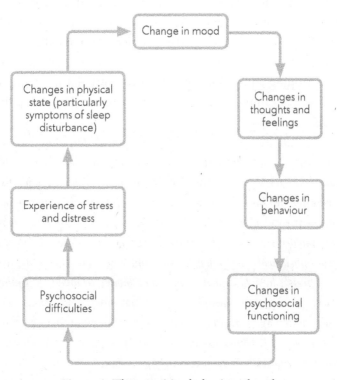

Figure 4: The cognitive behavioural cycle

You can see from this example how the cognitive behavioural cycle influenced all aspects of Malik's life. The starting point was activation of his underlying beliefs. In individuals who also have a biological vulnerability to develop a mood disorder, the cycle could also start with a disruption in circadian rhythms or a change in their physical and emotional state. No matter what the starting point, once the cycle begins, the changes and difficulties that occur are similar for each individual. Mood shifts in turn lead to changes in how that person thinks, feels (worsening depressed mood or depression compounded by anxiety or irritability, etc.), behaves and functions. This pervasive effect on a person's functioning and quality of life is demonstrated in Figure 4. Another example is given below for you to follow using the diagram.

Duncan was a 42-year-old businessman. His business was struggling financially (stress). *Duncan was worrying about this and was not sleeping* (physical symptom). *However, with this reduction in sleep he noticed he was feeling rather better in his mood* (mood change); *he became optimistic that he could solve the problems of the company by increasing the cashflow through a few 'quick deals' and some 'creative thinking'. He thought he was 'a genius': he had a plan to use some money to invest in a mink farm* (changes in thoughts and behaviour), *and would cover this venture by 'generating' some additional resources from his family income. He would use his own salary to place bets at the local casino. Duncan became increasingly preoccupied with these schemes and spent less and less time at home. His wife was frustrated that he was not around much, and that when he was, he seemed 'distracted'* (change in psychosocial functioning). *He decided not to tell his wife about the casino as he thought she would 'worry too much' and 'be a wet blanket'. The mink farm scheme failed, and Duncan lost increasing amounts of money at the casino. His mood shifted from elation to irritability, and one of his employees took out a complaint against him because he had been rude and angry with her during a meeting. His problems were compounded when his wife confronted him with the household bank statement: they had a large overdraft and the bank manager wished to see them* (psychosocial difficulties). *As the tensions at work and at home continued and the financial problems of his company and his personal overdraft got worse, Duncan began to feel tense, worried and depressed* (stress and distress).

You may now wish to see if you can apply this model to your own recent experience of mood swings, both the ups and the downs. To help you, a blank copy of this diagram is included in the Appendix.

The aims of cognitive behavioural therapy

CBT aims to teach individuals to intervene at key points in the cognitive behavioural cycle. It encourages individuals to cope with mood swings by helping them to:

- understand their biological and psychological vulnerability factors, particularly their own underlying beliefs and how these influence their well-being;
- identify and understand the nature of stress, particularly events that activate underlying maladaptive beliefs or events that disrupt their social patterns (social rhythm disrupting events);

- use self-regulation to reduce distress (such as the early symptoms of a mood swing), stabilise their mood and reduce high-risk activities such as excessive use of alcohol or illicit drugs or irregular adherence to medication;
- use self-management strategies to overcome intense mood swings by altering their active responses and identifying and modifying unhelpful automatic thoughts;
- develop an action plan to deal with early warning signs and symptoms, so that they have a greater chance of averting an episode of mood disorder;
- develop problem-solving skills that can be applied to a number of issues, such as overcoming the negative consequences of a 'high', and improve their day-to-day functioning and quality of life.

Reading this description may lead you to think there is too much to do, which in turn may make you feel anxious. However, there are a number of issues to bear in mind. First, remember that CBT is a *step-by-step approach*, so you only need to look at one issue at a time. Second, CBT is a *flexible approach*: not everyone reading this book will want or need to achieve all the aims on the list. Third, the advantage of using this book is that, if you choose, you might use it for a while, then have some breathing space before tackling other issues. Fourth, and very importantly, CBT recognises that everyone is different and that you will need to decide which of these aims concern you most. Finally, you will be in the best position to judge which approaches work best for you.

To help you think through your own needs, you may like to look back at the list of aims above and identify those that are really important to *you* and which *you* may want to work on. Again, it is really helpful to write down your list of priorities.

A note of caution

The next three parts of this book examine some of the cognitive and behavioural techniques that you may use to tackle some of your problems. Most of these techniques are also used in a course of CBT when a therapist and client work together. Some of you reading this book will find working alone easier than others. Practice and regular revision of the techniques described undoubtedly helps. It is a good idea to review the aims of each part of the book and then to read through each section a few times, perhaps making notes on the key points. Try to be clear in your own mind what each technique is about before testing it out in practice. Remember, there will be an element of trial and error, so it is useful to look on each attempt as an experiment. If something doesn't work out as you hoped, try to review exactly what happened and what you can learn from this. Could you adapt the technique to increase the chances of the 'experiment' succeeding next time? This approach is more productive than simply giving up and thinking the techniques won't help you.

Even with supreme effort you may struggle to use every technique effectively. Please do not be hard on yourself if you find some things difficult. This does not imply that you are less able than other individuals or that you have failed. Not all techniques are equally helpful for all individuals. Some people may simply find it hard to keep going on their own and may decide to seek professional support. Again, this is entirely appropriate. There is no rule that says a person has to solve all of their problems by themselves. This may be particularly true if you have a long history of mood disorder, if you have very intense swings or if your problems have proved difficult to handle in the past.

Lastly, this book does not to try to cover every aspect of every problem that every individual with a mood disorder has ever experienced. Some issues have been omitted because I did not think we could deal with them in a self-help book. The obvious example of this is the management of psychotic symptoms and deliberate acts of self-harm, as individuals with these invariably need more intensive support and treatment. Other issues have been left out because of the constraints of space or because of my own ignorance. I anticipated that you would not want to plough through a book of two thousand pages, so you will appreciate my decision regarding the former. On the latter point, I can only emphasise that this is an evolving area of clinical and research work and I still have many things to learn about mood disorders and their management.

CHAPTER SUMMARY

- The term 'cognitive' is applied to automatic thoughts and underlying beliefs:
  - ° automatic thoughts are situation-specific;
  - ° underlying beliefs are silent rules we apply across many similar situations.

- The cognitive behavioural model of mood disorders suggests that:
  - ° An individual's emotional response to an event is dictated by their automatic thoughts about that situation.
  - ° The content of the thoughts is determined by a person's beliefs about themselves and their world. Unhelpful automatic thoughts demonstrate common patterns of cognitive distortion.
  - ° Underlying beliefs develop from early learning experiences. Maladaptive beliefs operate like prejudices we hold against ourselves.

- Situations that activate maladaptive beliefs generate unhelpful automatic thoughts that in turn affect an individual's emotional and active responses.

- These responses may precipitate further difficulties in how a person functions, leading to psychosocial problems, stress and distress. The end point may be changes in physical state as well as further emotional disturbances.

- The cognitive behavioural cycle can be precipitated by:
  ° activation of underlying beliefs;
  ° circadian rhythm disruption or other physical changes that lead to sleep disturbance.

- Once the cycle is established, all aspects of an individual's life are affected.
- Cognitive behavioural therapy (CBT) aims to help people identify and manage the causes and consequences of the cognitive behavioural cycle of mood disorder.
- Not everyone will find the techniques described in this book easy to use or helpful.

PART TWO

LEARNING HOW TO COPE: UNDERSTANDING MOOD DISORDERS AND IMPLEMENTING BASIC SELF-MANAGEMENT

Aims of Part Two

At the end of reading Part Two of this book, I hope you will have gained a greater understanding of mood disorders and the key elements of self-management by:

- learning about life charts, symptom profiles and risk lists, and developing personal versions of these documents;
- learning how to identify reliable sources of information that will help you to become an expert on your problems and developing your skills for spotting misinformation or fake news about bipolar disorder;
- developing an understanding of self-monitoring of mood and activities;
- reviewing how to distinguish between normal and abnormal moods and behaviour;
- learning about the principles of self-regulation and developing a regular pattern of activities that is acceptable to you;
- understanding additional approaches that may further improve your self-regulation, e.g., reducing your use of alcohol and stimulants;

- learning how to identify and overcome common barriers to medication adherence.

6

Becoming an expert on your mood swings

In the first part of this book, we reviewed what is known about different types of mood swings and the stress–vulnerability model. We now need to use this information as a framework for exploring your personal experiences of mood swings. In this chapter, we will try to understand the pattern and nature of your mood swings and the stressors or other factors that may affect their frequency. Next, we will try to identify what other information you need to extend your own knowledge and understanding of these problems. Lastly, we will look at how you might increase your skills in distinguishing myths from facts. This is increasingly important because rumours and misinformation spread across social and other media just as rapidly as facts and accurate information about bipolar disorder and other health-related topics.

Constructing a life chart

To understand your mood swings and to develop approaches that should give you more control over what happens to you in future, we need to explore your past experiences. Figure 2 on p.18 shows the differences in severity and nature of the various mood disorders. This may have given you some insights into your own pattern of mood swings. To get a more detailed, individual picture we need to construct a chart that shows the number and sequence of episodes and the nature and duration of each one. Information on the influence of life events or medication changes can also be added to this picture. This may seem a tall order; so, to help you understand this approach, I will work through an example.

On the three charts, Figures 5a–c, the horizontal line represents a normal mood state. Using this as a reference point, the further the curve goes away from this line, the more severe the episode. Highs are represented by curves above the line; lows go below the line. The width of the curve gives an indication of the duration of each episode. The closer the curves are together, the more frequent the episodes.

Gabrielle is now forty years old. Her most recent mood swing was last year, when she was admitted to hospital with mania. Gabrielle had been feeling stressed by her job for a few months, and a month before the onset of the episode, she had stopped taking the lithium that had been prescribed for her. The episode lasted for four months.

This was not Gabrielle's first mood swing. Her first episode had been when she was aged twenty. At that time, Gabrielle experienced an episode of depression lasting six months that immediately followed the break-up of a two-year relationship. Gabrielle received antidepressants for nearly a year from the beginning of this episode before stopping the drugs of her own accord.

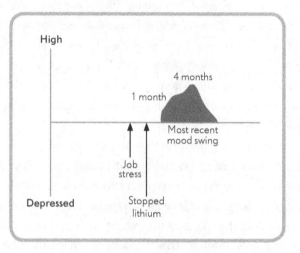

Figure 5a: Gabrielle's life chart

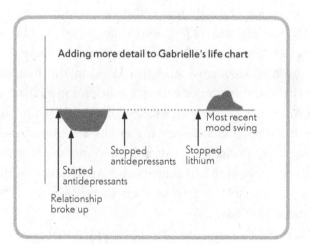

Figure 5b: Adding more detail to Gabrielle's life chart

Between her first and most recent episodes, Gabrielle identified two other episodes of depression of six months and twelve months' duration, one episode of hypomania (one month) and one other episode of mania (three months). It was not until her first 'high' that Gabrielle and her doctor recognised that she had a bipolar disorder. Following this diagnosis, she was prescribed lithium. One other mood swing occurred about two months after stopping lithium; another occurred shortly after moving to a larger home and being promoted at work.

As you can see, the chart gives some important insights into the pattern of Gabrielle's mood swings and factors associated with their onset. It is useful to review key events or experiences for at least three months prior to the onset of each episode. Note that positive life events, such as moving home and being promoted at work, may be as stressful as negative ones, such as the break-up of a relationship, if only because of the disruption of social routines that can go with them.

The vast majority of individuals affected by mood swings who have constructed a life chart tell me they have found the exercise invaluable, and that drawing the frequency, severity and duration of episodes is helpful in understanding the nature of the problem. So often, it is while doing this that the links between life events and mood swings or between changes in medication and mood swings, first become apparent. Many individuals have no idea that there is any predictable pattern to their mood shifts until they examine a life chart.

Gabrielle's history may be less complicated than your own, but do not let this deter you from trying to draw your

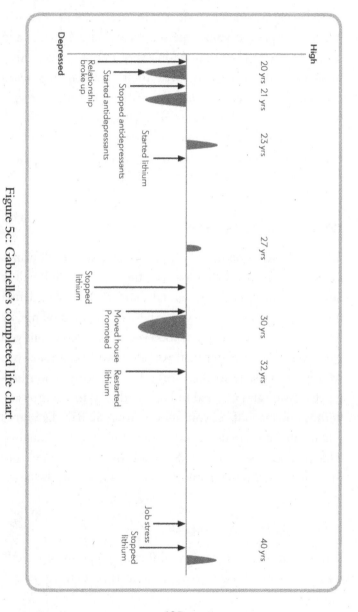

Figure 5c: Gabrielle's completed life chart

High

Depressed

20 yrs 21 yrs 23 yrs 27 yrs 30 yrs 32 yrs 40 yrs

Relationship broke up

Stopped antidepressants

Started antidepressants

Started lithium

Stopped lithium

Moved house Promoted

Restarted lithium

Job stress

Stopped lithium

own life chart. The chart does not have to be perfect; it is meant to represent your experiences in a visual format and does not have to be accurate in every minute detail. Also, many individuals need to revise their charts as they recall additional information about the nature and timing of episodes or recognise links between events and mood swings.

If you find it difficult to get started on your life chart, the following ideas on overcoming some of the common problems encountered may help you.

What is a 'normal state'?

Some individuals do not feel they ever experience a 'normal' mood state. If this is true for you, the reference line will at best represent a relatively neutral state. To help you define this, think of a time before you experienced mood swings, or when you (and the people who know you best) thought you were well or a lot better than you are now. In this state, you were probably able to think more clearly, to function better than you can now, and to cope with day-to-day stressors without major shifts in your mood. You will have had times when you felt more depressed or times when you felt higher. This may not be a perfect definition of 'normal state', but this can be used as the midpoint to help you to start the chart.

When was the first episode?

It is not surprising if you have difficulty pinpointing exactly when your mood swings began. This is particularly true if you have a very long history of a mood disorder. The first contact with the mental health services may come to mind most readily, but it may be hard to recall less severe episodes of depression or contacts with primary care services. If you are having problems here, a simple way forward is to put a question mark next to the first high or low period on your chart to indicate that the date and duration are not certain. Even if some information on the chart is uncertain or incomplete, it is useful to include some representation of each episode.

Also, try to note when you first noticed that things were 'not quite right'. Many individuals recall that they knew 'something was wrong' from an earlier time in their life (e.g., in adolescence), long before their first contact with any health services. Recording this information on a life chart may help in detecting stress factors and identifying successful and unsuccessful techniques you used to cope with mood shifts.

What type of problems did you first notice?

Perhaps you can remember clearly when you first noted that 'something was wrong', but it was not described by you or anyone else as a mood swing. Again, it is better to include this information on your life chart rather than exclude anything that might be relevant. The primary aim is to create a graph that helps *you* understand *your* experiences. Some mood swings may be 'masked' by medical conditions or by the particular coping strategies used. For example, one person had glandular fever at the age of thirteen years. At the time, the 'low' that he experienced was not diagnosed as depression but was viewed as part of the physical disorder. In retrospect, it may be that glandular fever acted as a physical stressor that exposed his vulnerability to developing a mood disorder. Another person was regarded as having an 'alcohol problem' in her late adolescence. In retrospect, both she and her parents realised that she had actually used alcohol to try to alter her mood state.

What about unusual or 'atypical' highs or lows?

Again, the key point is to include information that aids your understanding of what has happened to you. You may need to work on ways to represent mixed states (where you have symptoms of depression and mania at the same time), such as drawing a curve above and below the line in the same place. Likewise, you may want to differentiate euphoric (elated) mania from dysphoric (irritable) mania. A simple way would be to put a letter 'E' or 'D' within the curve representing the high. In the end, you are in the best position to work out a coding system that works for you.

What if you are unable to remember when an episode was or how long it lasted?

While the life chart does not need to be perfect, it does help to have some indication of differences between episodes. The more detail you can give to the description of the pattern, the more readily you may be able to pick out key events or themes in what happens to you. If you find it hard to be specific, you may wish simply to estimate the intensity and duration of an episode in terms of mild, moderate or severe and short, medium or long.

If it is the actual timing of episodes that is causing you difficulties, it may help to add another line of information to your chart. This line is used to record key moments in your personal life (a house move, change of job, birthdays, etc.) or memorable moments that you can date in history, such as your favourite sports team winning the last game of a season or an important social occasion. Using the dates of these key events as guides may help you to place the mood swing as before or after certain events, or at least as occurring between certain dates.

How do you fill in the gaps?

You may find that, despite all your efforts, some information is missing. When a particular episode occurred or which medication you were taking and for how long, can be hard to recall several years later. Before setting out to find all these details, try writing down a list of all the information you know is missing. Next, go through the list and try to assess whether each item of information is really likely to extend your understanding of your problems. The aim is to make the list as short as possible. Be ruthless about this. Cross off anything that is not critical to your understanding. With each item left, write down why this information is so important to you (e.g., what aspect of your problems it might help you to understand). If there is a clear benefit to pursuing the answer, think of any other details you can recall about your life at that time. These may help you pinpoint a possible source of the missing information. For example, it may be that you want to identify the timing of a hypomanic episode because this was the only time you experienced a 'high' and you suspect it occurred shortly after going on antidepressants, but before you had ever tried a mood stabiliser. However, you cannot be certain about this, nor can you identify the sequence of events. Information about where you were living at the time, who you saw about your problems, who prescribed your treatment, and whether you are in contact with the same health services or living in the same place may help. This information can be used to identify someone who might be able to find this information, or a place where such information may be recorded. If you can identify a potential source, you will then need to think about how and when to approach the appropriate person or organisation for this answer. Try to be patient; it may take some time to track down the facts, and sometimes it simply is not possible.

Do not worry if the answer to a particular question is not available. The life chart is initially used to explore the past, but you can continue to use it to describe what happens to you from now on. Knowing what information has been useful in constructing your life chart so far will help you keep an accurate record of similar facts in future.

You may want to approach a person whom you trust and

who knows you well to see if they have any comments on the life chart you have drawn. They may be able to fill some gaps you have identified, or they may put forward a new perspective and bring other important issues to your attention. They may recall life events that preceded mood swings that you have not remembered or recorded, or be able to describe the severity of your last depression more accurately than you can. You may choose to show a family member your life chart, so that both of you can understand what it is like to be you and the types of stress you need to avoid or learn to cope with differently.

The Appendix to this book contains a blank life chart for you to experiment with and this is also downloadable from https://overcoming.co.uk/715/resources-to-download. This is only a guide; you may prefer to use a larger piece of paper or to construct a somewhat different chart that suits your own needs better.

When you have completed your chart, examine it carefully and answer the question: '*What have I learned about my mood swings and about myself from this exercise?*'

If you find it hard to answer that question, you may find the following pointers helpful:

- Do the frequency and type of mood swings suggest that you have a mood disorder? If so, what is the nature of that disorder?
- Is there any pattern to your mood swings? For example, do they occur at particular times of year, or following certain types of experience or activities?

- Are there any links between events in your life and the occurrence of mood swings? If so, are there any common themes to the life events?
- If you are taking medication for your mood swings, are there any links between changes in your medication and mood swings? Or between stopping medication and your mood swings?
- Over recent episodes, is there any change in the frequency or severity of your mood swings? If so, how have they changed? Are there any longer-term changes in your situation or activities that may have had any impact on this pattern?
- Which episode on the life chart was the least disruptive or had the least impact on your life? Which was the most disruptive or had the greatest impact? What was different about those episodes that made you select them?

The answers to these questions may help you gain a greater awareness of the factors that affect your mood state. You may already understand these issues well, but a life chart can still be very useful in drawing this information together and in communicating to others the key aspects of your own experiences.

Identifying your symptom profile

A common problem for individuals who experience mood swings is that they are not always certain whether they are experiencing a temporary shift in how they feel or whether they are at the start of a 'high' or a 'low' swing. It is important to be able to distinguish between normal reactions and extreme or unhelpful emotional reactions. Without this knowledge, it is difficult to feel any sense of control over your situation or to be confident about when to use self-management approaches.

To decide whether a mood change is the forerunner of a significant emotional shift (into an episode of mood disorder) requires some detective work. First, we need to know how many different types of mood swings you experience, e.g., depression, euphoric mania, dysphoric mania, hypomania, mixed states, etc. If you review your life chart, you should be able to identify the nature of your different swings. The next stage is to take a separate sheet of paper for each type of mood swing. Then, for each type of mood swing, try to recall and write down the symptoms you experience. These will include the feelings, thoughts, behaviours and alterations in your day-to-day functioning that you experience, along with any changes in your physical state.

If you are struggling to get started, try to answer the following questions:

- How does your life change when you are 'high' or when you are depressed?
- How do your views of yourself, other people, the world and your future change when you are 'high' or when you are depressed?
- What do other people notice about you during these episodes?

Do not worry if some features occur on more than one symptom list; this is surprisingly common. For example, some people feel irritable when they are high or low. The main thing is to try to develop as complete a picture as possible. If you find it difficult to remember some details, try to recall the symptoms from your most recent episodes, or explore other sources of information. You may wish to discuss what you are doing with a person you trust, as they may be able to help you to develop the list. You can also read through information given in the earlier part of this book or scan other materials that describe the common symptoms of mood swings. However, ensure you include on your list only those features that *apply to you*.

Some individuals prefer to write each symptom in a more personal way than the descriptions you read in books. For example, rather than writing 'irritability' you may wish to write: 'I am easily annoyed or irritated, particularly in interactions with family members.'

Finally, revise your list to ensure that it focuses on the features that occur *regularly* when you go high or low. It may help to rewrite the list with 'my common symptoms' listed at the top of the page and 'my less common symptoms' at the bottom of the page. On reviewing the list, is it possible for you to say which symptoms occur at an early stage and which come later in an episode? Put a star against any symptoms that are the 'early warning symptoms' that your mood swing is getting under way. We will explore these symptoms in more detail at a later stage.

Table 2: Symptom profile

Highs *Elated and irritable*	Depression *Very depressed and anxious*
My common symptoms are: 1. Increased energy★ 2. Disinhibited★ 3. Increased spending 4. Reduced need for sleep★ 5. Easily distracted 6. Very sociable	My common symptoms are: 1. Indecisiveness and procrastination★ 2. Feeling slowed down 3. Loss of appetite and weight★ 4. Social withdrawal★ 5. Poor sleep with early wakening★ 6. Lack of energy, feeling lethargic
My less common symptoms are: 1. Intense optimism 2. Increased punning and rhyming 3. Aggressiveness 4. Risk-taking	My less common symptoms are: 1. Pessimism about the future 2. Agitation about minor things when I talk 3. Feelings of guilt and worthlessness 4. Thoughts of death
★Early warning symptoms	

To help you construct your list I have included an example of a 'symptom profile' in Table 2. A blank copy is also included in the Appendix (see p.370) and can be printed or downloaded from https://overcoming.co.uk/715/resources-to-download.

It is particularly important to consult this list whenever you are unsure whether your emotional state has shifted into a mood swing. Rather than ignoring any changes in how you feel, or convincing yourself that nothing is wrong, you can review your symptom profile sheet and check whether what you are experiencing now mirrors information you have already recorded. This can help you reach an accurate conclusion about whether you are developing an episode of depression or a high. It can also be used to help resolve any disagreements with, say, a partner or a member of your family about whether you are okay or not. This information will also be useful when you are developing your self-monitoring and self-management skills.

Developing a risk list

The aim of a 'risk list' is to make you aware of the factors that may trigger your mood swings. If you review the events, experiences or behaviours that occurred in the months leading up to an episode of mood disorder, you may be able to identify common themes; or you may notice that similar stressors precede the onset of your highs as compared with your low periods. Again, do not worry if you have not yet been able to identify these triggers; remember that from now on you can start to note key events or activities on your life chart, so that in the future when you look back at it you will more easily be able to see potential links.

If you have noted some key issues in the months preceding some or all or your episodes of mood disorder, try now to list them under three headings:

- life events
- life situations
- personal actions.

Now go back to your life chart and check if any similar events, situations or responses, occurred at other times. Don't forget to include on your list major life events that can happen to anyone. Even events or situations that seem to be inevitable consequences of everyone's life cycle (e.g., leaving school or college, changing jobs) may still have relevance to your mood swings.

We are now going to use this list to try to determine what events, situations and activities put you at high risk of an episode of mood disorder. Later in this book we will explore ways to manage these risk factors.

Having identified a possible list of high-risk events, situations and activities, the next step is to see whether any patterns exist within each of these three categories.

- High-risk events often have a specific personal meaning because of an individual's underlying beliefs, or are important because they disrupt a person's sleep–wake cycle (as described in Part One, these are often social rhythm disrupting events).
- High-risk situations may be positive, such as

OVERCOMING MOOD SWINGS

anniversaries and parties, holidays and vacations, or negative, such as ongoing pressures at home or at work. We may not always know if these specific situations have activated some of your key underlying beliefs or led to a disruption in your social rhythms (e.g., staying up late for a party or changing your daily routines because you are on vacation). However, you may be able to identify recurring types of situation, such as 'extended periods of time away from home' or 'family celebrations', which could be the basis for a pattern.

- High-risk activities are often the most difficult for individuals to identify, as to start with you may hardly be aware of their influence on your mood swings. Typical examples are consuming alcohol or using illicit drugs; excessive intake of caffeine or other stimulants; or suddenly stopping prescribed medication. It is important to ensure that any high-risk activities that you record occurred *before* the start of an episode and were not symptoms of the episode itself.

To help you construct a risk list I have included an example (see Box 1) using the information in Gabrielle's history that we examined at the beginning of this chapter.

Identifying high-risk factors

Here are some additional tips if identifying high-risk factors is proving difficult.

WHAT DO I DO IF I DON'T SEEM TO HAVE ANY HIGH-RISK FACTORS?

There are two main reasons why you might not be able to list any high-risk factors. The first is that you have not yet identified the factors that were important in the past. This is very common: after all, at that time you did not have any reason to attend to such information. Research has only recently shown that events that disrupt your social rhythms may be important. However, you can start to learn more about your risk factors in the future through careful self-monitoring of events or changes in your activities and behaviour.

Second, you may be very sensitive to minor changes in your stress level. The term 'sensitive' is not meant to suggest any personal flaw; it can refer to brain activity, as discussed in the section of Chapter 3 on vulnerability factors. If you experience frequent mood swings, it may be that these are triggered by many small changes in your life circumstances or your behaviour rather than by fewer, more memorable, big events. Individuals who have frequent mood swings, without all the other symptoms of a mood disorder, often describe this pattern of fluctuations. As described later, in the section on 'unhelpful thoughts' in Chapter 9, monitoring shifts in your mood in response to day-to-day events and activities will probably help you determine if this is why you cannot identify any specific high-risk factors.

BOX 1   GABRIELLE'S RISK LIST

Risk factors

1   High-risk activities
    Not taking prescribed lithium

2   High-risk situations
    Ongoing job stress
    Getting promoted

3   High-risk events
    Moving house (social rhythm disruption)
    Relationship breakdown (specific personal
       meaning)
    Getting promoted (fits here also: is this related
       to worrying about expectations?)

Other important information

e.g. High-risk combinations
      Multiple major life events (moved house and
         got promoted)

e.g. Protective factors
      Not sure at the moment

HOW CAN I DETERMINE IF AN EVENT HAS A SPECIFIC PERSONAL MEANING?

To some of you, this question will seem foolish. The personal meaning and importance of certain life events may appear to be obvious. However, if we are to develop a list of events that will be used to alert you to the potential development of a mood swing, we need to know in detail why each event that you note was important to you. This will ensure that you don't only monitor repeated exposures to the same event, but that you are able to spot events that have a similar meaning and impact.

Chapter 5 on the cognitive behavioural model of mood disorders described the development of underlying beliefs and the influence of these 'silent rules' on our day-to-day lives. If you were able to identify some of your own rules as suggested in that chapter (by completing the sentences: 'I am . . . ,' 'People are . . . ,' 'The world is . . . '), you can now use these to ask yourself if one or more of the events linked to the onset of your mood swings was related to these beliefs. An example is given below.

Greg grew up with the belief that 'The world is not fair'. He became particularly upset when a reorganisation at work meant he had to move to a different office away from other managers of similar status to him. One of Greg's colleagues admitted to being mildly irritated by having to move, but seemed to adapt quickly. However, Greg became increasingly upset. His mind was full of thoughts that he had been 'picked on'. In the end he became so sad that his boss went to see him. His senior was stunned to find out the cause of Greg's low mood; he explained that he had given Greg the nicest office on the floor as a reward for his hard work.

If no relationship between the events and your beliefs is obvious, you may wish to try the following experiment. Write the event down at the top of a piece of paper and then try to imagine that it has just happened. What goes through your mind? Can you capture your automatic thought and write it down? Be as specific as you can. The next step is to ask yourself this question: 'And if that were true, what would that mean or say about me?' (If the thought relates to other people or to your world, simply replace the words 'about me' in the question with 'about other people' or 'about the world'.) Write down the next thought that comes to mind and then repeat this exercise, writing down the thought at each stage. Repeating the question three to four times usually brings you to the 'bottom line' which often represents your 'silent rule'. To show you an example of this 'downward arrow' approach, I have borrowed an idea from cognitive therapist Melanie Fennell (see Box 2 and her book). I particularly like her example because it explores the beliefs of a therapist. In this instance I have adapted her idea and applied it to myself!

If this approach does not allow you to tap into your underlying beliefs or to be specific about why the event has been important to you, it is still useful to include the event on your list as well as monitoring similar types of events. You can also return to this topic at a later stage, after you have explored how the themes in your day-to-day automatic thoughts may also reveal clues about your underlying beliefs.

BOX 2   DOWNWARD ARROW TECHNIQUE

Event: Just re-read notes of a book chapter I've written on self-help

Emotion: Anxious

Thought: That's terrible, no one will understand this, I've been no help at all

Questions to get to the meaning:

Supposing that was true, what would it mean to me?
↓
That people reading it won't benefit
↓
And supposing they didn't, what would that mean to me?
↓
That I had done a bad job
↓
And supposing I had, what would that mean to me?
↓
That I was a lousy writer
↓
Supposing I was a lousy writer, what then?
↓
Sooner or later I'll be found out
↓
And what does that mean to me, being 'found out'?
↓
It means that:
Everyone would know I was no good and despise the fact that I had this chapter published
and
My previous successes didn't really reflect my ability, they were pure luck

My silent rule: To think well of myself I have to succeed at everything I try

WHAT IF THE RISK FACTORS SEEM TO FIT INTO MORE THAN ONE CATEGORY?

You may have identified a list of events, situations and behaviours but have difficulty in putting these into the different categories. Do not be too concerned about this. If in doubt, you can include a factor in more than one box. For example, you go away for a long vacation (situation); when away you change your daily routines (social rhythm disrupting event); and on some evenings you drink more alcohol than you do normally (behaviour). Six weeks after your vacation, you experience a 'high'. You also know that travelling by plane to your holiday destination and drinking alcohol may both disrupt your circadian rhythms. Rather than trying to guess which high-risk category to put the information in, it is quite acceptable to include all of these factors on your risk list. For example:

- *events:* long-distance air travel, disruptions to daily routines;
- *situations:* being away from home for long periods;
- *behaviour:* staying up very late at night, drinking alcohol late at night.

HOW CAN THESE BE HIGH-RISK FACTORS IF THEY HAVE ALSO OCCURRED AT OTHER TIMES WHEN I HAVE NOT HAD AN EPISODE OF MOOD DISORDER?

Sometimes, you may be unsure whether to include an event on your risk list if it is not always associated with the onset of an episode of mood disorder. In general, it is better to include rather than exclude items; you can always put a question mark against them to show that you are uncertain about their importance. The aim of the risk is to alert you to occasions when you need to increase your self-monitoring to determine whether any early warning symptoms develop.

Alternatively, you might wish to consider whether any other (protective) factors were operating that reduced your risk of developing a mood swing despite the presence of a high-risk factor. For example, were you protected from developing an episode of mood disorder on one occasion because you were taking a mood stabiliser regularly, or because you had someone in your life who acted as a confidante and supporter? If this was the case, you could add another category, entitled 'potential protective factors', to your list.

Using information you recorded on your life chart, symptom profile and risk list, you can now check whether there are any differences in the types of high-risk factors that precede different types of mood swings. If you had difficulty completing the cognitive behavioural cycle (described in Part One), you may also wish to make another attempt now, using factors identified on your risk list and your notes on early warning symptoms for your mood swings.

The Appendix of this book contains two blank versions of a risk list for you to complete (see p.371–2), also printable from the website https://overcoming.co.uk/715/resources-to-download. As well as space for you to list the different high-risk factors you identify, there is an additional space for you to note other information that is important to you that does not fit neatly into the categories outlined. Some individuals prefer the second version of the list as it can be used to identify factors associated with different types of mood swings.

Even if you cannot identify high-risk factors, you may be aware of the early warning symptoms that mean you are in danger of developing an episode of mood disorder. Through practice, you may be able to detect these symptoms quickly enough to take action to avoid an intense mood swing. Furthermore, any links between events, situations or behaviour and subsequent mood swings may then become apparent.

Key information you need to become an expert

Research suggests that when an individual experiences a health problem, no matter what type it is, they tend (without realising it) to organise their thoughts about the problem according to five key themes. These are:

- *Identity:* What is the name given to my problem?
- *Cause:* What is known about the causes?
- *Timeline:* How long will this problem last? Will it recur?
- *Consequences:* What is the impact of the problem on my life?
- *Control:* How can my problem be controlled?

So far, we have examined the nature and history of your problems (*identity* and *timeline*). We have also reviewed the high-risk factors that may increase the likelihood of your experiencing a mood swing (*causes*). However, we have not reviewed in detail the impact on your life of having mood swings (*consequences*) and we have only just begun to explore the effects on your mood swings, if any, of taking medication or engaging with other interventions (*control*). Part One of this book included a brief review of the evidence for the effectiveness of psychological treatments (*control*), but we have not yet examined how you may implement or benefit from these approaches. Before moving on to use the self-monitoring and self-management techniques, it is important to ensure that you are confident of the *facts* about your own situation.

Gathering evidence to support your ideas about each of these five areas is not recommended simply because it will give you a detailed understanding of your problems (although this is very valuable). It is also important because of the influence of cognition on behaviour and vice versa, as discussed in Part One. A person's view of their health problem will influence how they handle that problem. Misconceptions may lead to the use of inappropriate coping strategies. For example, a person who thinks that their mood disorder will 'burn itself out' may avoid reading information that suggests this is not the case and reject medication prescribed to prevent a recurrence. A person's underlying beliefs will also influence how they view their mood swings. An individual who believes that 'I am weak' may take to the view that their mood disorder is caused by personal inadequacy rather than by the interaction between stress and a biological vulnerability.

To become a real expert on your mood swings you may need to challenge some of your own assumptions about your problems. To complete your own understanding, you may find it helpful to work through the following questions:

Identity

CAN YOU RECORD THE NAME GIVEN TO YOUR MOOD SWINGS (E.G., BIPOLAR I DISORDER)?

Reviewing the information from your life chart and symptom profile may help you do this. If you have noted a name, can you rate on a scale of 0 to 100 how confident you are that this 'self-diagnosis' is correct? If your rating is 60 or below, can you identify what the gaps are in your knowledge that are causing you concern? It may be that you can overcome these concerns by gathering additional evidence from the descriptions of mood swings in this and other books and/or by going over any information given to you by health professionals. If you need further information to come to a decision, when and where will you seek this information? (The more specific you can be about the date and the place the better.)

Cause

WHAT DO YOU KNOW ABOUT THE CAUSES OF YOUR MOOD SWINGS?

Vulnerability factors (such as a family history) that may apply to you are described in Chapter 3 of this book. Your risk list also identifies factors that increase the likelihood of your developing a mood swing. If you do not have information about stress or vulnerability factors, when and where will you gather information to help you understand the causes of your mood swings?

Timeline

DO YOU KNOW HOW LONG YOUR MOOD SWINGS LAST AND WHEN THEY WILL OCCUR?

Again, you may be able to answer this question using your life chart, the early warning symptoms listed in your symptom profile and your risk list. You may also wish to review the information given earlier in this book (Chapter 2) on the average duration of manic and depressive episodes and the likelihood of recurrence of a mood disorder. Can you estimate your own risk of a further mood swing? What evidence do you have for or against that prediction? If this question is difficult to answer, it may be worthwhile setting yourself a target about when and where you will seek further information.

Consequences

WHAT HAS BEEN THE IMPACT OF MOOD SWINGS ON YOUR LIFE?

To assess the impact of mood swings on your life you may wish to consider the following:

- *How has your day-to-day functioning changed?* This may include your ability to work, your ability to care for yourself or the effect on your life of persistent symptoms such as lack of energy.

- *What adverse effects have there been on your inter-personal relationships?* This may include tensions in any current relationships with family or friends, or unresolved issues relating to previous mood swings.
- *What adverse effects have there been on your view of yourself?* This may include lowered self-esteem or feelings of shame and guilt.

You may have noted some of this information when you reviewed what you learned from constructing your life chart. If it is difficult to answer the questions, you could ask another person if they have evidence of any negative consequences of your mood swings. You can then gather information to support or refute the views put forward. Alternatively, you could ask other individuals with mood swings about their experiences, or read personal, textbook or internet blog accounts of the consequences of having mood swings. You can then assess how many of the experiences described also apply to you and make a rating of the impact each item has on your life. It is important to make a realistic judgement as to whether every problem you can think of was a consequence of having mood swings, or whether some difficulties might have arisen in your life even if you did not have a history of mood swings.

Control

HOW CAN YOUR MOOD SWINGS BE CONTROLLED?

It is very important to seek out reliable sources of evidence when answering this question. Much of what is written on the treatment of mood swings represents opinion rather than scientific fact. Also, this is an issue where your beliefs and attitudes are very likely to have influenced your selection of the information to which you have given most attention. We will return to this topic in a moment and also in the chapter that explores any barriers you experience to taking medication. However, just to emphasise, this book takes a scientific approach to the question of control by asking you to experiment with a number of techniques that may help you manage your mood swings.

In summary, gathering evidence on five key aspects of your problem will give you a balanced understanding of your mood swings. Whilst finding this evidence will improve your ability to distinguish ideas and hearsay from *facts,* it is very obvious to everyone that the internet is awash with an over-abundance of information and misinformation (the so-called *infodemic*). So, it is useful to briefly discuss techniques to help you decide if information you come across represents reliable evidence or if it represents misinformation or 'fake news'.

Navigating the health infodemic

The internet has revolutionised the availability of all types of information, so it is unsurprising that individuals with mood swings increasingly source health information via online forums, websites or social networks. However, the benefits of such easy access to a wide range of ideas must be balanced against the risks of being misled by poor quality or unreliable advice. The major cause for concern about online communications is that there is only limited filtering or vetting of statements, so that myths are likely to spread just as rapidly as facts. Furthermore, scientific studies have shown that people don't assess the accuracy of an electronic or online message before sharing it! So, one thing I would encourage is that you make a promise to yourself that, before you forward messages or documents of any sort, you will take a few moments to pause, reflect and consider the source of this news. This simple process (called cognitive reflection) has been shown both to reduce the risk of spreading misinformation and to increase the likelihood that you will select and share accurate information.

One way to help individuals to cope with the health infodemic is to empower them to discriminate facts and myths. You may think this is unnecessary and that people can spot misleading ideas easily. Whilst some extreme statements very obviously represent misinformation and urban myths can usually be identified, more subtle forms of misleading ideas or misinformation are accepted as true on first reading. Also, if you are preoccupied by other things when you are reading online statements (i.e., you are multi-tasking or distracted), you may miss the clues that clearly mark the story out as misinformation. The worst thing about this situation is that the misinformation is likely to get stored into your memory bank unchallenged (and indeed may be stored with other memories that contain accurate information).

A novel way to help people to be more questioning about what they read online and in social media postings is to practise spotting misleading information by playing free-to-access online games designed to help people develop these specific skills. Many of these exist, such as Harmony Square (a game about fake news) and some of these games are specifically targeted at health-related topics. For example, Go Viral (https://www.goviralgame.com/en) is a game which offers a gentle and entertaining introduction to developing your skills for spotting misleading statements about coronavirus (COVID-19).

These games might help you develop your antennae for spotting erroneous information in general and help you sharpen your skills in evaluating evidence or spotting fake news. This will mean you are better equipped to start to review online material that is more important to you personally, such as information about bipolar disorders. The basic principles of going through online or social media statements about health can be organised into a checklist that involves the following steps: reviewing the credibility of the source (including reviewing the 'uniform resource locator' or URL, i.e., the global address of the website or document), fact-checking (including visiting websites dedicated to this purpose), finding out if the myth/story is reported by multiple trusted mainstream sources, considering the motivation of the source of this story (and asking who benefits from promoting those views), through to checking research references and the accuracy of original source materials.

The checklist helps you to take a filtering, vetting and verifying approach. This may well have long-term benefits, but it is heavily reliant on your desire to examine the reliability of information in an objective way. From the perspective of health information, it is helpful to consider in more detail how you might examine the source of information about bipolar disorder and how you might consider the quality of any information you access. So, the key questions are:

'Did you find the information yourself (e.g., via an online search)?' or

'Who shared the information with you and where did they get it from?'

Most people who search for health information online start by putting a few key words into a search engine and then go through the top ranked items that appear on the first page of the web search. Unfortunately, this does not guarantee that you have identified reliable fact sheets. To help people to identify more reliable websites, the World Health Organization, working alongside European health organisations, has produced a website called Health on the Net (HoN). This allows people to do searches about bipolar disorders that only identify sites that have high levels of credibility (which is defined by the trustworthiness of the source and the expertise of the contributors). Alternatively, when you do a web search you can check if the website has a HoN certificate. Another option is to use the NHS website in the UK or, e.g., the Medline Plus website (this is a website offering information for the general public that was developed by the national health institute in the USA).

Another way to consider the credibility of the source of any information you have found online is to check the URL. For example, if the ending letters of the URL say something like 'ac.uk' or 'edu', it often means the source of a document is a university or an academic research website. This does not prove reliability, but it is worth bearing in mind that nearly all academic institutions or national research organisations (the URL might include 'gov') can only put health information on a website after it has been carefully reviewed by independent experts. For other websites, you can check the 'About Us' and 'Contact Us' pages to look for background information about an organisation and make sure they have legitimate contact details. The latter may be useful if you want to follow up on any particular advice that was offered or want to question an aspect of the information. Clues that a source may be less reliable or that information may be inaccurate include unprofessional visual designs of documents or webpages, poor spelling and grammar or excessive use of all capitals or exclamation points. The latter may help to alert you to more emotive postings and may be a sign that someone holds a belief very strongly. However, even if a posting hints at intense emotions (in the writer), it is important to remember that this does not mean the posting is accurate; indeed such postings should probably be treated with a degree of caution.

Having completed this task, you can consider the likely reliability of different sources of information in rank order. The list produced here is only an approximate guide, but it may help you in your efforts to become an expert about your problems. The first level described represents the highest-quality information, whilst the items further down the list are probably less accurate (and need more checking):

- *Systematic reviews* published in evidence-based medical journals or in electronic form (e.g., the Cochrane Database). A systematic review draws together key information from lots of research studies. It excludes studies that were poorly designed or flawed, and then carefully assesses the outcomes for all the people who entered the studies. It will, for example, search out all the high-quality treatment studies for a particular disorder and then work out how well people do with or without each treatment. These are relatively new, so not every treatment for mood disorders has been reviewed yet.
- *High-quality, large-scale multicentre research studies* published in mainstream medical or psychiatric journals. These studies usually conform to the highest standards in research design, with independent ratings of an individual's improvement and subjects allocated to the treatment groups by a special procedure called 'randomisation' (like tossing a coin).
- *Textbooks, leaflets* from established self-help organisations and the *doctors, clinicians and professionals* who

have read this information. These sources of information are usually sound, but textbooks may be slightly out of date. Research moves on quickly, so by the time the textbook is prepared, published and read, the evidence may be slightly different.

- *Smaller-scale, randomised trials or research studies reporting on a series of people or a single 'case example'.* This information is often 'hot off the press'; it may indicate new treatments that will come on to the market, or what the next line of research will be into the causes of a disorder.

- *General review articles, information or statements by people with some experience of living or working with a disorder or problem.* These sources of information are often more accessible to individuals with mood disorders than other sources of data. However, they are open to bias and tend to be less evidence-based.

- *Articles and reports in the news media.* Unfortunately, media reports are strongly influenced by the individual writing the article or making the film. They may put a particular 'spin' on the information they present to make the report interesting or eye-catching. This can introduce biases or distortions.

- *Unattributed comments, remarks by friends of friends, 'favourite sayings' of family members or anecdotes.* These views may not be wrong, but there is no reason for believing that they are right, either.

- *'I just know!'* This is an idea that originates from you (i.e. you are the source). Alas, this is not an evidence-based answer. How do you know? What evidence do you have that makes this idea a fact?

It may not be feasible to try to acquire copies of systematic reviews or research reports; and even if you can get hold of them, many scientific publications may be full of jargon that you aren't familiar with and so they can be quite heavy going. However, if you do decide to look at some of these reports, there are a few additional things to consider. For example, it is useful to check if the article is described as 'in press' or if it has been made available by the researchers before it has been submitted to a science journal or read and checked by other expert scientists (a procedure called peer review). This is worth checking because some articles may be retracted after review by other scientists (because the other experts spot problems with the original study or the journal decided that the interpretation of the results that are reported was not clear or accurate enough). Likewise, always bear in mind that publications represent the best evidence available at the time (sometimes called BETs). This may be very important if you are trying to do your own search of publications. Sometimes the reports that are easiest to access free of charge are much older documents. So, do beware of this, as you don't want to invest all your hopes in articles that were published several years ago. Whilst they may represent the BETs in the 1980s, it is possible that those scientific ideas are now out of date.

Overall, to get useful summaries of the current consensus on key topics about bipolar disorder, you will probably find that recently published editions of textbooks and books dedicated to discussing mood swings or leaflets and information from self-help and other organisations will be most helpful and the information is a bit easier to digest. Doctors, professionals and others with access to up-to-date information may also be able to answer your questions about issues of concern to you, or to help you if you do not understand some of the items you have read.

The final step in helping you manage information and misinformation about your mood swings is to reduce the risk that you are inadvertently a source of inaccurate statements or ideas! Research suggests that sharing or passing on health and other information and messages can be modified by enacting 'information hygiene'. This means that when you view online materials or social messages that include ideas related to your health, you should ask yourself the following questions:

1. How does this make me feel?
2. Why am I thinking of sharing this?
3. How do I know if it's true?
4. Where did it come from?
5. Am I supporting someone else's cause or agenda by sharing it (and am I happy with that)?

As a simple 'rule of thumb', if you know something is false or if what you read makes you angry, then it probably makes sense not to share it (sociologists and experts in 'infodemiology' often suggest that fake news is spread because it generates more extreme emotional reactions). From the point of view of this self-help guide, I would encourage you to spend time reflecting on how information (from any source) fits with your own model of your problems and try to disentangle which bits you agree with or don't agree with, and how this links to your emotional response. This is a more useful approach compared with automatically sending the item to someone else when you are in a heightened emotional state. Also, even if you are in a settled mood state, be selective about sharing messages, emails or website addresses that include misleading information. Even if you know they report misinformation and your intention is to make fun of it, there is a risk that someone else who receives a forwarded message (from you or from someone else in the chain of those who received the forwarded message) might not realise it was inaccurate or unreliable.

CHAPTER SUMMARY

Becoming an expert on the facts about your mood swings will enable you to make informed decisions about how to manage your problems.

Becoming an expert on your mood swings involves five key steps:

- Developing a detailed understanding of your past experiences by constructing a *life chart;*

- Developing a detailed knowledge of your experiences of different mood swings by composing a *symptom profile;*
- Developing a detailed knowledge of factors that may precipitate your mood swings, particularly noting on your *risk list* information about:
  - high-risk events;
  - high-risk situations;
  - high-risk behaviours.

- Gathering evidence that allows you to answer five key questions:
  - *identity:* What is the name given to your experiences?
  - *cause:* What is known about the causes of your mood swings?
  - *timeline:* When might episodes occur?
  - *consequences:* What has been the impact of mood swings your life?
  - *control:* How can your mood swings be controlled?

- Developing skills to differentiate information from misinformation will help you identify and assess the reliability of online reports about bipolar disorder and its treatment.

7

Self-monitoring and self-regulation

The previous chapter explored some of the details of mood swings that have caused you problems in the past and the factors that may trigger these episodes. If you are to prevent major mood swings in the future, you will need to be able to apply that knowledge. You will also need to be able to identify any shifts in your mood, behaviour and thinking from one day to the next and be able to judge if these are normal or abnormal. This chapter begins equipping you to do this by examining methods to monitor your moods and activities, and then exploring some basic self-regulation techniques that may help stabilise your day-to-day mood state and functioning and reduce the risk of minor changes spiralling out of your control.

Monitoring your moods

We all experience fluctuations in our emotions, and it is not unusual for one's mood to change several times over the course of a single day. However, if you experience mood swings or a mood disorder these emotional shifts need to be closely monitored, for two reasons: first, to understand better the events and thoughts that precipitate mood changes; second, to learn to distinguish between mood shifts that may be the forerunner of a major mood swing or an episode of mood disorder, and those that are within normal limits. Knowing how to identify the latter is particularly important. Individuals with mood swings need to feel confident that they can experience a normal range of emotions without fearing that they are about to be plunged into a problematic episode. Furthermore, they need to be able to communicate the differences between their normal and abnormal moods to others. It is quite common for the friends and family of someone with a mood disorder to worry unnecessarily and express concern about the person's mental state every time the individual appears to be cheerful. A shared understanding of the difference between normal and abnormal mood shifts can help avoid or at least reduce tensions within these relationships.

A weekly mood chart is a useful tool that allows mood shifts to be identified and monitored on a daily basis. Once you feel comfortable with the process it may help to keep a monthly chart, as this will mean you can quickly review your progress over extended periods of time. The approach has some similarities to that used to construct a life chart, but the information is collected as you go, on a day-to-day basis, so tapping into much more subtle shifts in how you feel.

As with a life chart, a mood graph starts with a horizontal line across the middle of the page, which represents your normal mood state (sometimes called euthymia). In order to build your personalised mood graph, there are a number of key questions to be answered:

- Which moods need to be monitored, and what rating scale should be used to measure shifts in these moods?
- What are the boundaries of normal and abnormal changes in mood, and are there any associated changes in thoughts and behaviour (particularly sleep pattern)?
- What events or experiences precipitate the mood change?
- At what point in any mood shift do you need to intervene; i.e., can you identify your 'action points'?

Mood ratings

Before launching into a regular routine of rating your moods, it is important to decide which mood swings cause you most difficulties and need to be monitored. For some individuals this is an easy decision: they experience highs and lows that disrupt their life. However, as mentioned earlier in this book, others experience mixed states or dysphoric mania. In these states they are not elated but may report feeling unhappy or irritable at the same time as being overactive. So, they may wish to monitor depressions and episodes of being 'hyper'. The critical issue is to decide which mood states *you* need to monitor and to be clear how *you* define each of these moods. A key test of the definition is: Can you describe this mood state to someone else in a way they can understand?

Ideally you should aim to focus on only two or three key moods. Monitoring more than this is difficult simply because of the amount of self-monitoring you would need to undertake. If you feel the need to consider more mood states, it may help to list these different mood states in a notebook and to start by monitoring the two or three moods that are currently causing you most difficulty. After a few weeks, if it is helpful, you could then choose to monitor some of the other mood states on your list. As for how often you need to record a rating, some individuals find that their mood varies so much over the course of the day that it is helpful to re-rate their mood on two or three occasions over each 24-hour period. A morning, afternoon and/or evening rating may help you to detect changes in your moods.

Assuming that you have identified two key moods to monitor, we now need to construct a scale that best represents the range of variability in each mood state. If you are monitoring lows and highs, you may choose to have a 0 to 10 scale, where $0 =$ most depressed and $10 =$ the highest you've been. A normal mood state or euthymia would be represented by a score of about 5. However, some individuals (for example, those who experience mixed states) prefer to represent lows on a scale of 0 to -10 (where $0 =$ euthymia and $-10 =$ severe depression) and highs on a 0 to $+10$ scale ($0 =$ euthymia and $+10 =$ mania). The diagrams shown in this book use this latter approach (see Figure 6), but it really does come down to personal preference.

The next step is to define the 'anchor points' on the scale. Anchor points are defined points on the mood rating scale which describe how you are acting and reacting when you record a particular score. This is crucial as it will help you start to decide when your mood shifts from a normal to an abnormal state. A range of +2 to –2 could represent your normal day-to-day fluctuations, with scores beyond this range representing greater degrees of disturbance. To define the different points on the scale, you may wish to go back to your symptom checklist and see which symptoms occur commonly when you have a mild, moderate or severe mood swing. By the end of this exercise, you should be able to answer the questions: 'If you rated yourself as +6 how would you be in your mood? What activities or behaviour would you engage in?' or: 'If you rated yourself as –8 how would you be in your mood? What activities would you engage in?'

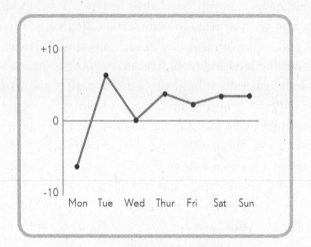

Figure 6: An example of a mood chart

If this exercise seems hard, you may find that you can develop a clearer picture of the anchor points after a few weeks or months of monitoring the variability in your own moods. In the interim, you may find it helpful to use the list I have provided in Box 3. You can adapt all or part of this list to describe your own situation and experiences.

Boundaries between normal and abnormal states

If you have begun to define the 'anchor points' on your mood graph, you may be able to decide quite quickly where the boundary lies between normal and abnormal reactions. However, it is best not to rely simply on your mood as the measure of 'highs'. This is because research shows that when an individual is going into a 'high' they generally do not attribute their positive feelings to the onset of problems. Almost invariably, it is only in retrospect that the individual realises that their mood shift was not a sign of well-being but a warning that they were about to lose control.

For this reason, it is especially important to include additional information to describe the boundaries between normal happiness and a 'high'. Again, for this exercise you will need to review your symptom checklist and possibly your life chart too. The important thing is to discover what changes in you accompany an upswing that ultimately progresses to a high. You may also wish to talk to someone you trust and who knows you well, as the two of you may then be able to gather the information that will help with this rating. If you are going to seek help, remember to try to listen to what the other person says to you without viewing their comments as a personal attack. You are discussing the symptoms that occur when you start to go high; they are not criticising you as a person, simply trying, with you, to construct an accurate picture of your mood swings.

Individuals who have used mood monitoring have also told me that it can be helpful to use the space at the bottom of the mood chart to note any other symptoms that they know can be associated with their highs or lows. For example, one person knew that when she was going high as compared to simply being happy, she would start to become increasingly preoccupied by religious ideas and her relationship with God. She decided that she would note this on her mood chart, as it helped her to distinguish normal from abnormal moods. Other individuals have suggested recording how many hours they sleep at night as sleep disturbance is often an early warning sign of problems to come. Both these options are valid and in Figure 7 I have shown what a mood graph would look like with this and other information added. However, if you find this diagram too complicated and not very 'user friendly', start by keeping a simple chart that is helpful to you. The crucial point is to tailor the mood chart to ensure it includes the information that *you* need at your fingertips. Simply getting into the habit of monitoring your mood state is an important first step. You can always develop a more complex version at a later stage.

BOX 3   ANCHOR POINTS

Mood Rating	Key characteristics
+10	Totally out of control, psychotic symptoms such as delusions that I rule the world
+8	Out of touch, not sleeping at all, taking major risks e.g. flying lessons
+6	Very overconfident, drinking excess amounts of alcohol, staying up late, not eating much, very impulsive e.g. buying items I don't need
+4	Very irritable, easily get angry if people try to stop me doing things
+2	Increased energy, don't need as much sleep, becoming disinhibited, arranging lots of social activities
0	Mood in balance, regular 7 hrs sleep, eating three meals a day, contented, good balance of pleasurable activities and tasks
−2	Rather flat mood, start to withdraw from people, sleep a bit erratic
−4	Reduced appetite, start to lose weight, concentration very poor
−6	Anxious, starting to avoid everyone and everything, feeling guilty about things I've done in the past
−8	Thought of suicide, keep seeing images of my funeral, not eating, virtually no sleep
−10	Very slowed down, can hardly move around, not talking to anyone

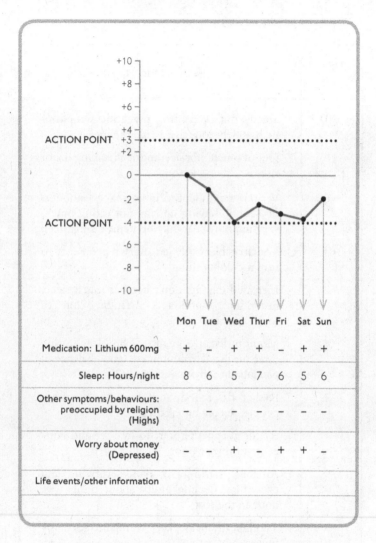

Figure 7: Mood graph including additional information

The final point in constructing a mood chart is to make sure that the anchor points are spread out evenly. There must not be a sudden leap from normal to abnormal. It is more helpful to see each point on the mood scale as part of a continuum, representing a gradual change from the point before. This means that you can then identify in advance what is likely to happen next if you do not take action (see Box 3). The reason I suggest defining 'anchor points' carefully is because I have been caught out using this system in the past. I once had a client who was keeping a mood diary, but we did not clearly identify what each anchor point on the scale represented. I did not realise that for her, +4 (out of 10) was feeling happy, but +5 was mania. Not only did the anchor points on this mood graph fail properly to represent the changes in mood and behaviour that she experienced, it gave us no time in which to act to prevent her going into mania.

Other factors

You may also decide to include on your mood chart information about medication, life events or other stressors. This can be helpful if you are finding it hard to gather information relevant to your risk list. Many women have commented that recording their menstrual cycle on the mood chart helps them to gauge the impact of hormonal changes on their emotional state.

Action points

Ideally, you should aim to have about six anchor points on your mood graph ranging from normal through to abnormal experiences of a specific mood state. The next issue is to decide at what point you need to intervene to stop your mood spiralling into dangerous territory. For example, you may have defined your normal range for ups and downs as between +2 and −2, and identified that at +6 you are hypomanic and at −6 you are bordering on an episode of depression. In that case, the points at which you may need to take action are probably +3/4 and −3/4. The first level of action may simply be to increase your self-monitoring and reduce any stressors. By +4/5 or −4/5 you may need to intervene more actively, for example, changing an unhelpful situation or recording and challenging your own unhelpful thoughts.

Noting action points may enable you to intervene early enough to prevent your normal mood variations developing into more major mood swings. The intensity of the action you need to take will obviously depend on how severe your symptoms are or how much your daily functioning is impaired. If you think you may be unable to take action on your own, it may be useful to share the information in advance with other people who may be able to help you. We will discuss the content of your action plan later in this book.

Lastly, mood charts can also be used to monitor responses to changes in treatment or circumstances. These graphs are more reliable than simply trying to recall how you have been over an extended period of time, and again provide evidence rather than impressions about your progress. A blank copy of a mood chart is provided in the Appendix on p.373.

Monitoring your activity levels

Many individuals report difficulty in developing their awareness of mood shifts and find that monitoring their activity or energy level is a more sensitive measure of their mental state. This is quite common and indeed, the increased recognition of the interplay between moods and activity and energy was a major reason that the criteria for diagnosing bipolar disorder were changed. So, for instance, individuals who are very aware of this link may note that they become overactive in the early stages of a 'high' or underactive when they feel 'low'. Others find monitoring activity levels is a powerful tool for stabilising their day-to-day mood.

Assessing one's daily and weekly activity schedule is a technique used in many time-management courses. The added value of using this approach if you experience a mood disorder is that you can also explore the links between activities, thoughts and emotions. Activity scheduling is widely used in CBT for depression, but its use in individuals with mood swings often needs modification to ensure that the changes in activity that help overcome depression do not lead the individual into an upswing.

Activity scheduling

At its most basic, an activity schedule is a written record of how you have spent each hour of your day. Simple as this may seem, the information recorded can further develop your understanding of how your mood changes in response to how you spend your time or how your current mood influences your activities and the way you behave.

To construct an activity schedule, you need to draw out a blank timetable to cover 24 hours a day for every day of the week. Dividing your waking time into hourly or two-hour slots works quite well and usually allows enough space to record key activities. Obviously, you don't need as much space to record events during the night, so only allocate a few boxes to the time between going to bed and getting up. Over the course of a week, keep a brief note of what you actually did in each period of each day. Next add two ratings to each activity: a P rating to show how much pleasure or enjoyment you got from each activity, and an A rating to record what sense of achievement you got from undertaking that activity. As with the mood chart, use a 0 to 10 (or 0 to 100) rating scale, where zero means 'no pleasure' or 'no sense of achievement', while the top rating on each scale represents a very pleasurable activity or a great sense of achievement. Sometimes the P and A ratings will be similar (e.g., when you feel pleased with yourself after doing something that you found difficult, such as giving a talk to a group of people). But at other times, the ratings will be quite different (e.g., taking a relaxing bath may be very pleasurable but may not give you any sense of achievement;

while clearing rubbish out of the garage may give you a great sense of achievement, but may not be very enjoyable).

When undertaking activity scheduling it is important to use your *current* level of functioning as the standard for the P and A ratings. For example, going out to meet a friend may not seem much of an achievement when you are your normal self. However, when you are depressed this may take considerable effort on your part and should be rated accordingly. Also, it is helpful to try to apply the P and A ratings as soon as possible after the activity, so you are gauging your immediate response. This approach ensures that the record is an accurate reflection of your situation. If you carry the schedule around with you, it will only take a moment to make these notes. An example of an activity schedule is shown in Figure 8. A blank schedule is also included in the Appendix on (see p.374).

When you have been monitoring your activities for about fourteen days, look back over your schedule and examine the range and pattern of your activities, and try to pinpoint those activities that you most enjoy or those that give you the greatest sense of achievement. As the pleasure rating is also a measure of one aspect of your emotional state, you may also be able to establish links between your activity levels and your moods.

To help you think about how to assess the information you have gathered, take another look at Figure 8 and then try to answer the following questions:

TIME	Monday	Tuesday	Wednesday	Thursday	Friday	Saturday	Sunday
12 midnight to 6 a.m.						Didn't sleep stayed up listening	
6–8 a.m.						to music P-9, A-5	
8–10 a.m.	College	College	College	Skipped college and went			
10 a.m.–midday	College P-5, A-7	College P-6, A-6	College P-7, A-5	shopping with	Got up late so missed		
midday–2 p.m.	Food shopping P-5, A-5	Bought Joe a birthday present P-7, A-6	Visited neighbour for coffee P-7, A-6	Jane and Sue P-5, A-7	college P-4, A-2		
2–4 p.m.	Tidied house P-6, A-4	Tidied my study P-8, A-9	Went to bank to sort my grant out P-4, A-8	Late lunch with Jane, Sue and Michael P-7, A-5	Lunch and drinks with		
4–6 p.m.	Went to launderette P-4, A-4	Afternoon nap P-7, A-3	Visited college library	Early trip to cinema P-7, A-6	Joe and Mary P-8, A-6		

6–8 p.m.	Evening in watching TV P–5, A–4	Evening watching favourite series on TV P–8, A–4	to get references for essay P–6, A–8	Night out with bowling club – drinks followed by		
8–10 p.m.	Bed at 10 p.m. P–6, A–2	Bed at 10 p.m. P–7, A–2	Wrote a few notes for my essay P–6, A–7	disco til	Disco in town til after midnight	
10–mid-night			Gave up and went to bed at 11 p.m. Watched TV for an hour P–7, A–3	early hours P–9, A–5	P–10, A–6	
MOOD CHART RATING	+2	+4	+5	+6	+6	+7

Figure 8: Rosa's activity schedule

- What is Rosa's *general level of activity* – very demanding, appropriate, low? (How full is each day?)
- What is her *pattern of activity* – very regular, mixed, disorganised? (How does the activity in one day compare with the next?)
- What type of activities does Rosa *enjoy?* (What are her P ratings?)
- What sort of activities give her a *sense of achievement?* (What are her A ratings?)
- What do you notice about Rosa's *sleep pattern?* (Check times of getting up and going to bed.)
- Is Rosa's sleep pattern associated with any general changes in her *mood state?* (Check mood chart ratings included at bottom of activity table.)

You may now like to apply the same questions to your own schedule, adding the following three questions:

- Is the schedule for the time period you are looking at typical of your day-to-day life? If it is not, you may wish to repeat this exercise when you are involved in your usual routine.
- If this is a typical schedule, do you have a regular pattern of sleep, do you eat at regular times, and are there any regular patterns to your social activities? This will provide a basis for the exploration of social rhythms that will be discussed shortly.
- How do the ratings on your schedule compare with your ratings on your mood graph?

This last question is particularly useful if you experience both highs and lows, as in some circumstances it may help you to become more aware of how and when your mood swings become a problem. Let's look at Rosa's schedule and her mood chart to explore how this might be done. If you look at the pattern of activity on the Wednesday, you will see that Rosa engaged in a number of activities she enjoyed, and her mood chart reflected that she was definitely feeling in a positive frame of mind. On the Thursday, Rosa did lots of activities with friends and was out socialising and drinking alcohol late into the night. By the end of the week, her positive mood state was approaching a level where she needed to take action.

While we do not know just from looking at the charts whether Rosa's increased activity was a cause or an effect of her starting to go 'high', you can see that the activity schedule may give clues about activities that are 'overstimulating' or high risk. Some individuals find it helpful to monitor activities S ('stimulating') or HR ('high risk') and again to measure the degree of S or HR on a 0 to 10 (or 0 to 100) rating scale. If you are not sure if an activity is overstimulating, you could try the following exercise:

- Briefly describe the actual activity.
- Write down your mood and energy (or activation) levels immediately before engaging in the activity.
- Re-rate your mood and energy levels immediately after the activity.

As with P and A ratings, the ratings for mood and for energy or activation may differ. Some individuals report that stimulating activities are more likely to push them into the 'danger zone' where a high may begin than simply engaging in lots of activities that they enjoy doing. Undertaking this type of rating may help you to see if you are vulnerable to highs if you repeatedly engage in stimulating activities. An example is given in Box 4.

BOX 4   MONITORING ACTIVITIES TO EVALUATE IF THEY MAY BE TOO STIMULATING

Actual activity	Mood and energy before	Mood and energy after
Swimming	Mood=+4 Energy=+5	Mood=+4 Energy=+3
Meeting at social club; dance with four other friends	Mood=+4 Energy=+5	Mood=+5 Energy=+8

Ratings: mood −10 to +10; energy level 0 to +10

One final point that is worth mentioning relates to the use of electronic self-monitoring devices. Some of these indicate that they will record your activity levels. However, you will need to check exactly what a device is actually recording for activity. For instance, on most devices, activity refers either to number of steps per day or it may note the amount of time per week spent in moderate or vigorous activity. So, the likelihood is that these devices may capture your physical activity, but not the full range of your daytime activities. Likewise, this issue is not necessarily solved by using self-monitoring apps that ask you questions about your mood and activity, etc. Whilst electronic mood ratings are similar to those recorded on the self-monitoring sheets used in this section, the questions about or recording of activity tend to be very general, and don't, for example, differentiate between different types of activity that may relate to your exercise level, your day-to-day tasks (routines such as cleaning your teeth, washing, dressing, etc.), any activity related to employment or your must-do tasks or your pleasurable activities such as hobbies. In sum, the information collected by most of the devices or apps is not really specific enough to be useful for this particular type of self-monitoring (as you need to specify the activity and your P and A ratings).

Monitoring your sleep patterns

Most activity schedules, such as the one shown in Figure 7, allow you to record the time you go to bed and the time you get up. If your sleep pattern is fairly stable, these ratings may be sufficient to allow you to monitor if you do actually go to bed and get up at regular times (and to demonstrate that you get a similar amount of sleep each night). However, many people who experience mood swings are aware that both their daytime activity and their night-time sleep patterns can be irregular and easily become disrupted. If you do have an irregular sleep pattern or experience very disturbed night-time sleep, then you may also notice that this impacts negatively on your mood state and it may even make your thinking sluggish or you may find you are less able to challenge negative thoughts. For readers who believe this description applies to them, or for those who are unsure, I would recommend that it is likely to help if you collect additional information about your day-to-day sleep patterns.

Some of you may wear activity monitors, have digital watches or other commercial devices that record your sleep pattern (or at least record times when you are in bed and not moving much). These offer a quick way for you to review your sleep pattern. However, other people don't use such devices or, as with activity patterns, they want a more detailed record. One of the best ways to get an overview of your sleep patterns is to keep a sleep diary for four to six weeks and then review if there are any ways of predicting how long you will sleep for on a night-to-night basis or when your night-time sleep will be disturbed. As there are different types of sleep disruption, you may wish to keep details about the following:

1. What time did you get into bed? (Note – this may not be the time that you began 'trying' to fall asleep, which is explored in other questions).
2. What time did you try to go to sleep?
3. How long did it take you to fall asleep (time difference between questions 1 and 2)?

4. How many times did you wake up during the night and how long did each awakening last (on average)? Is there a time of night when you waken from your sleep for a longer period of time than any other awakening? (You may also be interested to add together the time periods when you were awakened from your sleep, to calculate the total time you spent awake and the total time you spent asleep when you are in bed.)

5. What time did you wake up (finally) in the morning?

6. What time did you get out of bed for the day?

7. On a 0–10 scale, how would you rate the quality of your sleep last night?

8. Any other comments or observations (e.g., do you think there was a reason for the rating you made for sleep quality last night, did you take any over-the-counter sleep medications or did you take any prescribed medications?).

This may seem a long list, but usually you can answer these questions quite quickly, and it really does help to have this information if you have irregular, unpredictable or poor-quality sleep.

If you find it more difficult to review the diary by looking at written numbers, you could make a graph that includes the key items from the sleep diary (e.g., time you went to bed, time you went to sleep, time you wake up). Alternatively, you could use the sleep monitor on a digital watch or mobile phone which often generates a graph or chart to show the key elements of your sleep pattern over the course of a week. These options may give you a visual picture of whether there is a persistent problem in one specific element of your sleep routine, if the whole picture is very variable, or if there is one bit of your sleep that particularly impacts on the quality of your sleep.

To try to help you get a better idea of how this information is helpful, I have created some sleep charts in Figure 9. To simplify things, I only show a summary diagram for each sleep pattern, but hopefully you will be able to see how these different profiles can be identified by keeping recordings about the key sleep questions that were listed.

In Figure 9, we can see that Pattern A is a common sleep profile for people who find that the amount of sleep they get is their major concern (e.g., the overall duration is too short and/or accompanied by lots of night-time awakenings). Pattern A is associated with poor sleep quality ratings and many people report that they feel lethargic and struggle to start their planned activities the following day. Pattern B is also a problem because people don't get enough sleep, although their insomnia tends to occur typically in the early hours of the morning. Pattern C is described by people who find that their biggest problem is the timing of when they go to sleep e.g., getting to bed after midnight, and then still being asleep at about 11.30 a.m. the next morning. This type of sleep timing problem may be accompanied by very long duration of sleep (hypersomnia). Pattern D shows yet another problem, which occurs when people report a big difference between their sleep patterns over the weekend compared with weekdays. This can happen to many

Figure 9: Different sleep patterns that may be unsatisfactory and can then affect daily mood and functioning

Sleep pattern	Time of going to bed, going to sleep, waking up and getting up....					
	9pm	Mid-night	3am	6am	9am	Noon
Pattern A						
Pattern B						
Pattern C						
Pattern D						
Weekday						
Weekend						

Pattern A: This person goes to bed at 9pm but is awake for two hours, then their sleep is disturbed throughout the night, and the total sleep time is too short.

Pattern B: This person goes to bed at 10pm and goes to sleep almost immediately. However, they wake up in the early hours, lie in bed (worry) during the early hours of the morning and then get up. The total sleep time is too short.

Pattern C: This person goes to bed after midnight and sleeps for many hours, often not getting out of bed till noon the next day. A major problem is the timing of going to sleep and waking up.

Pattern D: This person shows different patterns on weekdays compared with weekends. The weekday pattern is reasonable in that they seem to get uninterrupted sleep and it is of adequate duration. The pattern of the person's sleep at weekends shows they spend more time after they go to bed still awake (looking at social media or watching TV) and then sleep for much longer on Saturday and Sunday night, getting up much later than weekdays.

Key to diagram: In bed, but awake   In bed and asleep

individuals, especially those who are not following a regular daily schedule.

A more detailed understanding or picture of your sleep patterns or problems over a month or so will allow you to find out how your sleep influences your mood and activities. All this information will be useful in helping you decide which different techniques to try to help to improve your sleep self-regulation.

Self-regulation

Having developed your self-monitoring skills, the next step is to modify some of your activities to try to help stabilise your mood and reduce the risk of more extreme swings. The intervention used to promote stabilisation is called *self-regulation*. The idea behind this approach is that more regular patterns of behaviour seem to help stabilise circadian rhythms and reduce the likelihood of unpredictable shifts in mood and activity levels. To apply self-regulation to your own life, you need to select events that occur on a daily or weekly basis and try to develop a regular pattern to them.

Some individuals find that self-regulation of their sleep–wake cycle, which is also referred to as rest–activity rhythms, on its own helps them feel more settled and better able to cope with their moods. However, others will need to extend their efforts to examining and then modifying their thinking. As these changes may be accompanied by mood shifts, the combination is often referred to as cognitive-emotional regulation, and we will address these issues in Part Three of this book.

Using your activity schedule

Initially, you have used your weekly activity schedules to monitor your daily activities and your mood and achievement ratings. As we found for Rosa, you may have been able to identify aspects of your own schedules that improve or worsen your mood over a day or a week. In order to begin self-regulation, we need to examine a series of your activity schedules. This will enable you to understand your pattern of activities and to assess the impact of any changes that you make.

Start by laying three or four schedules out in front of you. As you glance through them, ask yourself the following questions:

- Do you think that your schedule is reasonably balanced?
- Is it very demanding or very empty?
- Are your activities organised or disorganised?
- Are your activities both demanding and disorganised?

Disorganised schedules with no regular patterns of activity are indicative of irregular social rhythms and may lead to circadian rhythm disruption. Likewise, demanding schedules may lead you to feel stressed or overstimulated, either of which can trigger an episode of mood disorder.

If you are not sure how balanced or regular your schedules are, you may like to read the following paragraphs and then review your schedules.

DEMANDING SCHEDULES

Problem: A demanding schedule can be defined as one that includes more than four significant events or activities on most days of the week, particularly if there is no regular pattern to the activities. Note that a pleasurable activity, such as lunch with a group of friends, counts as a major activity!

Possible intervention: If you do seem to have a lot of busy and demanding days, it is worth reviewing whether you can make some changes. For example, can you adopt a slightly slower pace and spread out potentially stimulating activities over a longer period of time? Also, can you include more calming activities in your schedule, or increase the number of activities that you do alone? This is particularly helpful if you find being with friends very stimulating. You could also consider seeing fewer friends at one time, perhaps just one or two together, as a larger group is likely to be more activating. Again, the byword is *balance*. Friends may help lift your mood when you are down, so I am not suggesting you avoid this important source of reinforcement altogether. However, too much activity and too many social engagements will not benefit someone at risk of an upswing.

DISORGANISED SCHEDULES

Problem: Common signs of a disorganised schedule are a large number of unfinished activities and the lack of any regular pattern to your days. You may also have relatively few high A ratings, suggesting that you don't often feel a great sense of achievement. In looking over your schedule, note how regular your daily routines are. For example, what time do you eat each meal, and on how many days do you eat three meals? How often and at what time do you get exercise or meet with other people? What time do you go to bed or get up, and how many hours do you sleep each night? It is also worth noting whether you do any or all of these activities on your own or with other people.

Possible intervention: The first intervention to make if you have a disorganised schedule is to try to develop regular times for getting up and going to bed, for eating meals and meeting people and having periods of relaxation. If you can establish such routines, you will then probably find it easier to decide which other activities or tasks you wish to include in your schedule and how much time you can allocate to each additional task.

Disorganised or overdemanding schedules are common, but even if your schedule does not fit with these descriptions, there are three key components to self-regulation that you may find helpful:

REGULAR ROUTINES AND FORWARD PLANNING

Many people find it helpful to plan their schedule for each day beforehand. I usually encourage individuals to sit down in the evening and plan the whole of the next day to ensure that they are not trying to fit too much (or too little) into their schedule. Given that stable patterns of activity reduce the risk of circadian rhythm disruption, it is worth introducing predictable routines for frequently recurring activities, such as mealtimes, etc. Do not despair at this thought; no one is trying to remove the fun and spontaneity from your day-to-day life, but you will benefit from some stability in your basic activities.

To gauge how well you are managing this approach, you may wish to keep a record charting your regular activities – this will give you instant feedback. The graph is similar to a mood chart, but this time you put the hours of the day along the vertical axis. Your first aim is to eat three meals a day regularly and to keep the time of each meal to within about an hour (e.g., lunch between midday and one o'clock). Your second aim is to try to develop regular habits around sleep. Again, you should aim to go to bed, or to get up, within a band of about an hour; but it is not the exact time you retire to bed or get up that is critical. The two most important elements of a regular sleep pattern are trying to go to bed at about the same time each night and regularly getting the amount of sleep that you need.

A self-regulation chart showing a week's record of basic sleeping and mealtime patterns is shown in Figure 10.

If you have difficulty in limiting the number of activities you plan to do, you may need to learn to prioritise. First write a list of all the activities and tasks you believe you need to complete in the coming week, followed by the deadline by which each needs to be completed. Can any of these tasks be put off, or can anyone else take responsibility for their completion? Please try not to give yourself a hard time if you ask others to help. Your mental well-being is more important than trying to prove you can cope better than someone else

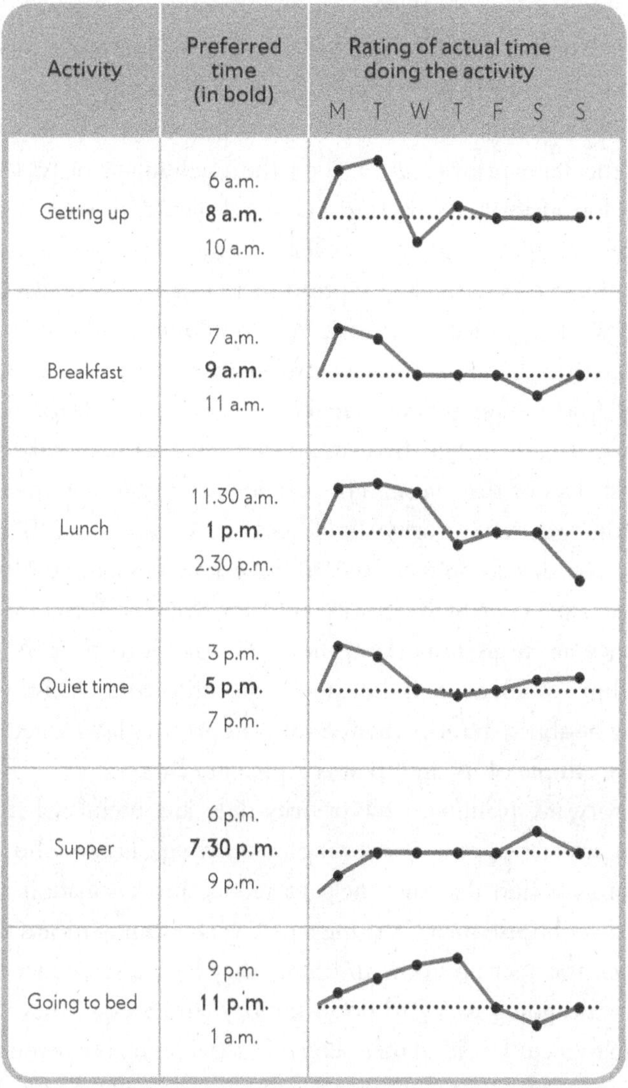

Activity	Preferred time (in bold)	Rating of actual time doing the activity M T W T F S S
Getting up	6 a.m. **8 a.m.** 10 a.m.	
Breakfast	7 a.m. **9 a.m.** 11 a.m.	
Lunch	11.30 a.m. **1 p.m.** 2.30 p.m.	
Quiet time	3 p.m. **5 p.m.** 7 p.m.	
Supper	6 p.m. **7.30 p.m.** 9 p.m.	
Going to bed	9 p.m. **11 p.m.** 1 a.m.	

Figure 10: A self-regulation chart: monitoring routine activities

or that you can do the impossible. Retaining responsibility for a task, becoming stressed and then spiralling into a mood swing will not benefit anyone, least of all you.

Having reduced the list as much as possible, try to identify all the high-priority tasks, then the medium-priority, then the low-priority. Next organise an 'A' list of all your high-priority tasks, written in order of how important it is to complete each task. Then spread them out across the days of the week in order of priority. You should *not* aim to include more than one or occasionally two high-priority tasks in each day. Also, remember not to make the rest of each day too busy – particularly if you have important tasks to undertake on most days of that week. The activities that you identified as medium or low priority should now be written on a 'B' list; and you should only go back to these activities *after* you have dealt with your high-priority tasks for that day. Remember, if they are really important, they will make it to your 'A' list within a week or so. If they don't make it to your 'A' list, you may be able to remove them from your priority list altogether. An example of 'A' and 'B' lists is given in Box 5.

Forward planning and priority lists are useful whether you are at risk of a downswing or upswing. Those who are depressed find that they help to reduce procrastination and fend off hopelessness. Writing a note each evening means that when they get up in the morning, they have a sense of what they are going to try to do in the day ahead. Also, they can plan to include within their schedule activities that they usually enjoy, to try to lift their mood as much as possible. This tends to reduce their anxiety and help them get started each day.

On the other hand, those who are worried about going 'high' often find that they can retain greater control if they have a plan of what they are trying to achieve and can structure their day so that they are not easily distracted or don't try to cram in more and more activities. If you are bordering on going high, it is also valuable to do two things. First, show your plan to someone else, to get feedback on whether it is sensible or overambitious. Second, plan your day and stick with your plan: do not add activities because you feel good.

BOX 5   A AND B LISTS

Activities and tasks to do:	_A list:_
Pay the rent	Pay rent
Go to the housing association weekly coffee morning	Go to doctor
	Take kids to swimming
Take the kids to swimming lesson	_B list:_
Visit doctor to have blood test	Housing association (go next week)
Fetch copy of next month's theatre programme	Fetch copy of theatre programme (delay this – I've got to go past the theatre next Thursday anyway)
Make an appointment for a dental check (due in three months)	Dental appointment (not urgent)
Wash the car	Wash car (ask Jack)

With practice, you can start to plan your schedule for a week in advance. There are many advantages to this longer-term planning. For instance, you can develop a list of things you want to do during that week and ensure that they are spaced out over the seven days. This is especially important for those activities that you enjoy or those that you find overstimulating, which you can spread out to ensure that you get the maximum benefit and the minimum disruption from them. It is also a good way of monitoring the regularity of your basic activities, such as eating, sleeping and exercise or relaxation routines. With time, you will hopefully develop a more realistic approach to what you can or cannot do in the time available.

STABLE ACTIVITIES = STABLE MOOD

Having established more regular routines and social rhythms, the next step is to develop a balanced programme of daily activities. To attain balance, you will need to make a regular assessment of the activities in your schedule. There are three key areas to consider:

- *Your overall level of activity:* In judging whether your overall activity level is appropriate, try to assess the quality as well as the quantity of the activities you engage in. Quality is probably more important than quantity, and more rewarding in terms of both pleasure and sense of achievement.
- *Appropriate activities for different mood states:* When you are feeling elated or possibly going high, you

may need to increase the number of calming activities that you include in your schedule. When you are depressed, on the other hand, you will need to add activities that you enjoy or that can help lift your mood.

- *The balance between solo and joint activities:* It is important to try to include a mixture of activities that you do alone and activities that you do with others. Again, your mood state may dictate when it is better to pursue a higher level of interaction (when you are down) or a lower level of interaction (to avoiding overstimulation when 'up'). These aspects will be considered further in a moment.

It is useful to review your planned schedule at the end of each day and see if you managed to complete all the tasks you had listed for it. This will allow you to decide if you are still putting too much or too little into your schedule. If you do not complete the tasks you set yourself, ask yourself what the obstacles were. Did problems arise that interrupted your schedule? If so, how predictable or unpredictable were these difficulties? Or did you simply underestimate the amount of time you needed to complete various activities? By answering these questions carefully, you can progress toward a realistic activity schedule that incorporates both the basic day-to-day tasks that you need to complete and the pleasurable activities that you want to include.

TRIAL AND ERROR

It may take some time to identify a balanced and realistic activity schedule that has regular social routines, but still allows you to feel you have control over your own life. Self-regulation does require an element of self-discipline, and you would not be human if you did not stray from your planned schedule from time to time. Also, it will take a while to determine the right mix of activities for you and to be sure about which activities genuinely help you improve your mood state.

The best way to cope with these uncertainties is to view the whole process as an experiment. Try out different schedules and keep notes on which you prefer, and which give you the most stability in your mood and functioning. Most importantly, don't judge your new, more regular schedule too soon. It will usually take a minimum of two to three weeks to feel comfortable with your new routines, particularly if you are attempting to reduce the level of activity and stimulation in your day.

Sleep routines

People vary in the length of sleep they need each night in order to function well the next day. We also know that the amount of sleep needed and the timing of when people go to bed and get up may vary according to many factors, not least age. However, despite these potential differences, there is scientific evidence that healthy sleep probably lasts about 7–8 hours per night and that people who consistently get less than 6 hours sleep per night may be more likely to experience physical and psychological problems. Interestingly, very variable sleep patterns can also be associated with poor health. As such, averaging 7 hours sleep per night but only sleeping 4–5 hours per weeknight and then sleeping 10–12 hours on Saturday and Sunday nights (like Pattern D in Figure 9) is not a healthy sleep pattern. More recently, scientific studies have shown that the circadian rhythm disruptions that occur more often in individuals with bipolar disorder may be characterised by a change in the timing of onset of sleep and of awakening and that this abnormality of the timing of sleep may result in prolonged sleep (so-called hypersomnia).

Individuals who experience mood swings may report a wide range of sleep patterns from regular 7-hour per night sleep patterns, to shortened sleep time or poor-quality sleep (common characteristics of insomnia), through to hypersomnia. However, sleep irregularities of any type may trigger or follow on from mood shifts, so trying to develop more stable and predictable sleep patterns is to be recommended.

The key to a healthy sleep pattern is to begin by developing a regular and foolproof system for when you go to sleep and when you get up. This system will never be perfect, particularly as mood disorders are often accompanied by sleep disorders; but the more stable and regular your sleep routine, the easier it will be for you to try to minimise the impact of any sleep disruptions.

The first goal is to try to settle into a regular time of going to bed and of getting up in the morning. In clinical settings, we often begin by setting a regular getting up time, as other changes (like needing to go to bed earlier) often follow on from that. However, we can carefully monitor the impact of this change in clinical settings in a way that is not possible at home. So, it is okay if you prefer to start by modifying your bedtime routines. Many people using self-help techniques tell me they prefer to start by establishing a regular bedtime that is achievable for them (probably between 10 p.m. and midnight is a good time slot to aim at). If you kept a sleep diary and found that you have been going to bed well after midnight and haven't been getting up until very late in the morning (or even the early afternoon), implementing earlier bedtimes and getting up times may need to be done in a gradual way. For example, you could start by shifting forward the time you go to bed and the time you get up by 20–30 minutes per week until you are regularly getting to bed before midnight and regularly getting up earlier. These first steps are trying to reduce your sleep duration to less than 9 hours. Further, to stabilise circadian rhythms and avoid the negative effects of too much variability in sleep duration, it is important that you stick with this new sleep timetable for 7-days per week and that weekends are not accompanied by an extended 'lie in'.

For those whose sleep diary showed that they are getting to bed before midnight, but that they do not get off to sleep for more than 30 minutes or that their sleep pattern is disrupted, then there is a need for slightly different tactics. For instance, you can review what you are doing in the hour or so before you go to bed and what you are doing when you get into bed. Ideally, the hour or so before going to bed should become 'winding down' time. So, the key things to avoid are too much eating or drinking (particularly avoiding alcohol or caffeine), too much loud music and too much stimulation – including watching exciting television programmes. If you need activity in the hour before going to bed, then it is worthwhile experimenting with more calming or relaxing activities, such as listening to soothing music, taking a gentle stroll, or perhaps a warm bath. If you like a drink at bedtime, make it a warm, milky one. When you get to bed, try to ensure your bedroom or sleeping area is conducive to sleep. Is the bed comfortable, is the room temperature to your liking, is there enough fresh air circulating, is the lighting low enough and is the space quiet enough? Next, try to use simple relaxation techniques to help you get off to sleep. With practice, these simple interventions may help you develop more healthy sleep routines.

Some people like to engage with social media, read or watch TV when they get into bed. This habit is likely to delay the onset of sleep and be associated with lots of night-time awakenings. So, more than any other issue, this one is really worth trying to change. For example, can you put your mobile phone or other devices on sleep mode, or better still, leave smartphones and tablets outside the bedroom altogether? It is important to avoid the temptation of answering texts or emails or participating in other electronic messaging. This is partly to ensure you are beginning to relax, but also to avoid the stimulation or the possibility this activity will stir up negative emotions. If you share your bedroom or you must have your phone or other devices to hand, can you attach blue light blocking filters to the screens of these devices as this will change your exposure to evening or night-time blue light. This will help reduce negative effects of blue light on your melatonin hormone production (and somewhat reduce negative effects of these devices on your rest–activity rhythms). Alternatively, you can change the light exposure setting for your devices by downloading a programme from the internet (these are often free and allow you to change the amount of blue light emitted by your devices for set time periods such as 9 p.m. to 7 a.m.). These approaches can also be used for TVs. If you can make the bedroom a TV-free zone then so much the better; if this is not feasible, then asking the person using the TV to consider using headphones (alongside fitting a blue light filter) may help. Of course, none of the techniques is foolproof, but it is worth trying a few experiments to determine whether some of these approaches increase or decrease the length of time it takes you to fall asleep once you are in bed.

If you find that on some nights you cannot get to sleep and are lying in bed awake, then scientific studies suggest that simply remaining in bed may not help. This is partly because you run the risk of becoming anxious in response to negative automatic thoughts about not being able to sleep, which is likely to generate a vicious cycle that worsens any insomnia. To combat this, you might get up and go into another room and read a book, or distract yourself from worrying thoughts, etc. However, if your inability to go off to sleep does not change (or your mood state worsens) then, rather than persist with this approach alone, you may want to consult a mental health professional, or to find out if it is possible to access a specialist in CBT for insomnia (CBT-I). This is suggested because the use of sleep restriction (getting up and not just staying in bed at night if you cannot get off to sleep) by people with mood swings might risk triggering a hypomanic or manic episode. Whilst this risk is estimated to be very small, it is better to seek advice before using this technique on a regular or prolonged basis.

If you manage to get off to sleep at a regular time and sleep through the night, the next step is to try to get up at a regular time. To start this process, set an alarm clock for the same time each day, *including* weekends. Even if you are tired, try to stick with this routine. To ensure that you sleep well at night, it is best to avoid taking naps during the daytime. Even if you have a poor night's sleep, dropping off during the day tends to lead to a further poor night of sleep.

If you are waking up throughout the night, then it is worth trying one or two experiments to see if this can be resolved. The problem may be reduced or resolved by, e.g., turning off social media or reducing your intake of caffeine, nicotine, spicy food and alcohol. Many people do not realise that the stimulant effects of caffeine may last for many hours after their last cup of coffee. So, it is worth considering changing from caffeinated to decaffeinated drinks from about midday onwards, and monitoring if this change helps you. Likewise, although small amounts of alcohol may initially sedate you, alcohol disrupts sleep patterns and will probably make you wake up more during the night. If none of your experiments appear to help, then you may wish to consult a health professional. For example, some people with mood swings, especially if they are overweight or clinically obese, may experience breathing problems when they are lying in bed, and these lead to their sleep being interrupted by repeated awakenings (a condition called sleep apnoea). There are several interventions that can help with this problem, but you would need a professional to help in setting up any treatments. Obviously, other physical conditions, especially painful joints or arthritis, etc., may cause people to wake regularly during the night, and these conditions should be discussed with a clinician to alert them to the fact that you are experiencing sleep difficulties because of these other problems, to see if this can be addressed.

Most people who follow these basic guidelines usually find the self-help interventions help overcome simple, common problems that were preventing them getting off to sleep and staying asleep or having a regular sleep pattern. However, some people find that when they get into bed, their mind becomes filled with negative thoughts, or they wake up before dawn and don't know how to cope in the early hours of the morning. If this happens to you, the following simple tips may help; if they don't, you may wish to consult a specialist self-help book on sleep or to talk to a doctor or clinician.

If your mind is full of *anxious or negative thoughts,* you can try:

- distracting yourself by imagining pleasant and relaxing scenes;

- using relaxation techniques (such as a breathing exercise described in the following pages of this chapter);
- using mindfulness techniques such as body scan or mindful meditation (these are described in Chapter 9);
- writing down your concerns (a notebook may be preferable to electronic media in this instance) and planning to review them in the morning;
- imagining placing all these concerns in a 'worry truck' and sending the truck to a garage that does not open until after you get up the next morning.

If you *wake early*, the advice is different depending on whether you are feeling positive or negative about yourself and your situation. If you are feeling slightly high and your mind is full of bright ideas, it is actually better to try to stay in bed and try to relax until it is time to get up.

If you must do something, you could make a simple note of your ideas *for a maximum of two minutes*, then try to use relaxation and distraction techniques that calm you down. Try to stick with your self-regulation programme, as too much stimulation too early in the day may increase the risk of going into an upswing in your mood and being overactive.

If you wake up and feel very depressed and negative, you can try to relax or to distract yourself and see if you can rest. If this does not make you feel any better, it may help to get up and do something active, i.e., to try to engage in some distraction activities. If this pattern of early wakening occurs regularly when you are depressed, it is good to plan for this situation ahead of time by designing a schedule of things you can do on your own when there is no one else awake. This might include simple tasks in your home that keep you occupied; other options are reading books, playing music that you enjoy and that may lift your spirits, or watching a video that you like. It is also worth having the telephone numbers of people you can contact at such times if you cannot shake off your feelings of unhappiness.

If none of the above strategies work, it is worth consulting your doctor about what else you can try, and/or whether a short course of sleeping tablets is required to get your sleep pattern back on track. Alternatively, it may be that the sleep irregularities are a warning sign of disrupted rest–activity rhythms and it may mean that interventions targeted at all elements of your mood swings are needed (these are discussed in the next section).

Additional approaches to effective self-regulation

Developing regular and predictable rest–activity rhythms can be achieved by applying the daytime mood and activity self-help techniques described and by more careful monitoring and self-management of sleep routines. However, there are other aspects to effective self-regulation such as attending to the following:

- diet and exercise;
- stimulus control; and
- relaxation.

Some general information and advice on each topic is offered here to help you work on these areas.

DIET AND EXERCISE

No one can tell you how to lead your life. However, if you have mood swings that cause you significant problems, there may be some modifications to your lifestyle that are worth considering. It is well recognised that physical illness can put your body under stress and precipitate mood swings in individuals who are at risk; for this reason alone, it is worth paying attention to your general health. This may start with scheduling three regular meals each day as part of a process of stabilising social routines, as discussed above. You do not have to follow a strict regime, but you might try to pay more attention to what you eat and drink and, e.g., try to limit your intake of unhealthy foods. You might begin by making a commitment to exclude junk food from your diet. There is no evidence that 'E factors' or food additives directly affect the frequency or severity of mood swings, but they may have some effect on some people; so, reducing your intake of these substances is a reasonable choice to make. Some nutritionists and diet experts simply encourage people to try to the apply the '80:20 rule'. Namely, try to limit your indulgences in sweets, treats or less healthy food and drink options to about 20 per cent of your weekly food and calorie intake. If you try to consume a healthy diet for the other 80 per cent of the time, you will probably benefit from this regime, or at least there will be minimal risk of harmful effects. Also, and I am sure you know this, try to keep an eye on portion size. This contributes significantly to weight gain across all age groups, because nearly everyone underestimates what a 'normal' or healthy portion size of proteins, vegetables, fats, carbohydrates or sugars looks like.

If you are not sure whether such dietary changes will be of any benefit to you, you can always monitor the effects of including or excluding these foods on your mood and level of activation. In addition, you can judge whether changing your eating habits helps you to gain or lose any weight.

Similar ideas apply to exercise. News outlets, social media and health information websites have expressed concerns that people are becoming increasingly sedentary. This has led to public health pronouncements that say things like 'sitting is the new smoking' (meaning the negative effects on health are comparable to the effects of nicotine). So, if you are not keen on exercise, perhaps you could begin by trying to be more active when you are indoors and, for example, even standing up more during the day is helpful (e.g., when answering phone calls or when using laptops). Likewise, if you spend a lot of time sitting down, then set up a reminder system so that you get an alert every 45–60 minutes to prompt you to stand up and walk about for a few minutes and do a few stretches. Scientific studies have shown that even this simple change in behaviour can bring many benefits.

Scientific studies indicate that adults should ideally aim to undertake 150 minutes of moderate exercise per week. However, remember that doing something is better than doing nothing. So, setting a more modest goal, such as an hour a week of moderate cardiovascular exercise – just enough effort to make your heart and lungs work a little harder – can be helpful to your general fitness. Furthermore, once you start moving more, the positive benefits are often immediate, with individuals noting an impact on their mood and general sense of well-being. As you become fitter, you could consider a greater commitment to an exercise programme, perhaps joining a regular group at, say, aerobics or going jogging. Of course, given the many different forms of exercise available, people often ask what activity might be best to pursue. But, as one American expert (called Steve Blair) observed, 'the best form of exercise is the one that you will do and keep doing'.

Many people find that wearing a digital activity monitor can help them achieve their healthy lifestyle goals. Many of the wrist-worn devices also link to websites, so that you can add information about food intake, body weight, etc. Also, there are apps available that guide you through the development of new exercise regimes. For example, Public Health England has produced a free app called 'Couch to 5k' which has proved popular as it helps people who are doing minimal exercise to build a routine to enable them to run five kilometres without stopping after about six to ten weeks.

There are also digital and online programmes specifically targeted at individuals with bipolar disorders which include ways of monitoring your mood swings and medication intake. So, it is quite possible to combine the goals of carefully monitoring mood swings and their impact on your life whilst at the same time recording the impact of healthy living on your sense of well-being. Some individuals who have used the CBT self-help programme tell me that combining this with the digital or other apps has provided them with new insights into the links that operate regarding their food intake, physical well-being and mood stability, etc.

Lastly, if these changes to diet and exercise are difficult to pursue alone, it is always worth trying to find someone else who also wants to eat a healthy diet or take more exercise. This does not need to be someone who experiences mood swings, it may be a friend who wants to change their eating habits or get more exercise and feel physically fitter. However, sharing your goals and discussing your successes together means you can encourage each other to stick with your plan. Likewise, joining a local exercise class or gym may mean that as well as increasing your fitness levels, you may make some new social contacts.

STIMULANTS AND STIMULUS CONTROL

Before discussing substances that contain stimulants, I would like to comment briefly on some other aspects of stimulus control. In the preceding pages, I have indicated on several occasions that there may be disadvantages to meeting with large groups of friends if you are at risk of going into a 'high'. Individuals who only ever experience downswings are often encouraged to seek the company of others; however, those who experience highs as well as lows have to be more cautious, as at certain times they may find social situations overstimulating. Other activities, too, can be equally 'high risk' when on the edge of an upswing. Taking part in exciting activities that incorporate an element of risk, like rollercoaster rides or go-kart racing, may be a trigger as well as a symptom of going high. Sometimes visiting the cinema to see a thriller or action movie may start to push you further toward a high; lively music can have the same effect. There are no set criteria by which to judge in advance what you will find overstimulating, but it is important to be aware of such possibilities. As discussed on p.116, generating a list of these activities and avoiding them when you are at risk of a high, is a sensible approach.

As part of your efforts to lead a more healthy life, you may decide to cut down on your caffeine and nicotine intake. Caffeine is found in coffee, tea and many soft drinks. Cutting down on soft drinks may also reduce your intake of sugar and other food additives. The main reason for encouraging you to reduce your intake of all of these substances is to allow you to understand your body's 'baseline state' – that is, how it feels and functions before you take in any substance that may affect it. If you wish to understand the effects of life events, behaviour and medication on your mood swings, you need to be able to make these judgments without other factors clouding the issue. It is not easy to cut down on nicotine and caffeine, but a gradual reduction will help you make important and accurate assessments of how you are feeling. For example, knowing the difference between feeling 'edgy' because you are starting to go high and feeling like this because you have too much caffeine or nicotine in your system is important if you are trying to decide what action you need to take. Likewise, symptoms of caffeine withdrawal may feel like the early stages of becoming depressed.

Alcohol and illicit drugs also have powerful effects on your mood and energy levels. The more you can reduce your intake of these substances the better. Even if you know someone with mood swings who has tried these substances without adverse effects, there is no guarantee that you can try them yourself with any safety. Some individuals feel that using these substances helps them treat their own symptoms, but the reality is that all of these substances can destabilise your physical and emotional state and push you into a severe mood swing or an episode of depression or mania. There is no getting away from the fact that the use of alcohol and drugs represents high risk; if possible, if you do use these substances, you need to have a plan for harm reduction.

Harm reduction involves two key elements. First, you must tell the doctor or clinician what you use, and how much. They may be able to help you reduce your intake. Even if you don't want that help at present, telling your doctor what's going on means they can avoid prescribing medication that might interact with these substances. Such interactions can have very unpleasant and serious physical consequences, so the least you can do is to protect yourself against these problems. The second element of harm reduction is to consider whether you can cope without alcohol or drugs, or at least reduce your intake. If you do wish to cut down, you will first need to assess your use (e.g., by recording how much and how often you use the substances on your activity schedule, or in a diary). The recommended highest levels of alcohol intake each week are 22 units for women and 28 units for men. (Indeed, recent studies suggest these levels should be reduced to a maximum of 14 units.) One unit of alcohol is equivalent to a single measure of spirits, a small glass of wine or half a pint of lager or beer.

The next step is to assess what action you can take as part of a personalised 'harm reduction' programme. It is usually easier to reduce intake of alcohol or drugs gradually rather than stopping suddenly. In addition, gaining the support of other people will probably help you, particularly when you feel stressed or are finding it hard to keep your 'harm reduction' programme going. It is unlikely that this programme of reduction will proceed without any hitches, so it is important not to give up and view your attempt as a failure simply because you hit difficult times. Try to plan one day at a time and keep reminding yourself of the positive benefits of trying to control your use of these substances. A similar harm reduction approach may also help individuals who are 'addicted' to gambling.

LEARNING TO RELAX

In order to reduce the risk of feeling stressed or high, it is helpful to learn about and regularly use relaxation techniques and consider trying meditation. There are many different methods of relaxation, and you may well need to try a number of approaches before you find the one that suits you best. Also, the increased interest in mindfulness has led to more people trying out different meditation techniques (we will discuss mindfulness in Chapter 9). Having found a suitable technique, it is a good idea to do it regularly so that you are familiar enough with it to employ it even when you are feeling stressed.

You may not realise that exercise, such as a 30- to 40-minute stroll or even a physical workout, can be used as a relaxation technique. Some people prefer these active approaches, as opposed to the more generally accepted muscle relaxation or controlled breathing exercises. Others find that gripping and releasing stress balls, playing relaxing music or receiving a massage is helpful. Relaxation tapes, learning to meditate or using methods described in books on relaxation are also recommended. Three simple techniques are described here:

- *Ten by ten:* This technique uses word repetition and can be helpful if you simply need to distract yourself from a particular thought that is preoccupying your mind. Take a positive word such as 'calm' or 'relax'. Repeat it to yourself ten times. Do this slowly without allowing other thoughts or ideas to intervene. Repeat this exercise ten times during the day or every hour if you are feeling stressed.

- *Controlled breathing:* Some people prefer to use the controlled breathing technique when lying down. However, if you feel tense in a crowded place, you could try to find a quiet space and simply stand still and focus on your breathing. Stand straight upright with your shoulders relaxed. Breathe in deeply and slowly through your nose over about four seconds.

Pause after taking this breath and imagine oxygen reaching the extremities of your body, your toes and your fingers. Slowly and gently breathe out through your mouth for about the same length of time. Continue to stand tall and to breathe slowly in and out. Allow your mind to clear. If this is difficult, imagine yourself in a pleasant, quiet place, e.g., lying in a hammock on a beach. Continue the exercise for a few minutes until you feel calm and relaxed. This usually takes three or four minutes.

- *Progressive muscular relaxation:* This exercise involves tensing and relaxing groups of muscles in your body. Some people like to develop a set sequence of muscle relaxation starting with the toes, but again personal choice is important, and it is worth experimenting with what works best for you.

- Begin by tensing one particular set of muscles, e.g., the foot muscles. Contract the muscles for about five seconds, then relax over about ten seconds. Dwell on the feelings as the muscles relax and imagine a positive warm glow spreading up your leg and into your body. Repeat this with the next muscle group until all the muscles of the body have been contracted and relaxed.

These three techniques are relatively easy to follow and usually begin to take effect quite quickly. You may prefer one approach over the others, or you may find that you like to use different techniques at different times. The most important element is confidence. Becoming familiar with a technique and knowing it works is more important than which particular technique you choose.

PLANNING FOR CHANGE

Self-regulation is easier to maintain when you are in a stable environment, but many individuals experience changes or disruptions in their routine. These changes are often planned and viewed as positive, for example, when they involve visiting people you like or travelling to new places. However, if you are at risk of significant mood swings you do need to plan ahead to make sure that the inevitable changes in your routine do not threaten your well-being. One simple precaution you can take is to avoid travelling at night if at all possible. This will reduce the risk of sleep disruption. If night travel is the only option, it is sensible to avoid alcohol or caffeine and to try to sleep during your journey. If your trip involves a significant shift in time zones, you may wish to consult a doctor or clinician in advance about how to adapt to your new situation as it is possible that your sleep–wake cycle and circadian rhythms will be disrupted.

Even when you find yourself in a new situation it is worth trying to retain key elements of your self-regulation routine such as sleep–wake times, mealtimes, exercise and quiet time or opportunities for engaging in relaxation techniques. The main principle is to enjoy your new situation and experiences while at the same time avoiding dramatic changes to your usual rest–activity routines. Don't make rigid plans that stifle the opportunities to have fun, but don't throw away everything you've gained from self-regulation for the sake of a few days or a few weeks of doing something different. There is a temptation to take a break from activity scheduling when going on vacation, but it is actually quite a good idea to do some forward planning for your holiday itinerary and to keep a record of what you actually did each day. In the end, this only takes a few moments out of the day, but it allows you to gauge how you are coping and whether you need to modify your planned schedule.

CHAPTER SUMMARY

Self-management involves two key elements: *self-monitoring* and *self-regulation*.

Self-monitoring involves:

- mood charts
  - developing a *mood graph* that charts changes in two key mood states;
  - carefully monitoring changes in mood, thinking and behaviour against defined *'anchor points'*;
  - identifying *'action points'* where early intervention may avert major problems;

- activity schedules:
  - monitoring and recording day-to-day activity on a *weekly timetable;*
  - *rating pleasure and achievement* for each activity;

- *reducing high-risk (HR) or over-stimulating (S)* activities.

- Self-monitoring can be extended to include more detailed recordings of sleep patterns
- Self-monitoring also includes understanding the links between
  - mood and behaviour
  - sleep and daytime activity patterns
  - rest–activity patterns and thoughts and moods

Self-regulation involves:
- using activity schedules to develop *regular patterns* for sleeping, eating, exercise, social activities and calming activities or relaxation;
- reducing excessive demands on your time and *improving the organisation or predictability* in your daily activities;
- planning a *realistic and balanced approach* to your day-to-day life that retains positive experiences but reduces the potentially negative effects of chaotic schedules and excess use of alcohol or stimulants.
- Self-regulation also demonstrates how mood, what you do, and physical state are linked.
- Self-regulation may stabilise mood and rest–activity rhythms and reduce the risk of minor mood shifts escalating into major mood disorders.

8

Biting the bullet: Sticking with your medication

Part One of this book discussed the use of medication in the management of mood disorders, and we noted that mood stabilisers are a mainstay in the treatment of bipolar disorder. However, about half of all the people prescribed these medications stop taking them at least once, against medical advice, and many others express ambivalence about taking tablets. In my experience, the decision about whether or not to take long-term medication causes considerable difficulty to many individuals. They struggle particularly with the sense that as medication is being used to stabilise their mood they are deprived of control over their own lives. In recognition of the problems experienced by many in coming to terms with medication, I have called this chapter 'Biting the bullet'.

If you are currently being prescribed medication but are not sure if this chapter is relevant to you, try answering these two questions:

- Do you ever have difficulty taking your medication as prescribed?
- Do you ever try to cope on your own without taking your medication?

If you have answered yes to either of these questions, you have clearly (intentionally or unintentionally) omitted some of your medication at some time. You may therefore find it useful to look at why others do not take their medication and explore simple ways to try to get the best from your own treatment.

Why don't people take their medication?

There are many different patterns of adherence to medication. Some individuals take everything they are prescribed in a regular manner; others regularly miss out part of the total dose; others show 'cycles of adherence', taking the treatment regularly over many months when they feel ill, but becoming less strict when they are feeling better; some individuals take none of the prescribed medications. Interestingly, research suggests that both total adherence and total non-adherence are rarer than some form of partial adherence. The reasons given by individuals for *not* taking some or all of their medication fall into three broad categories, which I will now look at in turn.

Treatment regime

A common barrier to medication adherence is lack of knowledge about the treatment. For example, many people do not realise that they need to continue with the prescribed medication even after they have stopped having symptoms. Other problems are a complicated treatment regime and medication side-effects. (I have included a table of common and more serious side-effects in the Appendix – see p.377). It is interesting to note that research suggests many individuals are prepared to tolerate minor side-effects if they believe the benefits of treatment outweigh the negatives.

Lifestyle

This is essentially a question of how chaotic or organised a person's daily routines are. A person with a chaotic life-style may not have developed a regular pattern of taking medication as part of their daily schedule or may regard the whole process as a hassle. Without some sort of 'cue' to remind them, they often forget to take their medication.

Attitudes and beliefs

Many of the people who report not taking their medication give as a reason their belief that the treatment will not help or that the medication prescribed is not the right approach. Some believe that the threat posed by their mood disorder (their susceptibility to relapse and the likely severity or consequences of an episode) is less than that posed by treatment.

In particular, individuals with mood disorders report that they dislike taking mood stabilisers because they do not wish to be reminded of their long-term problem on a daily basis, and do not like the idea of medication being used to control their mood. Others report that they have a negative attitude toward prescribed treatment for any health problems, and always prefer to try to cope without medication. In yet other cases a relative or friend influences the person's attitude toward the prescribed medication.

Along with some colleagues, I have been involved in exploring attitudes and beliefs about medication in people with bipolar disorders. These projects examined adherence patterns across different age and demographic groups, and also across different phases of bipolar disorder, including acute episodes and periods when people felt emotionally stable. Furthermore, we looked at beliefs that helped or hindered medication adherence in individuals with bipolar disorders compared with individuals with chronic physical health conditions that showed a fluctuating course, with periods of being ill interspersed with periods of better functioning (a pattern that mimics mood swings).

We found that rates of medication adherence were not predicted by age or sex or other social characteristics of people with bipolar disorders. Furthermore, adherence levels in individuals with bipolar disorders and those with long-term physical conditions were very similar and were *not* strongly predicted by the medications or side-effects. The best way to predict medication adherence was to look at the balance between two main types of beliefs. First, so-called necessity beliefs which are linked together by the idea that there are benefits to the treatments offered (e.g., people may decide that treatment is essential to reduce the negative consequences of mood swings, etc.). Second, concerns about treatment (e.g., that medications are all potentially harmful) or other issues that act as barriers. Individuals with long-term mental or physical health problems are likely to begin and continue treatment if they judge their personal need for treatment (because of the threat posed by the problem) to be greater than their concerns about potential adverse effects or are sufficient to overcome any perceived barriers.

Our research showed that medication adherence is influenced by the way individuals with bipolar disorders weigh up the necessity of treatment versus their concerns. Unsurprisingly, we demonstrated that the balance between these two different types of beliefs was not fixed in any individual but changed over time. When individuals were acutely depressed, they were more likely to believe in the necessity of medication and their concerns were not at the forefront of their mind. However, when they felt well, their attention shifted away from the necessity for medications and it was increasingly focused on any negative consequences of taking the medication or perceived barriers to treatment.

You may want to consider the balance between necessity beliefs and concern beliefs when you are trying out the strategies described in the following pages. You are more likely to be accepting of medication (i.e., higher belief in necessity, lower levels of concerns) when you are beginning to feel unwell or are acutely unwell and the most challenging time for maintaining your adherence is likely to be during periods of recovery. Furthermore, you are not alone in having beliefs that vary over time. We found that about 40 per cent of people with a long-term mental health or physical health condition describe ambivalence about taking medications (e.g., high necessity combined with high concerns).

To assist you in planning how to begin to use your self-help techniques, it is useful to consider how all these different influences on medication adherence combine together. To help understand this, the links between these factors are shown in Figure 11.

Self-management of adherence

The interventions that you can use to improve your own medication adherence follow logically from the description of the key reasons, outlined above, as to why people do not take their prescribed medication. The approaches also try to target all the elements of the model shown in Figure 11.

Knowledge

If you are not clear about what treatment you are being offered, how often you should take it, or other aspects of the regime, it is hardly surprising that you are at high risk of not keeping up with your medication. The crucial questions are: Is the treatment regime understandable? Is it acceptable? Is it manageable?

UNDERSTANDABLE

Individuals are less likely to take the prescribed medication if the information they have about the disorder and its treatment fails to fit together in a coherent manner. You need to check three issues to test whether the treatment you are being offered makes sense.

- First, you need to record what you know about your current symptoms.
- Now record your own views about what these difficulties mean to you.
- Next compare these ideas with the advice and information you have from clinical consultations or other sources of information.

Do these three components (symptoms, meanings, information from others) fit together? If not, which aspect seems unclear or causes confusion? If you are finding it difficult to answer this question, you may like to work through the checklist provided in Box 6. Having the answers to these questions overcomes many basic problems related to adherence.

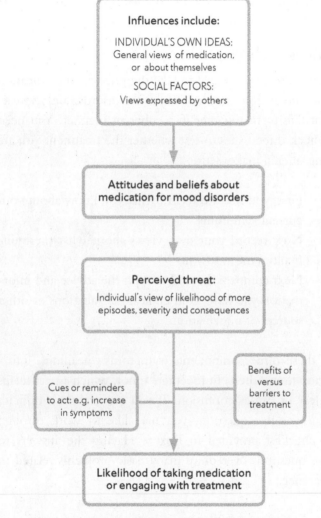

Figure 11: Factors influencing why someone might or
might not take medication

BOX 6   A CHECKLIST OF QUESTIONS TO ASK ABOUT THE DISORDER AND ITS TREATMENT

- The diagnosis

  What is the diagnosis and what does it mean for my future?

- The prescribed medication

  What is the name of the medication?

  What type of medication is it (e.g. mood stabiliser, antidepressant)?

  What dose will I need, and will any blood test be required?

  Does it matter what time I take my medication? Do I take a double dose or not?

  What common side-effects are there?

  What should I do if I get them?

  Are there any dietary restrictions, can I take other medications, and/or can I drink alcohol with this treatment?

- Treatment benefits

  Why do I need medication?

  How will each medication help me?

  How likely is it that I will respond to this medication?

  How soon should I feel better?

  How long will I need to stay on medication?

  How will I know if it is working?

  If the medication does not work how quickly can I stop taking it?

  Are there other treatments that could achieve the same benefits?

ACCEPTABLE

The next issue is whether the medication regime is acceptable to you. Are there any side-effects that are so unacceptable that you need to discuss how to reduce them, or are there are different medications available that you might tolerate better? Alternatively, do you need evidence that the medications are safe in the long term before you feel happy to take them on a regular basis?

If any aspects of your treatment are not acceptable, it is important to try to resolve the difficulties identified in collaboration with your clinician. It will really benefit you if you take some responsibility for overcoming the issues identified and play an active and constructive role in this problem-solving process. The key aspects that you need to consider are:

- What specific problems make the regime unacceptable to you?
- What alternative approaches can you suggest to overcome any barriers identified?
- How can you work with the clinician to improve the acceptability of the treatment?
- How will you both know when the treatment becomes acceptable? What would be different?

MANAGEABLE

Finally, you will find it easier to stick to the treatment prescribed if the regime is manageable. If it involves a number of medications, it is possible that you will have difficulty in remembering which treatment to take in what dose at what particular time of day. It is always worth asking whether the regime can be simplified so that it is easier to fit it in to your daily routines. Some people also find they can stick more closely with the prescribed treatments by keeping a written record of their medication regime on a flash card (a piece of paper the size of a credit card) that they always carry with them. Others use a pill box or dosette which allows them to check whether they have taken each dose.

Behavioural strategies

Overcoming any misconceptions about your treatment regime and correcting any unacceptable aspects helps many individuals. However, if you still find that your adherence to medication is erratic, you may wish to experiment with the following approaches.

PROMPTS

You may be able to set up a simple system of reminders to help you stick with your medication regime. For example, you could lay your tablets out next to the alarm clock each night with a glass of water, or stick a note on the bathroom mirror reminding you to take your mood stabiliser when you get up or set the alarm on your wristwatch for the time of your next dose.

REINFORCEMENT

If you share your home with others, can you ask someone else to remind you when to take your medication or to check that you have done so? Not everyone will wish to use this approach, some people preferring to keep control of the treatment. However, others report it actually benefits their relationships, as other family members are reassured that the medication regime is being followed and also feel they are making a small but helpful contribution.

SELF-MONITORING AND SELF-REGULATION

As discussed in the previous chapter, any regular activity can be incorporated into a daily schedule and the time of day you take your medication is an obvious candidate for inclusion in your forward planning. In addition, if you know your activity schedule is going to change at some point, you can take the opportunity to rehearse what to do in advance. For example, Deborah's regular routine was to take her medication at breakfast (about 8 a.m.). However, when she enrolled on a training course, she knew she would have to leave home at 7.30 a.m. for most days in the next week. To cope, she decided to place the tablets next to her alarm clock and modify her routine for a couple of days in advance of the change.

Another advantage of including medication adherence in your self-monitoring and self-regulation system is that you can identify and plan to cope with situations when you are at high risk of not taking your tablets. For example, Alex was a businessman who was away from home for two or three days most weeks (we will meet Alex again later.). He noted that he frequently forgot to take a supply of mood stabilisers with him. It quickly became obvious that being away from home was a 'high-risk situation' for non-adherence. With the help of his partner, Alex instituted an 'action plan'. This simply required that they both checked his travel bag each week and made sure he kept a supply of mood stabilisers in it on all occasions.

WRITTEN TREATMENT PLANS

If these simple strategies are only partially successful you may prefer to take a more systematic approach to your adherence problem and draw up a treatment plan. This may include other aspects of treatment as well as medication adherence. Importantly, it also acknowledges the benefits of following this regime, the likely problems you will encounter, and the suggested methods for overcoming these barriers.

When constructing your plan, try to be specific about the barriers you encounter, then write down as many alternative ways of overcoming these problems as you can. From the list of potential solutions, you then need to assess how feasible it is for you to undertake each option and also how likely it is to work. Include the best two or three options on your treatment plan, and then monitor how helpful these approaches are over the next few weeks. Over a few months of experimenting with different strategies you should be able to overcome some if not all of the barriers. Box 7 shows an example of a treatment plan, and the Appendix contains a blank copy for you to complete yourself.

BOX 7 MY TREATMENT PLAN

My treatment plan is to:

- Take the following prescribed medication:

Name of medication	Dose	Frequency
Fluoxetine	20mg	daily
Lithium carbonate	400mg	morning and evening

- Have contact with the following professionals

Name of person	Frequency of contact
Dr Foster	every 8 weeks
Janet (Community Worker)	every week

The benefits to me of this approach are:

- Medication helps me feel more stable
- Being more stable allows me to plan ahead
- Medication keeps me out of hospital
- Having Janet to talk to really helps me solve my problems

The barriers to my sticking to this approach are:

- Several college friends, especially Morris, ask why I take medication
- I keep forgetting to take the evening dose of lithium
- It's difficult getting to the community centre for appointments with Janet
- I worry that the antidepressant (fluoxetine) will send me high

The ways I might overcome these barriers are:

- I could read up on meds and try to explain things to Morris or give him the Bipolar UK leaflet on bipolar disorders if he's really interested
- I'll start using a pill box and put a note by the mirror in my study to remind me about the evening lithium (also ask if it is possible to take all the lithium in one go)
- I'll ask Janet if we can meet at the centre down the street as it's a lot easier for me to get to. She also does home visits, so perhaps that's an option
- I will monitor for early warning signs of depression and ask Dr Foster at my next appointment about the use of fluoxetine

Cognitive strategies

If behavioural approaches do not help, it may be that your problems are more strongly linked with your views about mood disorders and the pros and cons of taking medication. Below are some ideas on interventions that may help you tackle these difficulties. Other techniques for tackling unhelpful thoughts are described in Chapter 9 of this book.

EXAMINING THE EVIDENCE

To start to tackle your ambivalence towards medication you need to return to a common theme in this book: namely, being clear about the facts about your mood disorder, as opposed to your personal beliefs or the views of close family or friends. The particular facts to consider here relate to the threat to your well-being of rejecting the prescribed treatment. To do this, you could seek out information from any carefully conducted research on mood disorders (for example, from one of the sources at the top of the list on p.356). From these reports, it is possible to draw clear conclusions about the likelihood of further episodes of mood disorder, and the likely severity of those episodes, in individuals who do or do not receive medication. Research suggests that individuals with a history of significant mood disorder experience more severe episodes more often if they do not take medication than is the case if they do take medication. If you fit into the group who are likely to do better with medication, the next – very critical – issue is trying to come to terms with these facts. Unfortunately, when faced with painful facts most human beings do one or more of the following:

- They ignore them or try to put them out of mind.
- They deny that their problems are the same as those described.
- They challenge the quality of the information.
- They argue that they are the exception.

If this pattern sounds familiar, it is because we discussed these mechanisms when looking at how our belief system affects how we view our world (see p.80). But you have made a positive start: the very fact that you are reading this chapter of the book suggests that you accept you may have a problem. The next step is to agree the nature of the problem and how best to deal with it. The first step towards improving your adherence is to acknowledge that your negative attitudes or beliefs could be hampering your engagement with treatment. The next step is to try to help you suspend your negative attitudes and beliefs for long enough to test out some of the approaches to improving adherence. To start this process let us try two experiments.

First, a thought exercise:

What if the person you cared most about in the world had a mood disorder and came to you for advice about whether they should accept treatment? They have read up on the subject and have established the following facts:

- *They have bipolar I disorder and have noted that this has a 95 per cent chance of recurring at some point in their life.*
- *They also belong to a group of individuals who are at risk of having severe episodes that have very negative consequences for them.*
- *The treatment available reduces the risk of further severe episodes by more than 50 per cent.*

If that person came to you for advice, what would you tell them to do? Are you absolutely certain you would tell them to try to handle the situation on their own and not to accept or even give a 'trial' to the treatment offered?

This scenario is used simply to try to get you to check whether you are applying 'double standards'. Are you expecting things of yourself that you wouldn't expect of others? If so, are there any ways you can be kinder to yourself? For example, if you believe 'I should try harder to cope with my mood swings,' trying harder can also be 'reframed' as 'trying harder to stick with medication as well as using self-help techniques to cope with my mood swings'.

The other experiment involves checking the evidence that medication has never helped you.

- *First, take a close look at your life chart. Were periods of adherence associated with more or fewer episodes of mood disorder?*
- *Now look at your mood charts. Can you identify any additional stability or benefits offered by adherence to medication?*

If you are unsure whether medication has helped or there is any evidence that medication has been beneficial, you may wish to try out some of the following approaches.

TICS AND TOCS

Some individuals say that they genuinely think they would like to stick with medication and frequently think about the benefits of treatment; unfortunately, they just can't bring themselves to take the tablets at the vital moment because at that point their thinking becomes flooded by reasons not to do it.

The thoughts that encourage adherence are called TOCs (task-orientating cognitions), while the thoughts that prevent engagement with treatment are called TICs (task-interfering cognitions). In reality, many of the TOCs will be driven by beliefs about the necessity for taking medication, whilst many of the TICs will be associated with concerns. This is useful to note, as it means that you may be able to identify key themes in the TICs that you can discuss with your prescriber at a later appointment.

BOX 8 EXAMPLE OF TIC-TOCS

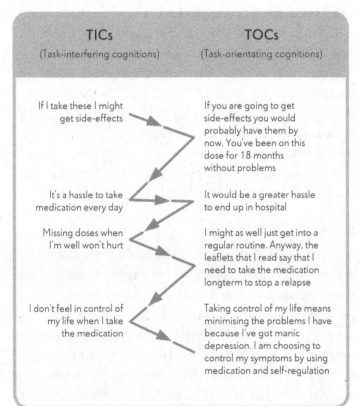

TICs (Task-interfering cognitions)	TOCs (Task-orientating cognitions)
If I take these I might get side-effects	If you are going to get side-effects you would probably have them by now. You've been on this dose for 18 months without problems
It's a hassle to take medication every day	It would be a greater hassle to end up in hospital
Missing doses when I'm well won't hurt	I might as well just get into a regular routine. Anyway, the leaflets that I read say that I need to take the medication longterm to stop a relapse
I don't feel in control of my life when I take the medication	Taking control of my life means minimising the problems I have because I've got manic depression. I am choosing to control my symptoms by using medication and self-regulation

Usually, TICs become more frequent as the moment when the medication is to be taken draws near, while TOCs are more common at other times. TICs are a form of negative automatic thought, and negative thoughts are more likely to occur when you are faced with a specific situation, such as taking medication. TOCs, by contrast, often occur at times when you reflect on your overall goals and aims in life. So: record TOCs whenever they come to mind; then keep this list to hand so that it is ready whenever you are feeling ambivalent about taking medication and are overwhelmed by TICs. The intervention requires that you counter every TIC with a TOC! If a TIC occurs when you are about to take medication, try to counter it with a TOC from your list. Your goal is to end each series of thoughts with a TOC. If you can do this, it may help you stick with your original plan to take medication. Box 8 demonstrates an example of TIC–TOCs.

COST-BENEFIT ANALYSIS

A cost–benefit analysis is a useful way of weighing up all the pros and cons of treatment. The exercise requires you to think about all the advantages and disadvantages of taking medication and the advantages and disadvantages of not taking medication. (In this approach costs represent the negative outcomes, not the actual financial price of the medication.) Box 9 shows an example of a cost–benefit analysis sheet completed by Geoffrey. A blank cost–benefit analysis form is provided in the Appendix.

BOX 9   GEOFFREY'S COST–BENEFIT ANALYSIS

Advantages of taking lithium	*Disadvantages of taking lithium*
• Treatment keeps me out of hospital • My family are less worried when I'm on lithium • I know I'm doing everything I can to keep my illness under control • It seems to be working for me; I've been free of episodes for two years	• I hate blood tests • I've gained weight as a side-effect • Lithium can be toxic; you can get kidney damage if the blood level is wrong
Advantages of NOT taking lithium	*Disadvantages of NOT taking lithium*
• I have fewer things to carry around or remember • I'm in control of me, not the tablets	• There is a greater risk I'll have a relapse • I might have to go back into hospital which may jeopardise my job • If my wife finds out she'll be upset • The doctor has expressed concern for my well-being if I don't stay with medication • Once when I was depressed, I wanted to kill myself – it was very frightening and I don't want to go through that again

What do you notice about the completed analysis? Two things may come to mind. First, very occasionally a similar item appears in more than one column. For example, one advantage of taking lithium was that it reduced the risk of hospitalisation. Being admitted was also a potential disadvantage of *not* taking lithium. Second, the benefits of adherence (the advantages of taking lithium, plus the disadvantages of not taking lithium) outweighed the costs. Geoffrey had not realised before completing his own analysis that he had more to gain than to lose by staying on a mood stabiliser.

If you wish to increase your own medication adherence you will have to work hard to identify the benefits of treatment. If this is difficult, you might wish to seek the opinions of other individuals who have struggled with similar problems. This may also suggest to you additional ideas or actions that reduce the disadvantages of adherence or the advantages of non-adherence.

TACKLING NEGATIVE AUTOMATIC THOUGHTS

If using TOCs or cost–benefit analysis does not help, it may be necessary to make a more detailed exploration of your negative thoughts about medication. To begin this process, you need to *recognise* and *record* each specific automatic thought. Next you need to pause and *review* this thought. Finally, you need to *respond* to this thought. This strategy of '*recognise, record, review* and *respond*' is useful for tackling the thoughts that occur in many difficult situations. However, it takes some time to feel comfortable with this approach. Do not worry if you make several attempts before you are able to go through this process without a hitch.

Approaches to automatic thoughts that are more resistant to change are described on pp.244–50. Below are some tips to help you work on your negative views of medication, followed by a worked example.

- *Recognise and record:* Can you write down in your own words your negative automatic thought about taking medication? Try to write down exactly what went through your mind, without modifying it. Now rate how much you believe this thought on a scale of 0 to 100 and rate your emotional reaction.

- *Review:* This negative thought represents the first idea that came into your mind. However, this does not mean that this idea reflects the facts. It is useful to try to establish the accuracy or helpfulness of your automatic thought. First, can you review the evidence that supports this idea, and then any evidence that goes against this idea? Next, can you review any alternative ways of thinking about this situation? Finally, in what way is this idea helpful or unhelpful to you (are there advantages or disadvantages to maintaining this view)?

- *Respond:* The final component of testing automatic thoughts about medication requires two actions. First, rerate your belief in the original thought (using the same 0 to 100 rating scale) and your current emotion. Second, decide what else you may need to do.

For example, you may wish to gather more evidence to support or refute your idea. Alternatively, you may wish to design an experiment where you record information about your progress prospectively to test out your idea more fully.

Let's take the example of Alex (who we met earlier) again.

Alex was a businessman. He had noted that when he was away from home he often did not take a supply of mood stabilisers with him, so he tried to overcome this problem by keeping an additional bottle of lithium tablets in his travel bag at all times. However, he reported that despite this he was still at high risk of non-adherence when he went away to business meetings. By monitoring this problem Alex was able to identify some important cognitive barriers to adherence.

Alex's situation and mood: 'Sitting in my hotel room on the morning of an important meeting about a contract for a new piece of work for my company. Taking the pill box out of my travel bag. Feeling anxious.'

Recognise and record – thoughts included:

- 'This is an important job, my boss stressed it was important that I did this well, I really must be on the ball.'
- Negative automatic thoughts: 'The tablets might slow me down and then I'll make a mess of this.'
- Belief in thought: 85/100.

Review: Evidence FOR – thoughts about the negative effects of medication included:

- 'I read somewhere that lithium can slow down people's thinking and that it can make you confused.'

Evidence AGAINST – thoughts about the negative effects of medication included:

- 'I've been on lithium for 13 months and I don't feel slowed down.'
- 'I haven't messed up previous meetings; my work has been of a high standard even while I've been taking lithium.'
- 'The only meeting that went really badly occurred on a day when I didn't take my lithium!'
- 'Confusion only usually occurs if the blood level is in the toxic range; my last test was fine.'

Alternatives included:

- 'I may just be putting all my worries on to the tablets, when really I'm just anxious that the meeting should go well.'
- 'I'll ask my doctor when I get back to town if there is any evidence that I have been slowed down by the lithium. If it was really true, maybe he could recommend another mood stabiliser.'

Advantages and disadvantages included:

- 'Focusing on this thought is not advantageous to me at this moment. I need to be planning my meeting.'

Response:

- Belief in original automatic thought: 40/100.
- Mood: less anxious.
- Action plan: I will read the Bipolar UK leaflet on lithium and its side-effects when I get home, and if I'm still concerned, I will contact Dr Foster and ask to discuss my worries at our next appointment.

A last comment

As a psychiatrist involved in the treatment of individuals with bipolar disorder, I am tempted to write twenty pages on why I think you should try to stick with any medication prescribed. However, CBT has taught me that persuasion is much less successful than helping individuals discover for themselves why they are ambivalent towards medications. Also, it is important to have a choice of strategies to test out. If, despite the techniques outlined in this chapter, you are absolutely unable to convince yourself to keep taking your medication, I would like to suggest three things for you to do:

- Always tell your clinician. Some may struggle more than others to show 100 per cent respect for your decision (particularly if they are concerned about the consequences for your mental health), but they need to know.

- For your own well-being, never stop your medication suddenly. Always reduce medication slowly over several weeks or months (preferably under the guidance of a clinician). Suddenly stopping your prophylactic treatment may significantly increase your risk of relapse.

- Re-read the section in Part One of this book on the 'no treatment' option (p.60). It is also worth monitoring your progress in medication-free periods, particularly noting fluctuations in your most common symptoms of mood disorder. ·

On a more positive note, if you do manage to maintain your adherence to medication, you may also like to negotiate with your prescriber to allow you to self-medicate to prevent mood swings developing into an episode of depression or mania.

CHAPTER SUMMARY

- About 50 per cent of individuals on long-term medication do not take all the prescribed medication.

- The most common reasons for not taking medication are:

- treatment issues;
- lifestyle issues;
- attitudes and belief about medication, especially the balance between beliefs related to the necessity for and concerns about taking prescribed treatments.

• Useful techniques for increasing adherence include:
  - *knowledge:* is the treatment regime understandable, acceptable and manageable?
  - *practical strategies:* prompts and reinforcement; self-monitoring and self-regulation; written treatment plans;
  - *cognitive strategies:* examining the evidence; TIC-TOCs; cost–benefit analysis; challenging negative automatic thoughts.

• If you stop taking medication:
  - always tell your clinician;
  - don't stop your treatment suddenly;
  - monitor your symptoms during medication-free periods.

PART THREE

SELF-MANAGEMENT OF DEPRESSION AND MANIA

Aims of Part Three

At the end of Part Three of this book, I hope you will have improved your self-management skills by:

- understanding the characteristic unhelpful behaviours and thoughts associated with depressed mood;
- introducing key behavioural interventions that can increase activities, reduce problems and improve your mood;
- learning how to apply cognitive strategies such as distraction and thought modification to develop a more balanced view of your situation and to reduce depression and anxiety;
- understanding the characteristic unhelpful behaviours and thoughts associated with highs;
- introducing key behavioural techniques to help you relax, maximise your self-control and avoid major problems;
- learning how to apply cognitive strategies such as active distraction and simple thought modification to develop a more balanced view and to reduce elation and irritability.

9

Self-management of depressive symptoms

For many individuals, simply undertaking self-monitoring and self-regulation as described in Part Two of this book will reduce the frequency or severity of mood swings. However, even if you are applying these techniques carefully, and have also worked hard to overcome barriers to taking medication as prescribed, it is still possible that you will experience some episodes of more extreme mood swings (beyond the + 2/ −2 ratings on your mood chart). These swings are usually accompanied by changes in your thoughts and behaviour.

The two chapters in this part of the book are targeted at helping you deal with these more extreme episodes and trying to restabilise your mood. The present chapter deals with depression; the next (Chapter 10) with mania and other types of 'highs'. Each chapter begins by looking at techniques to deal with unhelpful behaviours and then moves on to techniques for modifying unhelpful or dysfunctional thoughts. By tackling these two areas it is usually possible to improve your mood and general functioning. However, it is important to bear in mind that this division into thoughts and behaviours is slightly artificial, as they influence each other as well as influencing mood.

Dealing with unhelpful behaviours

In Part One of this book, we explored in detail the symptoms of depressive episodes and the vicious cycle of changes that may occur once depression sets in. The key unhelpful activities of individuals with depression are:

- *avoidance,* particularly of activities that give them a sense of pleasure or achievement;
- *withdrawal,* particularly from social situations that may offer support;
- *procrastination* – being unable to start or complete tasks or solve problems.

It is easy to understand how these difficulties increase individuals' negative views of themselves and further depress them. However, it is often difficult to break this cycle. Fortunately, building on previously learned techniques is a useful way to start. There are two main approaches:

- activity scheduling (including social interactions);
- step-by-step approaches to tasks and problems.

Activity scheduling

You may already have found activity schedules helpful in

planning your day and ensuring you take on neither too many nor too few activities. This strategy is especially important when experiencing a more severe period of depression. If you are finding activity scheduling difficult, here are some tips on how to cope with the most frequently reported problems.

UNABLE TO DO ANYTHING

If your energy level is low and you are inactive, you probably get up in the morning and then spend a long time thinking about doing things, worry about not doing things, and remind yourself of all the reasons why you can't do anything. These thoughts tend to increase feelings of depression and anxiety. To break this cycle, you have to take action. Having a plan of action for when you wake up is an important first step. It is also helpful if the timetable you have to start the day with is basic and simple.

It is best to plan a daily schedule at least one day in advance. Early evening is a good time to plan the next day; setting a fixed time to write the plan is even better. If this is really hard, can you get someone to help you in writing the plan? If no one is available at home, can you telephone someone on a regular basis to talk your plan through or get ideas?

At the end of each day, review your timetable and note what you have learned from your schedule. If you did nothing, did it actually make you feel any better? The usual answer is no. If anything, inactivity tends to make depression worse. So, it is worth trying to plan some activities for tomorrow.

Taking action has two effects. First, it can actually distract you and give you temporary relief from your negative thoughts and feelings. Second, and most importantly, you will feel better sooner if you keep on doing the things that have made you feel better on previous occasions.

If you are really struggling to do anything, perhaps you could try a short exercise to see if these questions help generate ideas of what to do next. Simply try to list two activities that you can:

- do on your own;
- do with other people;
- do early in the day;
- do in the evening;
- do at night;
- do which are free;
- do which cost money;
- do which help you use your brain;
- do which help you relax.

These ideas will generate a number of possible activities, some of which will overlap in several categories. For example, doing a crossword puzzle is something you can do alone, at any time of day or night, and will use your brain. This overlap is not a problem; in fact, one of my clients produced a matrix that she told me helped her pick just the right activity for any particular moment (see Table 3). I have included a blank copy of this matrix in the Appendix for you to complete if you wish (see p.381).

Table 3: Activity matrix

	Shopping with friend	Reading	Doing crosswords	Swimming	Running club	Watching TV	Going to the Theatre
Do alone		✓	✓	✓		✓	
Do with others	✓			✓	✓		✓
Early in the day	✓	✓	✓	✓		✓	
Evening		✓	✓	✓	✓	✓	✓
Nighttime		✓	✓			✓	
Free activity	✓	✓	✓		✓	✓	
Costs money				✓			✓
Uses my mind		✓	✓				✓
Helps me relax				✓	✓	✓	

What if you did some activities but didn't feel any better? This is actually more likely. The most common problem is not a lack of any activity, but a lack of positive activities that give any sense of pleasure or achievement or a lack of re-inforcement for what you did. It is essential to give yourself positive feedback for *anything* you do when you feel so low. Try to avoid self-criticism or discounting your efforts. If you had broken your leg, you would not expect to be able to do everything you usually do and would acknowledge the extra effort required in simply moving around on flat ground. Furthermore, you wouldn't expect to be able to run up a hill. It is very important to accept that depression is just as disabling as a physical injury. You must not expect too much too soon; but you can help yourself to recover by making gradual changes in your activities and thinking. Anything you are able to do is a valuable start. The next step is to include positive experiences in your schedule.

UNABLE TO ENJOY ANYTHING OR ACHIEVE ANYTHING

A frequent problem with activity planning is that individuals try desperately to keep up with their obligations but fail to consider their own needs. (This issue is discussed in detail in Melanie Fennell's book in this series, *Overcoming Low Self-Esteem*.) A schedule that includes no planned enjoyable activities or time for yourself is probably too difficult to maintain if you are already feeling down. Also, low energy and poor concentration may make it difficult to complete complex obligations. The goal is to set realistic targets and have a balanced plan of activities for your day.

Designing a more constructive schedule of activities begins with ensuring that any list of priorities (as discussed on p.167) includes pleasurable activities. You could start by making sure that your 'A' list of activities for each day contains an equal number of pleasurable activities and obligations. Many individuals report that when they feel depressed they are unable to think of any positive activities, so here are some questions that may help you:

- Can you list any hobbies or interests that you have?
- Can you record three things that you might enjoy doing?
- Can you list three things that you used to enjoy doing?
- Can you list three enjoyable activities that you always thought you might try in the future?
- If you talk to or observe other people, what activities do they engage in?
- Does the local library or community centre have any information on activities available in your area?

Some of the activities you note may be impractical or not manageable at present, but even so this list will give you some ideas of what you could try. If you are still struggling to get started, try reorganising the list of activities you have come up with in order of (a) how likely you are to enjoy it and (b) the probable degree of difficulty. Starting with an easy activity that offers average or above average pleasure, can you now add at least one of these activities to each day of your schedule?

You can of course include some basic day-to-day tasks and obligations in your schedule. However, it is worth following some simple guidelines that will help to reduce the stress associated with such tasks. As discussed previously, it helps to list all the tasks and try to delegate some to other people. Next, check through the list and select the simplest tasks. Include one simple task per day, gradually increasing to two and then three as you begin to feel better and more in control. The benefit of this approach is that it makes inroads into your obligations and gives you some success experiences – and it is vital that you have some positive reinforcement. Completing an essential task, no matter how small, fulfils the criteria for a success and can be rated as such. It is also useful to try to follow the completion of an obligation with some sort of reward, no matter how small.

An essential part of this approach is to allocate a fixed amount of *time* to a task. When individuals are depressed, they are slowed down in their thinking and their actions, so some tasks take much longer than they would normally. If, while you are depressed, you set yourself a target of cleaning two rooms in your home, the danger is that it will take much longer than expected, and quite possibly fill most of your day. This will leave you feeling frustrated, with a low sense of accomplishment and with no time for other, more positive experiences. Rather than improving your mood, it may make life feel very empty. In contrast, setting a target of two hours' house cleaning in the morning is much more manageable. No matter how slow your progress, simply sticking with the time allocated will be deemed a success. You can then give yourself positive feedback for your efforts; and, by identifying a clear time to stop, you are also enabling yourself to move on to other activities without feeling guilty. Furthermore, as your depression begins to lift, you will become more active, have more energy and be able to do more in the same amount of time.

The final stage in this approach is to review the list of more complex tasks and consider whether any obligations can realistically be postponed. If there are any important tasks that cannot be delayed or delegated to others, can you think of anyone who can help you to complete them? If the task is difficult but others cannot help, you may wish to follow the process described later in this chapter under 'Step-by-step approaches'.

UNABLE TO FACE ANYONE

Individuals who are depressed frequently say that they doubt whether other people like them or want to spend time with them. Negative thoughts such as 'I'm boring' or 'They wouldn't want to be with me if they knew what I was really like' are common. These thoughts are powerful and not easy to challenge. When they are combined with low activity levels, it is easy to understand how individuals become socially isolated. However, it is important to try to retain some contact with the outside world. Keeping in touch with people offers you an important source of support, and often provides valuable external feedback and reinforcement at a time when you are finding it hard to see yourself in a positive light.

It is not easy to make social contacts if you fear being judged by others or worry about letting people down by not being good company. However, remember that you can control the frequency of social contacts and the pace of change. Perhaps you could try to include one social interaction each day for the first few days, and then gradually increase to two a day by the end of the week. The duration of the contact can also be built up gradually as you begin to gain confidence.

As with other activities, getting started can be difficult, so:

- First, can you generate a list of the social contacts that you have previously enjoyed or that you think you might enjoy.
- Next, can you note the name of anyone who usually makes you feel good about yourself?
- Finally, has anyone actually contacted you recently to arrange a social activity?

The next step is to reorganise the list in order, with the least stressful social contact at the top of the list and the most challenging social event or engagement at the bottom. For example, the top part of your list may look something like this:

- Buy a newspaper and try to hold a brief conversation with the shopkeeper.
- Call Jane and have a chat on the telephone.
- Accept Rosemary's invitation to go to coffee (call beforehand and tell her I can only stay for 30 minutes).

- Take flowers round to Jackie who is at home recovering from the flu.

To help in the early stages, you could plan in advance (as in the third option here) to set a time limit for the interaction, as knowing the end point sometimes helps reduce any associated stress. You could also rehearse some topics of conversation or questions you could ask people so that you don't feel at a loss for words when you first meet.

Some individuals prefer to recommence their social interactions by talking to people they don't know well and by keeping the conversation light (talking about the weather, the news).

Others prefer to start by talking with or meeting people they trust and who know them well. There is no 'best approach'. Begin with the social contact that you feel most confident (despite your depression) you can undertake. As with other activity 'experiments', review your progress, examine any changes in mood, and gradually work your way through the list you have developed.

DEALING WITH SETBACKS

Although you will generally make progress in the right direction, if you follow the guidelines set out above, it is likely that some days will be harder than others. Still, though it may not seem like it at the time, we often learn as much from reviewing difficult days as we do from looking back over successful days. Examining some of the following themes after tricky days may help you identify why things did not go according to plan:

- *Being specific about your planned activity*: Your schedule is more likely to work if you are absolutely clear about exactly what you are going to try to do and what time of day you will try to do it. If you decide that you will phone a friend and try to arrange to meet, you need to decide in advance which friend to call and when you will get in touch. If there is any room for doubt in the schedule, you may find that you spend too much of your day procrastinating about what action to take. It is also useful to compare your planned activity with your actual activity. Did you manage to carry out your plan? If not, what were the barriers? Can you overcome these problems? Was the day better or worse than you had anticipated?

- *Becoming aware of fluctuations in your mood*: If you feel depressed and your plan did not help alleviate your sadness, it is all too easy to write the whole day off. However, by rating the sense of achievement and pleasure of each activity you will gather more accurate information. Even on a 'bad' day, it is usual to have some variation in your A (achievement) and P (pleasure) ratings. It is helpful to check whether you felt 100 per cent depressed for 100 per cent of the day or whether there were any variations over the day. Did any activities coincide with an improvement in or worsening of your mood? If a planned positive activity did not have the desired effect or outcome, can you work out why? Also, try to remember that each daily activity schedule is an experiment. You are trying to find a package of things that work for you. If an activity is not beneficial, how can you modify your approach or change the activity to improve your chances of success the next time you try it?

- *Acknowledging successes*: Often, individuals stick with their activity schedule, and rate their sense of pleasure and achievement at the time of completion of the activity as quite high, but then discount their ratings at the end of the day. Classically, such individuals start a review of their day by saying: '*Yes*, I did all those activities, *but* this schedule is nothing compared to what I should be able to do . . . ' It is important to try to fight this 'yes but' approach. The best way to overcome the tendency to discount your efforts is to set clear goals for each day in advance and to reward yourself for doing what you set out to do. Again, if you find this hard to do on your own, you may consider sharing your plans with someone and then getting their objective feedback on whether you achieved your goals.

- *Giving yourself a chance*: It may be hard to convince yourself that changing your activities will alleviate your depression. This uncertainty is totally understandable. There is no 100 per cent guarantee that these approaches will work for you. However, the opposite is also true: there is no reason to assume that they won't. No matter how doubtful you are, there is actually nothing to lose (and much to be learned) by trying them out. It is entirely appropriate to be sceptical about the benefits of activity scheduling. But healthy scepticism means that you suspend your negative judgement until you have completed a fair experiment, not that you turn your back on the whole idea.

Step-by-step approaches

If you are depressed, you may feel overwhelmed by the tasks you want to complete or the problems that you face. The key to coping is to focus on one issue at a time and to take a step-by-step approach. Plan the approach, rehearse how to overcome obstacles and then review your progress.

DEALING WITH COMPLEX TASKS

First, write the list of tasks; then put them in order of difficulty. Now, starting with the easiest task, see if you can break it down into smaller bites and make a note of each separate step you need to take. As you become more skilled at this approach, you can work your way down the entire list so that eventually you have generated several manageable steps for even the most complex task.

Having repeated the process for each complex task, you now need to decide which task you prefer to start on. Tomorrow, try to complete step one of that task; the next day, try step two; and so on.

Breaking a large task down into several smaller tasks makes it much easier to work out what barriers there are to progress. Furthermore, having worked out each step, you can rehearse how to undertake each task in your mind and begin to predict potential sticking points. You may also be able to try techniques for overcoming any hurdles. Box 10 provides an example to help you understand this approach.

BOX 10   STEP-BY-STEP APPROACH TO TASKS

Goal: To attend a daytime class at the community college

Steps:

1. Find out what the local college has on offer – walk down and get a brochure
2. Read brochure and choose possible courses
3. Check starting date and class times for three courses I might like to do
4. Make sure I can get a babysitter for class times
5. Call Joanne to see if she would like to go on a course as well
6. Come to a joint decision about which course
7. Go down to the college and sign up for the course
8. Attend first lesson with Joanne

DEALING WITH PROBLEMS

Unfortunately, being depressed does not relieve you of any other problems in your life. There is a temptation to avoid confronting problems; but, as most will not disappear, it is worth taking the same step-by-step approach to them. The critical first step is to turn each problem into a goal, viewing it as a target for you to aim at rather than a burden to overcome. This will help you begin to think about potential solutions. Having clarified your goal, can you now brainstorm all the alternative ways you can achieve this target? Next, go through each approach and work out the feasibility of each strategy. For example, what are the pros and cons of each alternative solution? What are the advantages or disadvantages of the approach for your current situation, for the future, for other key people in your life? What barriers are there to implementing that plan? Having considered the alternatives, try out the most promising approach; then review its success. If that approach did not work, move on to the next potential solution. Again, to help you with this I have worked through an example in Box 11.

Modifying unhelpful or dysfunctional thoughts

The most common automatic thoughts that accompany a downswing are negative thoughts about yourself, your world and your future (sometimes called the *negative cognitive triad*). The negative cognitive triad is associated with depressed mood, although negative predictions about the future are also associated with anxiety. As we shall see in the next chapter, irritability may also be a prominent emotion in highs and lows, particularly in response to perceived criticisms of what you do. Negative mood states can be alleviated temporarily by distracting yourself from the thought. However, to achieve lasting reductions in your depression and anxiety, it helps to be able to *recognise* and *record*, *review* and *respond* to your unhelpful automatic thoughts.

BOX 11   PROBLEM-SOLVING

Problem: Not enough time to work on self-management strategies

(Convert *problem* to a *goal*)

Goal: Increase the time available on a regular basis to review progress with self-monitoring

Alternative solutions:

1.   Stop doing self-monitoring if I haven't got the time
2.   Delay starting self-monitoring for a few months
3.   Get a babysitter or do a child minding 'swap' with Gemma for a few extra hours a week
4.   Create time by delegating other household tasks such as family shopping to Alan
5.   Set time to read each day at coffee instead of listening to the radio
6.   Schedule a set time in my diary (Friday at 10 a.m.), write it in for three months in advance, and try to give it priority

---

Having assessed the advantages and disadvantages of each approach, my preferred option is:

Do a childminding swap with Gemma – this will give me two hours on Thursday afternoon

---

My reserve plan is:

Set time to read each day at coffee

Recognising and recording automatic thoughts

It is not easy to identify thoughts immediately as they run through your mind and it will take some practice. The two key elements that will help are to note down exactly what you were doing when you noticed that your mood changed, then to record how depressed or anxious you felt on a 0 to 100 scale. If you describe in detail what you were doing, the time of day, where you were, who you were with, you may find it possible to recall what was going through your mind at that moment. If this is difficult, try closing your eyes and recreating the scene in your imagination. Ask yourself the following questions:

- What thoughts, memories or images do I have?
- What thoughts do I have about other people?
- What thoughts am I predicting they have about me?
- What do any of these thoughts say about me or my situation? About other people?
- If it were true, what does this idea mean about me? Or about others?
- What am I afraid of right now? What bad events or outcomes am I predicting?

Using this checklist of questions, you will probably be able to come up with some of the unhelpful thoughts that go through your mind. As with mood state, it is useful to rate the intensity of your belief in each thought on a 0 to 100 scale. Having rated your belief, pause to remind yourself that just because this is the first idea that came into your mind or the one you believe the most, this does not mean that it is necessarily the correct interpretation of the situation or event.

You may find that you have recorded several automatic thoughts. Before moving on to explore your thoughts it is helpful to make sure they accurately reflect your *immediate* reaction to the situation. You may be tempted to 'tone down' a statement to make it less painful. Unfortunately, techniques for modifying dysfunctional thoughts are probably more effective if you deal with the raw rather than the polite version. For example, 'I'm bad' or 'I'm no good' are clear negative automatic thoughts that would make you feel down, whereas 'I began to think I wasn't very nice' or 'I thought I didn't do that very well' do not convey the reality of the thought or the depth of feeling.

Reviewing your automatic thoughts

Having identified the automatic thoughts that are associated with your negative mood, it is important to follow a regular process of review. Rather than trying to tackle every automatic thought associated with your emotional response, try selecting the one that you believe most strongly, or the most extreme idea, and then review it in detail by working through the following stages.

EXAMINE THE EVIDENCE

You will be very well aware of evidence that supports your idea, but are you attending to any evidence that goes against your idea, or any contradictions? To examine the evidence, list all the information that is compatible with your view. Stick with factual evidence, not feelings, intuition or hearsay. Next, write down all the evidence that does not support your automatic thought. This will be harder, as such information is not at the forefront of your mind. To get started note anything that contradicts your thought, no matter how small. If you are still struggling, think about what you would say to someone else if they asked for your views of the evidence for and against the idea. You could also think whether you have any past experiences that support or refute your idea.

Having collected evidence for and against your automatic thought, is there any room for doubt that it is right? If you are still not sure, can you identify any sources of additional information that will help you reach a conclusion? What experiment could you do to test out the idea further yourself? Can you ask someone else how they would view this idea? If you conclude that there *is* room for doubt, it is appropriate to explore what other views could be considered.

CONSIDERING THE ALTERNATIVES

Having demonstrated that the first idea that springs into your mind may not represent the facts, the next step is to generate a list of alternative ways the situation *could be* viewed. Questions that may help include:

- What other views could I take of the situation?
- Would I view the situation differently if I felt better?
- Have I any experience of similar situations?

- How did I view those situations?
- What might someone else think in this situation, particularly someone who is not depressed?

This approach may generate at least one or two additional ideas that can again be examined to identify evidence for or against them.

ADDITIONAL QUESTIONS

In tackling your automatic thought, you may also question how helpful or functional it is for you to stick with this idea. Questions about this might include:

- Are there any advantages to holding this view? Are there any disadvantages?
- Can I identify any particular pattern of thinking errors, e.g., overgeneralisation?
- Am I taking all the responsibility for a situation? Can I take a more balanced view, where I take some but not all of the responsibility for what has occurred?
- Finally, if my original idea is an accurate reflection of the situation, what is the most constructive and helpful action I can take?

Responding to your automatic thoughts

Having examined your automatic thought, can you now re-rate how strongly you believe your original idea? By now, you are probably less convinced by it. Next, can you re-rate the intensity of your emotional response? It is unlikely that your depression or anxiety will have disappeared, but you may be able to rate your feelings less negatively. Finally, review the outcome of working through this process. What have you learned? Is there any other action you can now take to help you further in modifying this thought?

If there is no change in your mood state, consider whether there is any other powerful thought operating that you have not yet examined. If so, it is worth repeating the process, targeting this new thought.

Lastly, it is important to use these cognitive techniques alongside the practical techniques outlined in the previous section. The combination is likely to improve your mood state more than either approach alone.

It will take practice to feel comfortable with the process of challenging and modifying your automatic thoughts and coming up with more balanced views of your experiences. To help with this process, I have included an example of a thought record in Table 4.

A blank thought record is provided in the Appendix. Ideally, you should copy this template and use it regularly, keeping your automatic thought records for future reference. Reviewing several automatic thought records can enable you to identify common patterns in your dysfunctional thinking, such as jumping to conclusions or mind-reading (as described on p.87). The records may also reveal themes in the events or experiences that you find stressful, thus helping you to plan for the future. Also, these records may help you identify some of your own underlying beliefs.

Additional ways of understanding your thinking style

In the last decade, there have been some fascinating scientific studies that explore not just the links between the content of an individual's automatic thoughts and emotional responses, but also how their thinking patterns or cognitive processing style relate to their mood state. Many of these research projects suggest that one way to reduce the frequency and emotional impact of *repetitive negative thoughts* is to view them as a personal habit. This line of reasoning then suggests that, like other unhelpful behaviour patterns, it is possible to identify when these behaviours occur and to consider using some additional CBT techniques that aim to break this habit. To understand the techniques, we will begin by briefly reviewing some elements of the theory about repetitive negative thinking, especially rumination.

According to the late Susan Nolen-Hoeksema, who was an expert in psychology working at Yale University in the USA, rumination is 'a mode of responding to distress that involves repetitively and passively focusing on symptoms of distress and on the possible causes and consequences of these symptoms . . . people who are ruminating remain fixated on the problems and on their feelings about them without taking action.'

In sum, rumination is what is happening in your mind when you overthink a past event or situation and continue to brood about the problem, this type of 'toxic' thinking is likely to be associated negative feelings. This does not mean you should avoid thinking about the past, indeed done in a constructive way, this can be helpful. It is important to recognise that people who engage in reviewing past negative experiences and emotions often do so in the belief that they will gain insight into their life or a problem. For example, someone may reflect on a situation by first relaxing and then reconsidering the past event or experience and then engaging in thoughts and behaviours to ensure similar problems are less likely to occur in the future. This may involve using approaches such as decision-making, planning and problem-solving. In contrast, rumination differs in important ways from helpful re-living of experiences, such as reflection. Rumination is characterised by brooding about the negative aspects of a past event and replaying the problem over and over again, without ever moving on to consider constructive solutions. So, rumination is often accompanied by other unhelpful behaviours such as avoidance (which we discussed earlier in this chapter). Worrying is a very similar cognitive process to rumination, but it is focused on the future. Typically, the individual is making negative predictions about what will happen in the future ('what-if' statements) and this thinking style increases feelings of anxiety and fear about not being able to cope. Again, this may be associated with avoidance of situations.

Additional CBT techniques for understanding and managing repetitive negative thinking often consider this cognitive processing style as a 'bad habit'. We all have some habits that are less desirable or less adaptive than others, and many people have learned to successfully overcome unhealthy or unhelpful habits. One of the key approaches to helping you to understand the purpose and nature of rumination or worry is to use functional analysis (also referred to as the ABC technique). This is very similar to other CBT self-help techniques as it involves identifying what you were doing when you began to ruminate (referred to as the antecedents), and to record the behaviours and consequences of any repetitive thinking. To show you how to employ this technique, try to identify a time when you engaged in rumination, i.e., an occasion when you got stuck in a negative, distressing thinking loop (without being able to get out of it). Now try to recall and write down the following:

- What was the thought that set off your rumination (i.e., the initial thought associated with the past event or experience that you were brooding about)?
- When did you start thinking that? (date and time)
- How long did it last?
- What were you doing when you started thinking that?
- How engaged were you with the task or activity that you were doing at the time?
- What happened next and what were the consequences of thinking about that past event? (i.e., how did you feel, what was your emotional response, did ruminating help, etc.)
- What interrupted or ended this period of rumination?
- What might be the function (or purpose) of thinking about that past event? (i.e., in what ways did you think it was helpful to you, did you feel different after

engaging in the process, what had you hoped you would achieve from ruminating, etc.)

The above questions can help you identify time periods when you are at greatest risk of ruminating or worrying. For example, ruminating may be more frequent when you are only partly paying attention to your current situation or activities, e.g., 'half-watching' a TV show, or you are walking to the shops in the morning, and so your mind wanders to past events that upset you. Alternatively, there may be specific triggers to your rumination, such as reading an article about families, which sets off the process of ruminating about any problems you have, e.g., in your relationship with a sibling. What happened to end the rumination is also worth recording, e.g., was it the smell of burnt toast that pulled you back to the present, or did you manage to do something to break into the negative thinking loop (such as refocusing on an important task that required your full attention). As in other self-monitoring or self-management exercises, you may have noticed that the important questions start with the words 'what, how and when'. This is very deliberate as several clinical studies of CBT suggest that it is unhelpful to use 'why' questions when examining rumination. The reason for this is that 'why' questions simply feed into the entire process and reinforce the toxic brooding (as 'why' is typically the word that goes through a person's mind when they are brooding about an event in an unhelpful way and find themselves unable to engage with active problem-solving).

Once you start to recognise times when you engage in rumination, you will probably want to ask yourself the following questions:

- Has ruminating helped me make any progress towards solving the problem or in my decision-making?
- Has ruminating helped me to understand the problem (or my feelings about it) any better than I did before?
- Has ruminating changed my mood in a helpful or unhelpful way?

Invariably, people confirm that rumination is feeding into negative thinking and self-criticism and has not improved their problem-solving. So, the next step in overcoming rumination and its negative consequences involves trying to break into the negative processing style. Of course, many of you will use the self-help techniques for challenging automatic thoughts that have been described already. However, other options for overcoming repetitive thinking style focus more on the idea that you can reduce rumination by interrupting the cognitive process (to break the bad habit).

Having begun to recognise times when rumination is likely to occur, one way to tackle it is simply to select another activity that needs your full attention. For example, you might engage in a conversation with someone you care about and talk about a topic that is important to both of you, or you might engage in doing a task you enjoy or something that needs your full concentration like following a new recipe. Alternatively, if rumination is more likely when, e.g., you are walking to work or to the shops, you might play some music you are familiar with (and sing along in your head) or listen to a podcast or audiobook. Another option is to interrupt the rumination loop by simply engaging in self-talk and describing what task you are doing at that moment and thinking about the steps required to complete the task (e.g., if you are getting ready for the day, you might remind yourself of your immediate schedule and tell yourself 'I'm going to take shower, decide what clothes I'll put on and what time I'll leave the house', etc.). Essentially, these techniques are all aimed at shifting your attention away from the rumination and distracting yourself from an unhelpful habit.

Other interesting approaches to repetitive negative thinking can include giving yourself permission to set a specific time in the day when you allow yourself to brood for a short period (e.g., 10 minutes). You might need to practise so-called 'attention to experience' strategies, as they need to be used carefully and, for instance, you will probably want to set an alarm to signal the end of the 'session'. The main goal of these approaches is to help you understand that you are in control of rumination processes and that you can turn your attention on and off.

If you are not confident that you can control the habit through self-management, you may want to get additional help, especially to tackle prolonged rumination. Some people find that distraction and shifting attention are not as effective as challenging negative thoughts in changing their mood. However, it is often possible to use combinations of these approaches. There are some CBT therapists who are trained in rumination-focused CBT (RFCBT) and others who can guide you through the use of a wide range of 'anti-rumination' techniques. These include developing a list of other experiences that you might try that deeply absorb you (e.g., a sport or other outdoor activity or an indoor hobby).

All of the approaches outlined can help to overcome procrastination and avoidance, but many individuals also benefit from using techniques that reduce self-criticism (we will discuss this topic again in the final chapters of the book). These techniques can be useful because individuals prone to rumination and worry often start to criticise themselves for not being able to overcome this cognitive processing style on their own. Helping individuals become more self-accepting often begins by getting people first to identify feelings and thoughts of compassion and then learn how to bring compassion to a range of difficult situations. If you try out these exercises you will probably find that, at least initially, you are able to show lots of empathy and compassion for other people but that you are much less able to be self-compassionate. As we will discuss in the final pages of this book, learning to be as compassionate about yourself and accepting yourself as you are can help to reduce self-criticism and can be an additional way to prevent rumination from occurring.

Other techniques are available to help with repetitive negative thinking. However, as these overlap with mindfulness approaches, they are discussed in the next part of this chapter.

Mindfulness

Different uses of the word 'mindfulness'

Before describing how some elements of mindfulness may be used to overcome or prevent depressive symptoms, it is helpful to orientate readers to the ways in which the word mindfulness is used and to clarify how the term mindfulness will be employed in this book.

To briefly summarise, mindfulness describes a specific way of living and mindfulness is best understood as a process, i.e., it is a series of activities and events that you undertake to achieve a particular outcome (i.e., living mindfully). This means that, e.g., meditation, on its own, is not the same as mindfulness. Mindful meditation is only one component of mindfulness or mindful living. Also, to emphasise the point, practising mindfulness can involve many other activities besides mediation.

It should be noted that the mindfulness techniques that are used most often, and that will be described here, are mainly aimed at staying well or reducing stress, especially associated with depression. These approaches are not currently recommended for the self-management of acute hypomania or mania. There is a therapy that is called mindfulness-based CBT (MBCBT) and expert therapists have used it with individuals with bipolar disorder. However, some of these therapists suggest that inappropriate use of some mindfulness techniques could actually worsen hypomanic or manic symptoms. The scientific studies available seem to indicate that the risk of this happening is low and may be more theoretical than actual. However, it does indicate that if you do want to try mindfulness for all aspects of bipolar disorder you would be best to seek the input of an expert MBCBT therapist to help you get the benefits of this therapy whilst minimising any risks associated with its use. For information, I have included a reference to a textbook on MBCBT for bipolar disorder, but in the rest of this section of the book I will describe some of the ideas behind mindfulness and some self-help techniques you might find helpful.

WHAT IS MINDFULNESS?

Mindfulness is an ancient Buddhist practice which has gained increasing attention in western countries since about the mid-1980s. One of the main proponents of mindfulness, Jon Kabat-Zinn, states that mindfulness is actually a very simple concept. It means paying attention in a particular way: 'on purpose, in the present moment, and non-judgmentally'. Likewise, one of the best-known UK experts on mindfulness, Professor Mark Williams, describes that an important part of mindfulness is 'reconnecting with our bodies and the sensations experienced'. So, it seems that mindfulness raises awareness of thoughts and feelings as they happen moment to moment and it helps people to notice how those thoughts might be driving their emotions and behaviour.

The concept of mindfulness overlaps considerably with other CBT models. However, the practise of mindfulness differs somewhat from the other self-help techniques we have discussed so far. For example, mindfulness uses more meditation and focuses more on body sensations when you are doing daily tasks. Also, mindfulness is not so much about challenging negative thoughts as distancing yourself from them. For instance, mindfulness encourages individuals to note that their anxious or depressive thoughts are mental events and that these may go through your mind in a resting state. Mindful living would mean that you witness these negative thoughts, perhaps labelling them as anxious or depressive ideas, but you don't always try to challenge them. This approach can help people who struggle with repetitive negative thinking, as they become better at spotting the build-up of difficult emotions and thoughts. The goal is then to deal with the thoughts and emotions more skilfully, instead of just reacting to them or responding in ways that might make the problems worse. For some people, the approach described is very powerful, as it emphasises that thoughts are ideas not factual statements. For other people, different CBT techniques are more effective, such as a more detailed review of the thoughts, differentiating negative thoughts from other cognitions and more directly examining and modifying unhelpful thoughts. However, it is worth experimenting to see which approaches suit you best.

Books on mindfulness suggest that mindful meditation is a scheduled activity that is practised on a regular basis, often at a specified time of day on specific days of the week. The CBT techniques described in this book are also built into daily life so that they become a mode of living. However, the approaches differ, as other CBT techniques are tailored to different situations, whereas mindfulness tends to employ the same set of techniques without any changes. Lastly, the behavioural techniques used in mindfulness are about developing a focus on the present moment, whereas other CBT techniques promote adaptive behaviours linked to the past, present and future.

These similarities and differences are mentioned so that you understand that mindfulness may help you to develop a complementary set of skills to those you have been working on so far. The use of mindfulness is compatible with other CBT self-help approaches, but some of you may find that acute symptoms are not so easy to modify with mindfulness.

EXAMPLES OF MINDFULNESS SELF-HELP TECHNIQUES

The first step in using mindfulness is to try to be more aware of your thoughts, feelings, body sensations and to take notice of the world around you every day. There are many tasks and routines that people engage in that they carry out on 'autopilot'. So, becoming more mindful can start by focusing on the task in hand and trying to make sure you are fully engaged in the moment, e.g., brushing your teeth 'mindfully' would entail focusing your attention on the feeling of your feet on the floor, the brush in your hand, and your arm moving up and down. Mindful eating involves paying attention to the taste, sight and textures of what you eat. Likewise, if you take a walk or some exercise, you might leave your mobile phone at home or stop listening to music and instead focus your attention on your breathing and where your feet are in space as you move. Having done this, you might begin to pay attention to smells, sights and sounds in your environment, such as the trees or sky and the feeling of the ground beneath your feet, etc.

These basic mindful approaches to daily activities are often supplemented by body scanning and practising mindfulness meditation. The exercise called body scan asks a person to move their attention slowly through different parts of their body, starting at the top of their head and moving all the way down to the end of their toes. The idea is to try to focus on feelings of warmth, tension and tingling or feelings of relaxation in different parts of your body. This simple process offers useful training in attention and being in control of changing your focus and will raise your awareness of body sensations.

Perhaps the best-known mindfulness technique is mindfulness meditation. The goal is to engage in mental training practice as this can teach you to slow down your thought processes, let go of negativity and feel calmer in your mind and body. The longer-term aim is to practise this activity regularly, although it doesn't have to be daily if that is not practical. To help you get used to doing this meditation, you can start by trying a short, 5-minute session, then gradually increase this by 10 or 15 minutes each week until you can meditate for about 30 minutes at a time. Like the relaxation techniques discussed earlier in this book, it is helpful to get comfortable and to sit in a chair or lie down. Also, some of you may like to set an alarm to signal the end of a meditation session.

Although the exact meditation technique can vary, it usually involves breathing practice and focusing awareness on your body and mind and any sounds you can hear (including not only your breathing, but other sounds arising from the immediate environment). The most important skill to develop from this exercise is being able to consider your thoughts and emotions in a non-judgemental way whilst you are in a state of relaxation. If you find yourself getting caught up in your thoughts, such as beginning to ruminate about past events or worrying about future events, try to observe only where your mind went and then return to focus on your breathing and on the present. The key aims of this mindfulness meditation practice are that you learn to return your focus to your breathing, to stay in the present moment and not to be self-critical (e.g., don't get annoyed with yourself if other thoughts intrude into your mind).

With time, people report that they are able to relax and feel calm even if negative thoughts pass through their mind during their mindfulness exercises. It is suggested that meditation or other mindfulness techniques help people react to their thoughts in a way that is more detached – thoughts are experienced in a way that seems like you are overhearing a conversation that you're not getting involved in. This can obviously be very useful to people who are at greater risk of feeling stressed or experiencing a more extreme emotional response to their negative thoughts than other members of the general population.

Overall, mindfulness is as much about achieving a healthy, more stable mood state as it is about trying to intervene when someone is feeling distressed. If you decide to try these techniques, you need to be aware that, like other approaches discussed in this book, mindfulness techniques may sound simple, but it can take some time to master them. One reason for persevering with mindfulness self-help techniques is that they might enable you to develop additional coping skills, e.g., learning to choose how to focus your attention. These mindfulness techniques can alleviate some acute feelings of stress as well as preventing future downswings, but the benefit is mainly described for people who have experienced many previous depressive episodes and those who do not have severe mood swings or a bipolar disorder. Some individuals with bipolar disorders have reported that rumination-focused or mindfulness self-help techniques can be useful approaches to repetitive negative thinking processes and are very helpful in improving their mood in the short term. However, these benefits do not always persist longer term and some people report that they still need to use other techniques to modify their automatic thoughts to help them stabilise their mood.

In summary, adding mindfulness to other self-management techniques means that you may gain additional insights into how your mind works, extend your ability to control your focus of attention and change how you respond to automatic thoughts. Also, mindfulness helps you to be open and curious about yourself, your thoughts and the links to your feelings. Like the other CBT techniques described in this book, mindfulness can further improve your self-esteem and self-acceptance. This is important because not only can this reduce feelings of stress, it may build resilience against developing a depressive episode. However, until we have more scientific studies available, I would not recommend using mindfulness for hypomania or mania unless you had help from an expert therapist.

Hopelessness: A special case

If you are depressed, you may get thoughts that make you feel hopeless. Unfortunately, some individuals who feel intensely hopeless about their future begin to think that they cannot carry on. In order to keep yourself safe through these difficult times, it is important to remember that the automatic thoughts that are making you feel hopeless can be tackled through the same techniques as those used for anxiety or depression. What evidence is there for your thoughts? What alternative ways of viewing your situation are there? What activities could you undertake right now to alleviate these feelings, even for a short time?

If you really cannot overcome your hopelessness, it is important to talk to someone else. This becomes vital if you have any associated ideas about harming yourself. If these thoughts flood your mind and you are feeling too down to tackle them alone, please seek help.

Table 4: Tackling unhelpful thoughts in depression: The thought record

Situation or event	Emotion (rated 1–100)	Automatic thoughts (belief rated 1–100)	Evidence for and against the thought	Alternative view	Rerate emotion and belief in original automatic thought	Action or outcome
Susan, my best friend, didn't return my phone call	Anxiety 70	She can't be bothered with me any more 80	Evidence for, none Evidence against, Susan rings regularly and has been a real help and support for years I'm thinking this way because I'm down	I can't guarantee her son passed on the message, she might not know I called Even if she knew I'd called she might be very busy, and just not had a chance to get back	Anxiety 45. Thought 30	*Outcome:* I realise I'm thinking in a very negative way and I don't actually have the facts *Action:* Ring Susan again with a definite proposal for some time out to do

Sadness 80	She's probably out with more rewarding friends, i.e. she doesn't like me any more 65	Evidence for, none Evidence against, Susan told me only last week how much she valued my friendship Jane told me that Susan had been saying when they met how much she liked me	When Susan and I have ever had any difficulties in our friendship she's been the first to sit down and sort it out; she'd have said if she had a problem She is actually allowed to go out with other people!	Sadness 50 Thought 20	something we both enjoy If no answer by phone, drop by her house next Tuesday to check she's OK

Keeping going and seeking help

Even with practice, there will be times when it is very difficult to use the techniques described in this chapter. You may find it hard to focus on thoughts, to write things down or to take action. It does take an enormous effort to start using these approaches.

If you are struggling to implement these strategies, can anyone offer you support in your efforts? Even someone offering encouragement to try self-management approaches may help you get started. Other approaches to the management of depression, such as input from mental health professionals and use of antidepressants, are also important and will be discussed further in Chapter 11 on relapse prevention.

CHAPTER SUMMARY

Self-management of depression involves:

- Understanding *unhelpful behaviours* such as:
  - avoidance;
  - withdrawal;
  - procrastination.

- Using key *behavioural interventions* such as:
  - activity scheduling;
  - step-by-step approaches to tasks and problems.

- Identifying *automatic thoughts* particularly those focused on:
  - negative views of the self, world and future;
  - these thoughts are associated with depressed and anxious mood.

- Using key *cognitive strategies* such as:
  - distraction;
  - modification of unhelpful thoughts by examining the evidence, generating alternatives and devising experiments to test out ideas.

- Cognitive processing styles, such as rumination about the past and worry about the future, may represent unhelpful learnt behaviours that are associated with procrastination and avoidance.
- Mindfulness techniques offer insights into thinking processes and help individuals to learn how to control their attention. Using these techniques can lead to stress reduction.
- Being alert to feelings of *hopelessness*. This is a particularly difficult symptom to cope with. Additional help and support are needed if this feeling is persistent and intense.

10

Self-management of hypomanic and manic symptoms

When an individual experiences a 'high', their mood change is often compounded by difficulties in recognising that their actions are extreme and outside of normal boundaries. Also, they are easily distracted and unable to focus on the task in hand. This means that it is important to try to keep any self-management interventions simple. This chapter describes techniques to control unhelpful behaviours and basic strategies to modify unhelpful automatic thoughts. However, these techniques are most effective in the early stages of a high; it is unlikely they will be feasible if you are in the midst of a manic episode.

Dealing with unhelpful behaviours

The main difficulty for individuals who are experiencing a high is that they have too much energy, and struggle to exercise full control over their own actions, which may involve a worrying level of risk-taking or be open to mis-interpretation by other people. This in turn may lead to the individual becoming irritable with people who prevent them going ahead with what they want to do. The key unhelpful tendencies are:

- *distractibility* – inability to complete tasks;
- *risk-taking* – engaging in ill-judged activities through overestimating the gains and/or underestimating the dangers;
- *impulsivity* – acting without thinking things through, often associated with disinhibition;
- *irritability* – common in dysphoric mania, but also present in euphoric mania when actions are thwarted by others.

There are a number of strategies that can be tried to help reduce the adverse effects of these behaviours, but it is very difficult to use any of these techniques during a manic episode. It is therefore important to try to intervene as soon as the warning signs of a high are present, or at the latest during the hypomanic phase. The two basic approaches involve:

- keeping safe;
- maximising self-control.

If you do not feel able to control all of your actions or totally trust your judgement, it is worth reducing your exposure to 'risky' situations. Preparing plans when you are in a normal mood state that can be used when you are high is invaluable, as it is often difficult to put these approaches in place during a high without the help of others. Useful interventions include the following:

KEEPING SCHEDULES SIMPLE AND PREDICTABLE

Make a very basic, manageable and regular activity schedule. Even if you are full of energy, it is better to reduce rather than increase your planned activities from their normal level. Allow time between one activity and the next, as you are likely to find it difficult to retain your focus on each task. Don't skip eating or sleeping. Indeed, make a particular effort to include regular meals and regular times for going to bed and for getting up. Aim to spend at least 50 per cent of your daily schedule in a calm environment or engaging in relaxing activities. Try to avoid two areas:

- *Complex tasks or problems:* Keep your goals simple and delay any major obligations. If you do need to undertake simple tasks, try to persist with the activity until it is complete. Remember that when going high you are more easily distracted and at risk of starting lots of activities and finishing none. Push yourself to stay with each task before moving on to other things, no matter how attractive other activities may be. (This is the opposite advice to that for depression, where we used time limits.) If there are complex tasks that cannot be delayed, do not start them without recording a step-by-step approach and preferably enlisting the support of someone else.

- *Stimulants and stimulating people:* Try to avoid situations, substances or people that push you even higher. One of my clients designed a 'vroomometer', a chart listing activities that she was able to cope with at different stages in an upswing. She drew it up when she was in her normal mood state and found it invaluable in picking out activities that were safe when she was in the early and later stages of a high. An example of such a chart is given in Figure 12.

Having made your plan, try to stick with it. Even if you feel full of energy, don't try to add more into your day. The risk of inappropriate actions or problems is high and is better avoided. If when you review your day you do not feel you are using up enough of your energy, can you burn off some of it through exercise in a safe environment – for example, by swimming several lengths of a swimming pool? However, you must feel confident you can cope with that environment. If not, can you use an exercise bike or follow an exercise video in the confines of your own home? Try not to set endurance tests for exercise. It is better to attempt about half an hour per day and then review your schedule after four or five days to decide if any more exercise is likely to help calm you down and reduce your excess energy.

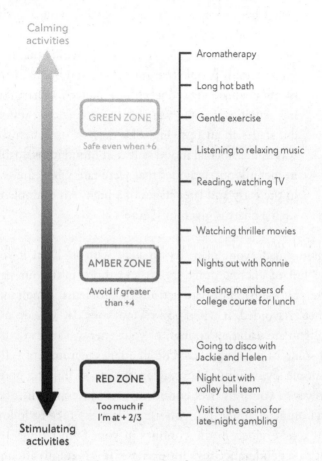

Calming
activities

Aromatherapy

Long hot bath

GREEN ZONE

Gentle exercise

Safe even when +6

Listening to relaxing music

Reading, watching TV

Watching thriller movies

AMBER ZONE

Nights out with Ronnie

Avoid if greater
than +4

Meeting members of
college course for lunch

Going to disco with
Jackie and Helen

RED ZONE

Night out with
volley ball team

Too much if
I'm at + 2/3

Visit to the casino for
late-night gambling

Stimulating
activities

Figure 12: An example of a 'Vroomometer'

CALMING ACTIVITIES

As well as avoiding activities that are stimulating, it is important actively to calm yourself. This is achieved by ensuring that you incorporate relaxation sessions into your day and also introduce other methods to reduce your level of arousal. For example, stay in familiar surroundings. You could even use a particular room in your home where you feel comfortable to take time out. Here you could lower the lighting or even sit in the dark for about an hour. Listening to relaxing music may help. Also, try to avoid exciting books or films if possible. A boring book is a good idea, particularly at bedtime! Slowly repeating simple phrases to yourself such as 'relax', 'calm down' or 'take your time' may also work.

SAFE THRILLS

If you do not seem to be able to resist seeking out excitement, try to identify safe pleasurable activities. For example, rather than taking flying lessons, can you get access to a computer that has a flight simulator programme on it? Rather than driving your car at speed, can you watch a video of a grand prix? These alternatives may seem less appealing, but it is important to remind yourself that the consequences are much less dangerous. If you feel compelled even to try these safer alternatives, limit your exposure to a maximum of about half an hour per day and preferably engage in calming activities immediately afterwards. Ideally, you should avoid even safe thrills if you are becoming manic, as the additional stimulation may have adverse rather than beneficial effects.

MANAGING SOCIAL SITUATIONS

As emphasised earlier, it is wise to avoid some social interactions, particularly those that involve large gatherings of people. If you do engage in social interactions, try to space these activities out over the course of the week and where possible keep the rest of your schedule regular and predictable. In any social interaction it is worth doing the following:

- If possible, sit down on a chair before you start talking.
- Sit upright and try to control your breathing.
- Work hard at listening to the other person's comments.
- Don't interrupt, no matter how keen you feel to join in.
- Wait for a gap in the conversation before speaking.
- Pause before you begin talking.
- Speak at a rate that seems slow to you.
- Do not use your hands as you talk – if necessary, try sitting on them!

Although you may feel very slowed down by this approach, it usually only just brings your activity and speech rate within normal bounds. If you are concerned that you have overcompensated and have slowed down too much, check this out with someone you trust.

MANAGING SOCIAL MEDIA: A SPECIAL SITUATION

Access to the online world includes social networking and opportunities for online spending. In some ways, it is slightly artificial to split these issues into two topics, but it seemed helpful to break the issues down into manageable bites. Having said that, readers should be aware that some of the ideas in the paragraphs on social media overlap with ideas in the section on online spending and vice versa. Some readers may find it helpful to review these special sections together to see how the tactics suggested can be transferred across these situations.

Managing your use of and exposure to social media is discussed separately to highlight that this use can be complicated for people with mood swings. The advice about the use of calming techniques, trying to pause and other approaches are all relevant to self-management of social media. However, it is worthwhile reviewing what we know about the use of social media by individuals with mood swings, and especially considering any concerns related to times when people are hypomanic or manic.

To help you to understand this topic more, it is helpful to start by highlighting that there is a small amount of research that has explored this issue. I need to mention that this is a new area of scientific study and that the findings from these studies are rather variable. For example, some research projects found an increase in the use of social media in those with bipolar disorder, especially associated with attempts to increase social connectedness, compared with other people. Other studies did not find such clear evidence of increased time spent using social media but found an increase in the use of some specific types of sites, e.g., dating websites. Furthermore, the use of these sites changed according to mood state in people with a bipolar disorder. As might be predicted, decreased use of such sites occurred during depression and increased use during upswings.

Another survey of individuals with mood swings showed that although they reported that they had more friends on social media sites than other members of the public, they also reported more problems with social media as well. For example, people with mood swings were more likely than people without mood swings to exclude or block social media contacts, were more sensitive to rejection or negative comments made via social media, and more likely to say they felt overexposed online (due to issues with the level of privacy). This research is at an early stage, but we should note that the studies do *not* suggest that people with mood swings should never use social media to connect with other people. Indeed, it is important to acknowledge that social media can be a source of support to individuals with mood problems. However, the research does indicate that it is worth being especially careful about which sites you sign up to and how often you connect, and that you consider how you might limit your use of social media or avoid its use during periods of overactivity or elation.

Overall, we need more scientific research before we can be certain about the best way to maximise the benefits and minimise the risks of social media for individuals with mood swings. However, you may want to think about the research I have mentioned and then consider if any of the findings apply to you. For example, it seems that individuals with mood swings are more susceptible to the negative effects of social media than other people. This may be because their views of themselves are amplified by their mood state and any negative comments (perceived or actual) that are made to them via social media may be associated with worsening of depression or may lead to feelings of anger or irritation in mania or hypomania. Another finding was that, in an upswing, people can get caught up in their online interactions and lose sight of a rational perspective. Also, ill-judged comments to other people (that later lead to feelings of embarrassment) or making dubious contacts (that you later regret) are some of the reasons given by people with a bipolar disorder for excluding and blocking a larger number of their social media contacts than other people.

Professionally, I often recommend individuals take a break from social media when they are in an upswing (apart from connecting with close family and friends) and ask them to consider enlisting family members or close friends to help them stick with a plan to take a break. If you want to access social media during hypomanic episodes, then the ideal would be to find ways to be online, but in a less active or interactive way. For example, you could still watch video clips and gifs etc., without getting engaged in commenting on them and you could avoid using Twitter or Instagram, TikTok etc. As a precaution, and in advance of any upswings, you may want to check which search engine is rated as the best one for protecting your privacy and, if possible, use that one as your default search engine. This makes sense as initiating new social connections might lead to some of the problems or regrets noted in the previous paragraphs.

To help your friends or family to help you, you could discuss the issues that might arise and agree that you would review all the evidence about your activity and behaviour. Ideally, you would then jointly explore two key questions:

- Is your use of social media intruding or interfering with your daily life? and/or
- Is your response to social media contributing to a reduction in your well-being (you should agree in advance how you will assess this, e.g., does well-being refer to your mood state, the quality of your interactions with others, etc.)?

If the answer is yes to one or both questions, it is worth taking a 'holiday' from social media and maintaining contacts with other people through human interaction. Further, staying safe may entail time-limited talk time or text messaging that is restricted to family, friends, support group members and health professionals. If the answers to the two questions are unclear, then monitoring the amount of time you use social media (number of hours per day) and your emotional reactions to this use may help you work out the next steps.

Maximising self-control

If you are going high, you may be full of ideas and bursting with things you want to do. As a consequence, you can get frustrated and angry with people who fail to see the apparent brilliance of your plans or who try to stop you carrying out your planned actions. One way to reduce the risk of becoming angry is to try to increase your own control over your actions. The simple rule is: 'Control what you can control, and don't engage in behaviours that you can't control.' If you are unsure whether you can retain control it is better to delay things than to risk problems. To overcome your desire to act, you may wish to try the following ideas.

RECORD YOUR IDEA OR PLAN

You may be convinced that all the ideas you have are good ones and should be implemented. However, it is worth trying to contain your impulsiveness. The apparent brilliance of your ideas is not always a reflection of reality. Individuals who are going high tend to notice only the strengths of an idea and are not always able to focus on the weaknesses. To help you avoid getting into battles or risky situations, keep a notebook to hand where you can record your ideas. You can then return to evaluate these ideas after you have recovered from your high. It will also be easier to convince others of your good idea if you present your plan after you are back to your usual self. If you follow this approach, you actually have a greater chance of getting genuinely good ideas adopted, as they will not get lost in the mass of less viable proposals. You will also maintain your credibility as someone who does have moments of inspiration, rather than gain a reputation as someone full of erratic ideas.

BAN MAJOR DECISIONS

Maximising self-control primarily involves restraining yourself from doing anything that you may regret later. It is vital that you do not make any major decisions about your personal or professional situation. Not everyone you meet will know that you are not your normal self, and some may take your decisions at face value. It is important to avoid decisions that have major consequences for your future, such as beginning new relationships or changing jobs. Any important decisions that you wish to contemplate should be listed in your notebook for future consideration.

This approach means that no one is taking decisions away from you or denying you the opportunity to lead your own life. You are retaining control by taking the initiative and choosing to delay any irreversible decisions.

48-HOUR DELAY RULE

Professor Aaron Beck, the father of cognitive therapy, has developed many of the approaches used to help individuals with bipolar disorder. One of the important techniques he describes is the '48-hour delay rule'. He states that 'If it's a good idea today, it will still be a good idea tomorrow and a good idea the next day.' This is a useful approach to many situations, but can be particularly useful in avoiding impulsive purchases, especially of very expensive items that you would not normally consider buying. During the 48 hours you have the opportunity to reflect on your plans and most importantly to seek advice from others on the wisdom of your proposed course of action.

An additional way to prevent financial extravagance is to surrender control of your credit cards to a trusted friend or even to have an arrangement with your bank or financial adviser. Again, look at this as your attempt to take maximum possible responsibility for your actions, no matter what your state of mind. Getting help to prevent overspending will enable you to avoid some of the desperate financial problems that many other individuals have had to cope with after recovering from a high.

THIRD-PARTY ADVICE

Individuals who are high find it very frustrating to have people criticise any proposals they make and dismiss negative feedback as jealousy or lack of imagination. To overcome this, it is useful to identify in advance (i.e., when you are in a normal mood state) at least two people whose opinions you respect and whom you trust. You can then arrange to turn to these individuals when you are high to seek feedback on your ideas and planned actions. Having at least two people available offers a safety net in case you cannot contact one of them at the vital moment. If possible, you may even arrange that they regularly initiate contact when you are high and ask you to report any ideas you are considering acting on. They may be able to talk you through the pros and cons of your ideas or help you record them. They can encourage you to return to these ideas when you are back to your usual self.

ONLINE SHOPPING AND SPENDING: A SPECIAL SITUATION

Online shopping, gambling or gaming all present another special situation where enacting the 48-hour delay rule and getting third-party advice can be particularly important.

Most individuals are connected to the online world for many hours per day, often 24/7. This scenario combined with the repeated encouragement to buy 'must-have' items or to engage in other types of online spending represent significant challenges when people are beginning to feel disinhibited (which is a common feature of hypomania or mania). As one individual with mood swings commented, 'it is hard to resist shopping online, it would be like asking me to sit in a pub all day and never to have a drink!' Inevitably, prevention is better than trying to resolve financial problems (credit card debt, etc.) after the spending has occurred. There is no single strategy that will work for everyone but, as with use of social media during upswings, there are some approaches that might help. Most of these ideas reflect the techniques used for managing other problems during upswings, so hopefully you can transfer your skills between situations. Almost all these interventions work on the principle that being proactive will minimise the chance that major problems will arise and most aim to try to engage you with the idea of delayed gratification.

First, it is a good idea to do the following as soon as you can (ideally when you are quite well). On your smartphone, laptop, tablet and any other electronic media that you have, you should clear cookies from your search engines, download and activate 'ad blockers' and select a search engine that is most likely to protect your privacy (as was noted in the comments on social media use). Also, it would be beneficial to unsubscribe from those emails that essentially represent marketing letters and to unfollow any online sources that simply offer a platform to show you things you can purchase (especially websites offering things that 'you didn't know you needed'). The aim is not to make your life uninteresting, nor for you to miss out, rather these changes represent an acknowledgement that individuals with mood swings are at greater risk of 'emotional spending' than other members of the public. The goal is not to prevent you from ever making online purchase or spending money, but to try to make your spending purposeful and planned.

The second step is to try to make it harder for yourself to purchase items online. For example, you should check if your credit card details are stored on any shopping websites. It is a good idea to delete these. It won't necessarily stop you spending money on that website, but it may help reduce impulsive spending. In keeping with the 'delay rules' discussed in this chapter, if you do decide to make a purchase, it is helpful to let the item sit in the online shopping basket for about 48 hours (or ideally a week!). You can return to review the items in the shopping basket and if the purchase is a good idea and the item is needed, then you can continue to the buying stage. Before confirming making the purchase you might also enlist the help of a trusted friend or family member who can also review the planned purchase with you. There are some obvious questions to ask, for example: Can you justify the purchase to them and explain the need to make the purchase right now? Can your friend or family member offer useful insights regarding the benefits or risks of making the purchase?

If you are already aware that you are at risk of excessive online shopping, the third step might be to put in place some additional self-protection. For example, unsubscribe yourself from any 'buy-now-pay-later' schemes. Likewise, you might talk to your bank as they can actually block making purchases from or spending money on certain websites. Also, try to avoid browsing on sale websites. Ideally, find an alternative activity to distract yourself and try to avoid justifying your activity as 'checking out' websites to seek out value for money purchases. This is especially important when you are starting to tip into an upswing, as this represents a particularly risky time for making unnecessary, but expensive purchases.

A fourth step is to try to repair any 'damage' by reversing the spending. For instance, many online shopping sites allow returns to be made with a full refund of all your money (except sometimes you have to pay the postage cost). So, if an impulse buy has been delivered, you may have a second chance to rectify the situation by deciding against keeping the item and returning it. Again, if you have a trusted friend or family member nearby, you might get them to help you review purchases and decide if the items should be kept or returned. To make a decision, you might employ the two-column technique described later in this chapter to help you to undertake a review of the advantages versus disadvantages or pros and cons of purchasing the item.

As well as the above, there are some other general strategies to consider regarding how you plan any purchases. These really fall within the remit of financial management and good personal housekeeping but are worth re-iterating here. For instance, do you actually plan any of your purchases (big or small) in advance? If not, have you considered making a list of things you need (essential purchases) and things you want (your wish list)? You can even put these in rank order, as this all helps in reducing the likelihood of impulse buys. Next, do you know or can you estimate what budget is available for these additional purchases (e.g., how much money do you have to spare after you have paid all your monthly living expenses). If you stay within your spending budget for the next few months, can you purchase one of these items without going into debt?

The above tactics are ways to try to ensure you are making conscious decisions about purchases most of the time. Many individuals without mood swings have ended up with significant financial debts because of ill-judged internet shopping or failing to keep a record of how much money they have spent online. If you have mood swings, it is helpful to try to avoid these problems as the risk of practical difficulties (trying to pay back an overdraft, loan or credit card debt) may be compounded by the psychological stress of coping with problems that arise because of financial difficulties. Alas, these problems can increase negative thoughts about yourself, affect your sleep, cause arguments and worsen your mood state. As such, it is worth trying to think ahead and plan to avoid these problems, and if you are not sure you can manage this alone, then seeking help from advocacy groups or professionals is a good plan.

One final comment. All of the above ideas about self-management in relation to finances can be applied to the issue of gambling or spending money on online games (including the temptation of making within game purchases). I would encourage individuals who engage in online gambling or gaming to look at setting budgets and agreeing spending limits with the site they are using. Further, I would recommend seeking help at the earliest possible moment if you or someone close to you starts to consider that your online gambling or gaming habit is becoming risky. This problem may be related to the onset of a new mood episode, but it has also been shown that individuals with a bipolar disorder are more likely than other members of the public to develop a gambling addiction or other form of internet addiction. This may mean that this 'addiction' problem can, like alcohol and substance use problems, be an ongoing issue even when you are not experiencing a depressive or manic relapse.

Modifying unhelpful or dysfunctional thoughts

Being high is usually associated with positive but unrealistic automatic thoughts about your abilities and prospects for future success. Classically, individuals have an overoptimistic view of their world, in which they:

- overestimate the gains and underestimate the risks associated with any ideas;
- are totally focused on their own wants and needs;
- fail to attend to any negative consequences of their actions for themselves or others;
- experience angry thoughts as a consequence of their reduced tolerance of frustration.

Individuals who experience dysphoric mania also report negative automatic thoughts and irritability. (If this applies to you, you may find it helpful to use the approaches to unhelpful thoughts described in Chapter 9 on dealing with depression.) Techniques for modifying the automatic thoughts that accompany a high are outlined below.

Active distraction

If you are finding it hard to contain your wish to act on an idea, can you try to distract yourself from this course of action by thinking about other topics or by blocking the thoughts?

Selecting another focus for your attention is helpful provided you do not simply move on to the next 'big idea' that you have. Likewise, simply letting the first thought melt away is unlikely to resolve the situation, because your mind is working overtime and generating lots of new ideas. The critical element is therefore to distract yourself actively and to find a strong focus for your thinking that leaves no room for drifting back to your first automatic thought. Some individuals have particular images that they use; these may be relaxing scenes or sometimes visions of the bad outcomes that have occurred in the past. You will need to try this technique a few times to establish whether it works for you.

Another approach is 'self-talk'. Try repeating statements such as 'I can resist this urge,' 'I don't have to act on this now,' or simply 'Stop, it's dangerous.' Keep the statements simple and repeat them as often as you can until you feel more in control.

The two-column technique

If you are overactive and easily distracted, it is often too difficult to undertake a careful review of your automatic thought using the techniques described for depression. At best you may be able to push yourself to reflect on your ideas and to write down the pros and cons of any thought. However, it is important that the lists you compose bring in the information that is outside of your immediate focus of attention.

For example, when you feel high, you will tend only to see things from your point of view, or to see the enormous potential of the idea or the benefits of the scheme you propose. The critical aspect of the 'two-column' technique is to ensure that you pay attention to the alternative. Namely, for each positive statement you write down, you should immediately respond with a statement on the downside of your idea. To help with this approach, ask yourself the following questions:

- What *harm* might this idea do to *others*?
- What is the *destructive* potential of the scheme?
- What are the potential *losses*?

You will have to work hard to come up with answers, and if this proves difficult you may wish to consult others to help you in completing this task. For example, can you call on the individuals you have nominated for third-party advice (see above)?

Table 5 gives an example of the 'two-column' technique. Some blank copies of this form are included in the Appendix for your own use.

Modifying 'should' statements

A common accompaniment of a high is increased irritability. If this is not tempered it may spill over into anger. Given that you may also be less inhibited than usual, the whole situation may become dangerous. Prevention is obviously important, but you are only likely to be able to take full responsibility for your anger and irritability in the early stages of a high. Later, you are unlikely to be able to control your emotions and actions without professional support and recourse to medication.

Step one in averting difficulties is to keep a list of situations that you know 'wind you up' or frustrate you even when you are symptom-free. Ideally, arrange to stay away from the situations or people involved until you feel more settled and able to cope. If you find yourself in situations where you are becoming irritable and cannot immediately withdraw, there are two approaches you can try:

- engage in one or more relaxation or calming techniques;
- try to employ the social interaction skills discussed earlier in this section, particularly sitting down to talk and speaking calmly and slowly.

Table 5: The two-column technique for tackling
unhelpful thoughts when high

My idea: Give up work and use the money I get on leaving to buy a farm	
Reasons for acting on my idea (benefits to me, constructive aspects, gains)	*Reasons against acting on my idea* (risk of harm to others, destructive aspects, losses)
I've always loved the idea of living in the country	My wife prefers living in cities
	The children would have to leave school in the middle of their studies
I can learn a whole new set of skills and become a farmer	My wife and children would leave all their friends behind
	I don't know the first thing about running a farm
I'll be able to do what I want, I'll be my own boss and make lots of money for my family	There may be tensions at home. My wife would also have to learn new skills. If she doesn't want to do this, it will damage our relationship
	My wife and children might not agree to move to the country
	Farming is actually a very busy job and some tasks have to be done at set times, so I may have less freedom than I think
	Lots of people are struggling to make money in farming
	The thing I like best about the countryside is visiting it; that doesn't mean I would enjoy working there

Conclusion: I still think I want to live in the country, but I may not actually want to run a farm. Use 48-hour delay and contact Ruth and Mark (third-party advice).

Most irritability and anger can be traced back to your automatic thoughts. Thoughts that contain 'should' statements are particularly powerful: 'She should not talk to me like that,' 'He shouldn't try to stop me,' or 'I should be allowed to do what I want.' While you may not be able to follow a systematic process of exploring these thoughts in the heat of the moment, you can still try to reframe them in less emotive terms. For example, every time a 'should' statement goes through your mind, can you reframe it as 'I would prefer it if . . . '? This does not change the fact that you have a negative thought, but it may help reduce the intensity of your reaction and make the thought and your emotions more manageable. You could also try reminding yourself of the disadvantages or potentially negative consequences for you of acting upon your negative thought.

If you are still reasonably in control of your high, you may be able to review and modify your thinking as described in Chapter 9 on depression. Begin by noting the event or situation in which your negative thoughts arose, and the intensity of your emotional response. You may well find that many automatic thoughts that are associated with anger or irritability arise after someone has made a comment that you perceive as critical of you. Anger and irritability are often secondary emotions, arising in situations where your first response is that you feel hurt or upset. The good news is that you can stem your descent into irritability or anger if you can identify and challenge your initial negative automatic thought and deal with any hurt you are feeling.

Hidden behind the bravado that accompanies a high there may well be a fragile self-esteem that is easily wounded. Furthermore, many individuals report that as they come down from a high they feel quite depressed. This is an important time to be vigilant about comments you view as critical. You need to explore the evidence and examine the alternatives. Next, can you assess how accurate the comment is and also what would it mean if it were true? How could you change things if it were true? Finally, can you assess how sensitive you are being to other people's comments? If you are being oversensitive, how can you manage your reactions differently?

Here is an example.

Stevie was slightly high and feeling sociable, so they went into the canteen at work and sat down with some colleagues who were already chatting to each other. Stevie was mildly disinhibited and began talking across the ongoing conversation. One of their colleagues said, 'Please don't interrupt just yet, Stevie.' Stevie felt angry as they wanted to tell them about some interesting ideas they had. However, before telling the colleague what they thought of her, they decided to try to review the situation and work out why they felt angry.

- *Situation:* With colleagues; asked not to interrupt.
- *Angry thoughts:* 'She shouldn't talk to me like that. She made me look foolish.'
- *Initial automatic thought:* 'Maybe she doesn't like me. They don't want me to join them.'
- *Initial reaction*: Anxiety, hurt.

- *Stevie's response:* She actually smiled when she said, 'Please don't interrupt,' and she did say 'just yet'. The person they were listening to was just delivering the punchline of a joke.
- *Stevie's decision:* Try to stop mind-reading; also note I'm a little bit disinhibited and need to sit down before I speak.

Stevie self-rated the *perceived criticism* as 40 per cent but self-rated his *perceived sensitivity* as 75 per cent.

Keeping it simple; preparing in advance

In writing about techniques for managing highs I have tried to pay attention to the fact that you are likely to be more distractible and disinhibited than normal. I realise you will struggle to implement some of these approaches. This chapter has therefore concentrated on simple techniques, rather than complicated sequences of interventions. However, even simple techniques will be hard to use when you are going high, and will be virtually impossible once you are in the midst of a manic episode. So, the more you try out these skills when you are your normal self, the greater your chance of being able to use them effectively when you are going high. As with depression, the role of other approaches such as self-medication and professional support are considered in the next chapter, on relapse prevention.

CHAPTER SUMMARY

- Self-management of highs includes: understanding *unhelpful behaviours* such as:
  - distractibility;
  - risk-taking;
  - impulsivity and disinhibition;
  - low tolerance of frustration.

- Using key *behavioural interventions* such as:
  - keeping safe;
  - maximising self-control: controlling what you can control; delaying or avoiding what you can't control;
  - planning ahead to try to avoid negative financial consequences from engaging in online shopping, gambling, etc.

- Identifying *automatic thoughts* particularly those focused on:
  - overestimation of gains, underestimation of losses;
  - overoptimistic predictions;
  - excessive focus on the self.

These thoughts are associated with feeling elated, but also with irritable mood.

- Using key *cognitive strategies* such as:
  - active distraction;

- ° modification of unhelpful thoughts using the two-column technique; modification of 'should' statements by reframing.

- These techniques are best implemented in the early stages of a high, as they are unlikely to prove feasible during a manic episode.

PART FOUR

PUTTING IT ALL TOGETHER

Aims of Part Four

At the end of reading Part Four of this book, I hope you will have developed a plan for the future by:

- identifying and recording your own 'relapse signatures' for key mood states;
- developing a relapse prevention action plan including self-management, self-medication and early contact with key supporters, including professionals;
- identifying how to improve your view of yourself and develop a set of future life goals;
- devising a plan to encourage you to use cognitive and behavioural strategies in the future.

11

Relapse prevention

Before describing in detail the key elements of the relapse prevention package, I thought I would relate a story:

Ethan was a clinician working at a hospital that frequently carried out fire drills. The fire alarm was tested regularly on a Monday morning, but once a year there would be a full-scale fire practice with hospital staff required to follow the exit signs and congregate at various points in the hospital grounds. In order to cause the minimum disruption to the working week, the date and time of the annual fire drill were posted on notices around the hospital several weeks in advance. Despite this, Ethan failed to take note of the date. As usual, the Monday morning alarm went off. Ethan assumed it was the usual weekly test and of course ignored it. He was therefore extremely irritated when ten minutes later his teaching seminar was interrupted by a fire officer who was checking rooms to make sure everyone had vacated the building. The officer duly asked the seminar group to make their way to the assembly point in the hospital grounds. Ethan pleaded with him not to interrupt his work, explaining that he was very busy and had other priorities. What was more, Ethan said to the officer, he had worked at the hospital for years and knew what he should do if there was a fire.

If he was in any doubt, Ethan pointed out, there were laminated notices stuck on the back of each office door with details of the drill.

The fire officer listened patiently to Ethan's protests and then smiled. 'Well,' he said, 'if you have worked here for years you probably do know what to do if there's a fire. Our reason for carrying out this exercise is to make sure that you will all be safe if ever an emergency occurs. To reassure me that you will be safe, perhaps you could write down the key points written on the fire notice on the back of your office door and then talk me through the route you would need to take to get to your allocated assembly point.' Needless to say, Ethan didn't even try; as the students were only too aware, he didn't have the answers. With as much dignity as he could muster, Ethan followed the exit route and participated in the fire drill.

This story is used to illustrate a simple but crucial point. Ethan failed to notice the date of the full-scale practice despite the information being all around him. He also thought he knew what to do; he believed he knew what was written on the laminated information sheets that were within his gaze most days of the week. Ethan believed he knew what action to take if problems arose, to the extent that he did not feel the need for rehearsal.

You may recognise the parallels between this story and your own situation. You may think you know the risks and you may even know the symptoms that warn you of an impending mood swing. You have probably read about self-regulation and self-management. However, can you recall your early warning signs and symptoms and the key interventions, right at this minute? Can you write them down? Most importantly, there is a difference between knowing the theory and actually being able to take the appropriate actions. How confident are you that you can implement the actions required to stop things getting worse? Can you rate on a 0 to 100 scale (100 = totally confident) how confident you are that you can implement a relapse prevention strategy? If you score less than 100, you may wish to read on.

This chapter of the book is aimed at helping you ensure you are confident that you can implement a relapse prevention package even when you are having a difficult time. It is actually very helpful to think about relapse prevention as a fire drill. It emphasises that it should be a routine with which you are so familiar that you will be able to follow it under stress almost without having to think about the next step in the sequence.

Knowing your relapse signature

If you watch a television show regularly, you will become very familiar with the signature tune. You have heard it so many times that, if you hear the first few bars of the tune, you can probably sing the next few notes. You can confidently predict what comes next. The same principle can be applied to identifying times when you are at risk of experiencing a significant mood swing. 'High-risk' events or behaviour may act as triggers. Alternatively, you may not be certain about the likely triggers, but you may recognise the early warning symptoms of an episode. These two elements form your personal 'relapse signature'.

Triggers

In Part Two of this book, we explored 'high-risk' events, situations and behaviours and recorded those on a risk list. Look over that list now. Are there different risk factors for different mood swings? If you did not identify any risk factors when you first read Part Two, you may wish to go back to your schedules and charts to see if you can find any clues about potential triggers for mood disorders.

Any triggers should be recorded on paper, using a separate sheet each for depression and highs. You may wish to include additional sheets for mixed states or other problems such as rapid cycling.

Early warning symptoms

More than 80 per cent of individuals with a mood disorder can identify key symptoms that occur in the month or so preceding the onset of a full relapse (this period of time is called the *prodrome*). These prodromal symptoms constitute the second level of the relapse signature. They may provide the only warning of an impending relapse in those who cannot identify triggers. More often, the symptoms signal the progression of the relapse process to a dangerous phase where action will be needed to prevent an episode of mood disorder.

Identifying your early warning symptoms is easier to do if you can refer to your symptom checklist. You may already have starred the symptoms that occur in the early stages of each relapse (see Table 2 on p.115); if not, try to reorganise your list of symptoms into the order in which they usually occur. If this proves difficult, you could try to think about your most recent episodes of highs or lows and establish what the first changes were that you noticed. If you are still struggling, you may wish to seek help from someone who has observed you during your mood swings. They may be able to help you identify between three and six symptoms that occurred earlier on in each episode.

The next step is to examine the three to six symptoms you have identified. Try to estimate how long before the full relapse each of these symptoms occurs. Now try to decide which symptoms are the most memorable *at the time they occur*. Which are you most aware of, which are most out of keeping with the way you usually behave, which are the most severe? These symptoms are probably the most robust markers of an impending relapse and are the best ones to focus on.

Using this information, it is usually possible to identify accurately at least three symptoms from the prodromal phase of a high and three from the corresponding phase of a low that will alert you to the risk of a relapse. These constitute your early warning symptoms. In selecting the three key symptoms, try to exclude those that you are more conscious of in hindsight (e.g., feeling on top of the world when you are going high), and if you can, have three unique symptoms for each phase. If sleep disturbance is present in both phases, try to have three additional early warning symptoms on your list. Some individuals prefer to have four or five early warning symptoms. This is quite acceptable, but fewer than three may reduce the reliability of your relapse signature.

For mania, you may be able to identify early warning symptoms that only ever occur when you are at risk of relapse. This is not always possible for depression. You may find that there is a gradual worsening of your baseline level of depressed mood or concentration. If this is the case, try to clarify what degree of change in the severity of that feature would cause you concern.

Interestingly, the prodromal phases for any one individual are fairly constant, for both mania and depression. If you have identified that your early warning symptoms occur over a period of four weeks for one manic episode, there is a strong likelihood that the prodromal phase of any future manic episodes would be of the same duration. On average, the prodromal phase of hypomania or mania lasts for about three weeks, although the full range extends from a few days to about three months. The average prodromal phase for depression is actually slightly shorter than for mania (many people are surprised by this), being about two weeks, with a range of a few days to about five weeks. Despite the smaller 'window', with practice it is usually possible to institute an action plan aimed at averting a major depressive episode.

Frequency of monitoring

The final component of the relapse signature is to establish how frequently you should check for the presence of triggers or early warning symptoms. It is important not to overdo this – for example, you are unlikely to need to check every day. If the occurrence of the triggers or early warning symptoms is predictable (e.g., at certain times of year), you may decide to check for them once a month during the low-risk periods, increasing to once a week during high-risk periods. The presence of the first early warning symptom heralds the time for more intensive monitoring (such as daily or every other day). This allows you to establish whether any other early warning symptoms occur and to evaluate which interventions prove helpful.

Developing an action plan

The action plan is a written record of the strategies that can be used in response to the relapse signature. The interventions are usually listed in the order in which they will be introduced. The basic sequence includes increasing self-monitoring and self-regulation, followed by a selection of cognitive and behavioural self-management strategies. Ideally, you will be able to identify through experiments the specific interventions that you find particularly acceptable and effective.

Reviewing previous relapses

An additional route to identifying useful interventions is to review the details of your most recent relapses. What types of problems arose in implementing your action plan? Can you or anyone else identify ways in which you could prevent or reduce these barriers next time? If there are ways, it is worth adding those new strategies to your action plan. If no obvious practical barriers existed, you may need to consider whether any negative thoughts reduced your motivation to implement the plan. It may help to challenge these thoughts or develop some self-statements that will encourage you to put your plan into effect.

Self-medication

The next stage of an action plan may include self-medication strategies. The principles and potential benefits of self-medication are easily understood. The strategy allows a person at risk of mood disorder to keep an additional supply of antipsychotic, mood stabiliser or antidepressant medication in their possession. This gives the individual an early opportunity to increase the dose of a particular medication or institute a new course of treatment, in response to changes in their mood and functioning. The actual changes in mental state that would lead to self-medication and the exact nature and limits of any changes in the treatment regime, are agreed in advance with the prescriber.

Not all clinicians will agree to collaborate in this approach. They may be particularly reluctant if they have any anxieties about the safe implementation of self-medication, or if there have been significant problems with medication non-adherence in the past. Before including this strategy in your action plan, you will need to talk with your clinician to determine whether this approach is acceptable to both of you.

Setting up support systems

The last stage of the action plan involves working out how to mobilise support at the earliest appropriate time. Support may be enlisted from individuals in your social network and mental health professionals. If you can, identify about three individuals whom you could contact in a crisis. Having more than one option is obviously important, as this reduces the risk of your being left without support at the vital moment. Next, you need to ensure that you have contact details for each individual and are clear about their availability. With any clinicians or professionals, make sure you have established if they are available outside of normal office hours, or whether there might be different contact numbers you need for evenings, night-times or weekends. Your action plan may also include the name of anyone you trust whom you wish to nominate to be involved in key decisions about your treatment, or who you would like to take any major decisions on your behalf.

Communicating your action plan

Having recorded your relapse signature and action plan for each type of mood swing, you now need to decide who should receive a copy. Obviously, anyone who is mentioned in your plan, particularly as part of your support network, will need to have a copy, as will key members of the professional mental health network. You then need to decide whether to give a copy of the plan to any members of your family or friends who do not have an identified role in your relapse prevention package. Finally, you will require readily accessible copies for your own use. Ideally, note your relapse signature and key elements of your plan on a flash card (a piece of paper the same size as a credit card) which you can keep with you.

Examples of relapse prevention packages

Annie had a history of bipolar disorder. She had identified that episodes of depression were often associated with relationship difficulties and situations where she perceived she had been strongly criticised, let down or rejected. Not all such experiences were followed by depressive swings. However, the early warning symptoms that suggested she might go on to experience a major depressive disorder were: reduced energy and feeling slowed down (about four weeks prior to relapse); frequent bouts of crying for no apparent reason (three weeks); social withdrawal (one week); and early morning wakening (one week). As shown in Table 6, Annie's action plan started with increased self-monitoring in response to her low energy. If she experienced bouts of crying, she redoubled her efforts to institute self-regulation approaches such as scheduling pleasurable activities and social contacts with individuals who made her feel more positive about herself. This helped pre-empt social withdrawal. If she continued to slide into depression, she introduced more intensive thought modification strategies and also began treatment with an antidepressant. She arranged to bring forward her three-monthly outpatient clinic appointment.

Table 6: Annie's relapse prevention plan for depression

Triggers:	Activation of underlying beliefs about approval, being likeable, or perceived rejection
Early warning symptoms:	Lack of energy (−4 wks)
	Bouts of crying (−3 wks)
	Social withdrawal (−1 wk)
	Early wakening (−1 wk)
Frequency of monitoring:	Monthly if no triggers
	Every two weeks if triggers present
	Every three days if reduced energy
Action plan:	Increase self-monitoring
	Increase self-regulation − schedule at least 2 pleasurable activities/day
	Make 1 social contact/day plus visiting Jane and Rachel weekly (support)
	Use thought records to record and modify negative automatic thoughts
	Reintroduce antidepressants starting on fluoxetine 20mg daily
	Call Hardcastle Clinic (020 615 3982) & ask for appointment within 2 wks
Copies given to:	Dr Brown, Rachel

Alex had a history of recurrent mood swings. His three most recent episodes had occurred in the last three years and had been hypomanic or manic swings. He noted that the timing of the episodes was virtually identical: all three had occurred around Christmas time. At this time of year Alex was often busy trying to complete the annual reports for his company. He also received a substantial annual financial bonus. Alex drank more alcohol and got less sleep at this time of year as he attended a number of Christmas parties. The prodromal phase of the highs lasted about twelve days, usually starting with difficulty getting off to sleep and increasing irritability (first five days), being overactive and more talkative (six to nine days), being preoccupied by a desire to cut his hair (ten days) and excessive spending (one to two days). It is noteworthy that Alex reported one idiosyncratic symptom (desire to cut his hair) that recurred with each episode. Also, the excessive spending just about coincided with the beginning of the episode.

As shown in Table 7, Alex drew up a basic action plan that included setting limits on his spending to prevent any financial problems. He also agreed to consider taking time off work if his mental state did not settle after one week of his action plan.

Having examined these tables, you may wish to use the blank templates in the Appendix and try to record your action plans for highs and lows. Also, your action plans might be used as the starting point for discussions regarding an advanced treatment directive (which we discussed in Chapter 4).

Practice!

Without wishing to overemphasise the point, it is important to feel confident that you can institute your action plan when it is most needed. To do this, you will need to know in detail how to implement each planned intervention. These skills are best attained by using the different self-monitoring and self-management techniques on a regular basis. There is no substitute for such practice. Also, when you are experiencing early warning symptoms, try to view the introduction of the action plan as an opportunity to test out your skills and to examine how well your proposed system works. When the symptoms have finally subsided, take the time to review how effective your plan was. It is particularly useful to explore any aspects of the plan that were unsuccessful. Do not be afraid to make changes. It is important to feel able to revise or modify the interventions so that they meet your needs.

With practice and experimentation, you may eventually be able to avert major mood swings. However, if you do manage to avert a relapse, this is not the time to relax and stop using cognitive and behavioural strategies. Remember that upswings are often immediately followed by downswings. Also, the early phase of recovery from a downswing is a time of high risk for a further downswing. It is important to remain vigilant and to maintain your basic self-monitoring and self-regulation approaches even if you are in the recovery phase following a mild episode.

Table 7: Alex's relapse prevention plan for hypomania

Triggers:	Christmas time, increased pressure at work, increased alcohol intake, receiving Christmas bonus
Early warning symptoms:	Difficulty getting off to sleep and increasing irritability (−12 days)
	Being overactive and more talkative (−6 days)
	Desire to cut my hair (−2 to 3 days)
	Excessive spending (−1 to 2 days)
Frequency of monitoring:	Every 2 months February–September
	Every month October–January
	Every week mid-November to mid-December
	Every 2 days if sleep disturbed or irritable
Action plan:	Increase self-monitoring
	Increase self-regulation – reduce alcohol intake, try to reinstitute regular bed time, use A & B list, increase calming activities
	Set ceiling on spending (give credit cards to my wife)
	Reintroduce anti-psychotic medication (ring Dr Jones for prescription)
	Consider time off work if no improvement
	Call community Psychiatric Nurse (Jean 493 211, night-time on-call service 0341 876 430) for appointment within 5 days
Copies given to:	Dr Jones, Jean, my wife

CHAPTER SUMMARY

- An effective relapse prevention package includes information about your:
  - relapse signature: *triggers* and *early warning symptoms*;
  - *action plan:* self-monitoring; self-management; self-medication; mobilisation of support; early contact with mental health services.

- Each significant mood swing requires a separate relapse prevention package.
- When each package is complete, a copy should be distributed to selected individuals.
- Details of the package can be written on a flash card to allow you ready access to key information.
- The *frequency of monitoring* of the relapse signature should vary according to the potential risk of relapse. It is important not to be overconscientious, as this may increase your anxiety rather than enhance your sense of self-control.

12

Looking to the future

If you have managed to use the self-regulation and self-management techniques described in this book, you may already have been able to reduce the severity of your mood swings, or even prevent an episode of mood disorder. Controlling the symptoms that have disrupted your life is certainly important. However, your well-being is not defined simply by greater stability in your mood or the absence of symptoms of mood disorder. The next step is to overcome problems that prevent you from feeling at ease with yourself and in your relationships. Further, you will need to feel confident that you can cope with day-to-day problems and have a sense of where your life is going.

The final chapter of this book aims to help you to begin this process by looking at your view of yourself, aspects of your relationships with others and some of your day-to-day problems. Much of this discussion focuses on coping with the aftermath of previous mood swings or episodes of mood disorder. Lastly, it looks at setting goals for your future and suggests additional tips on how to be your own cognitive therapist.

Improving your self-esteem

When you feel down, it is common to have negative automatic thoughts about yourself. However, some individuals report that they never feel totally at ease with themselves. This low self-esteem or lack of self-confidence may be a lifelong characteristic, predating any mood swings; or it may have arisen as a consequence of having repeated severe mood swings and difficulties in coming to terms with behaviour during these episodes. In reality, many individuals with mood disorders have a long-standing fragile self-esteem that is further undermined by experiencing mood swings. There are a number of approaches to overcoming low self-esteem, and a detailed account can be found in Melanie Fennell's book, *Overcoming Low Self-Esteem*. Later I will outline some useful ways to begin the process, but first it is important to identify unhelpful strategies that in the long term appear to have more disadvantages than advantages.

Unhelpful strategies

If you lack self-confidence to start with and then have repeated experience of mood swings, it is easy to understand why you might employ various strategies to put painful thoughts about yourself at a distance. Unfortunately, there are some approaches that don't help individuals to cope effectively on a day-to-day basis. The three strategies that *do not* seem to help improve self-esteem are:

- trying to avoid thinking about what happened;

- trying to externalise the responsibility for the way you feel;
- trying to convince yourself that being slightly high will overcome your negative view of yourself.

UNHELPFUL STRATEGY 1: AVOIDANCE – 'IF I DON'T THINK ABOUT IT, IT'LL GO AWAY'

It is tempting to avoid thinking about previous episodes of mood disorder and refuse to look at any adverse consequences of your actions, for you or for others. While avoiding thinking about issues that make you feel unhappy about yourself may help you for a short time, there are two major problems with this approach. First, you are missing an opportunity to work out how to solve your problems and to reduce the chances of the same problems cropping up in the future. Second, to avoid thinking about what happened may mean avoiding any discussion or contact with individuals who knew about it and might comment. This will inevitably restrict your lifestyle and may actually mean you lose contact with some sources of support. In the long run, this may worsen rather than improve your self-image.

UNHELPFUL STRATEGY 2: REJECTING ALL RESPONSIBILITY – 'IT'S NOT MY FAULT'

You are not 100 per cent responsible for some of your actions when you are unwell. There are times when individuals with mood disorders are clearly no longer able to control their actions and responses. However, it is equally true that you cannot reject all responsibility for what happens to you. No matter how many other factors play a role, shifting the responsibility to 'the illness', other people, mental health professionals, the hospital or the treatment, without exploring what you may be able to do to help yourself, is counterproductive.

If you subscribe to the view that everything in life is totally beyond your control, you are in danger of giving up on your future. This would be a tragedy, as there are many areas of your life that you can positively influence. Furthermore, establishing what you *can* control will help you develop a more positive view of yourself. For example, you are not responsible for the fact that you get mood swings, and you may not be able to stop them happening. However, you may be able to learn how to recognise your problems early and seek help before your symptoms progress to a dangerous level. In addition, you can control other aspects of your life in spite of your mood swings.

Lastly, blaming everyone or everything else is unhelpful to your self-esteem. Even if other people or services have not always acted in your favour, you cannot expect to control how they react in the future. Ultimately you can only be sure of changing *your own* role or actions. The important aspect is to understand what you can control and what you cannot, and to be clear about your responsibilities and those of others. As discussed later in this chapter, your degree of responsibility will rarely be either 0 per cent or 100 per cent.

UNHELPFUL STRATEGY 3: 'WHO AM I?' – BASING YOUR SELF-IMAGE ON HOW YOU ARE DURING YOUR HIGHS

Individuals who experience mania often think that their ideal 'normal' state is not euthymia but the early stages of a high. At this point they feel more productive and active, and often get positive feedback from those people around them who do not know that they have a mood disorder. Alas, basing your self-image on a temporary state is unrealistic and unhelpful, for two reasons. First, there is a danger that you are focusing only on the good aspects of highs – what about the disadvantages? Don't forget that the early stages of a high do not last for ever. This phase usually leads to a manic episode or to a depressive swing. Both outcomes have considerable negative effects for you or for other people. Second, positive feedback or admiration from others will not last if those individuals also see you when you are so high that your thinking becomes chaotic, your mood unpredictable and your actions erratic. Their views of you will start to fit into the 'yes, but' category: 'Oh *yes*, he's capable of a fantastic work rate and can be the life and soul of the party; *but* sometimes he really loses control, the quality of his work deteriorates, and he goes too far and upsets lots of his colleagues.' A reputation of this kind is unlikely to help you feel positive about yourself.

Having highlighted some unhelpful strategies, we will now focus on approaches that may lead you in the long term to a more positive and stable view of yourself. To begin with we need to review the way you see yourself now, then look at how to cope with any negative consequences of recent mood swings.

Helpful strategies: Back to basics

The first steps in building up your self-esteem are:

- to develop a realistic view of yourself;
- to reduce your over-dependency on others' opinions;
- to try to build a positive self-image.

TRYING TO DEVELOP A REALISTIC VIEW

How well do you know yourself? You may feel bad about yourself, but, as we have discussed on many occasions earlier in this book, these feelings are often associated with negative automatic thoughts. To try to clarify in your own mind where any negative feelings come from, and how accurate any negative thoughts are, it is helpful to draw up a list of your personal strengths and weaknesses (a blank table for this purpose is provided in the Appendix – see p.389). To get started, here are a few questions that may help you:

- What do you like/dislike about yourself?
- What positive/negative qualities do you possess?
- What do other people like or dislike about you?
- How would others assess your strengths and weaknesses?
- What qualities do you like/dislike in other people? Do you share any of these qualities?

Try to be honest with yourself and to give equal attention to each question. Also, try to avoid global labels such as 'I'm a terrible mother' or 'I'm useless'. Even if you have such negative thoughts, try to be specific about why you have made this statement. This means exploring the evidence. For example, 'I lost my temper with my children over nothing,' or 'I have failed to deliver on promises I made to people.' Now try to check whether the list contains any statements based on single events or experiences. Are you certain these represent persistent personality characteristics? If not, why do you think they should be included (you may have a particular reason)?

Next, explore whether you have any evidence to support each statement on your list. If not, can you justify including this item on your final list? When you have reviewed and revised what you have written, ask yourself the following questions: What do you learn about yourself from your list of strengths and weaknesses? If you showed this list to someone you trust or who knows you well, would they agree that this is a realistic appraisal? If you are not sure, could you ask them? Finally, can you write a two- or three-line summary about yourself? Try to identify your key strengths and weaknesses and start your description by noting your good points. For example, 'I am reliable and hardworking and people like my sense of humour, but I can show a low tolerance of frustration and sometimes expect too much of others.'

You cannot change your self-esteem overnight. However, by working on the list, you can begin to explore the following themes:

- How can I build upon my current strengths?
- How can I reduce the frequency of any negative actions or thoughts related to my weaknesses?

- Which weakness is the best one to start working on?
- What new, positive attitudes can I introduce to build further upon my strong points?

Focusing on these issues will help you feel more confident about who you are and encourage you to begin to like yourself a little more.

AVOIDING SELF-CRITICISM

As well as developing a more accurate view of yourself, it is helpful to look at how you assess yourself on a day-to-day basis. By all means set yourself realistic and acceptable standards, and by all means assess whether you have lived up to your expectations. However, try not to be overly self-critical. There is a myth that self-criticism motivates people. My clinical experience is that it does the opposite. Individuals who constantly find fault with their own actions become demoralised and find it hard to keep going in the face of increased stress. Making constructive and encouraging self-statements, on the other hand, can help you achieve your goals.

To overcome self-criticism, see if you can reframe your criticisms into more helpful statements that encourage you, rather than demand that you do certain things. If your internal critical voice is very powerful, imagine that it is a parrot sitting on your shoulder that is making these criticisms. I often suggest this to people in my clinics, and I then ask them what they would do about the parrot. The more generous ones say they would make it fly away; those who are really fed up say they would shoot it. Whichever method you personally prefer, the goal is simple: silence the internal critic!

DON'T BE OVER-DEPENDENT ON THE VIEWS OF OTHERS

Some individuals, rather than experiencing persistent low self-esteem, say that their self-image varies purely on the basis of the feedback they get from other people. Fluctuating self-esteem is as damaging as continuously low self-esteem, as it makes you vulnerable to more extreme mood swings. While you should not ignore all feedback from others, it is important to see these comments in context. Ask yourself three questions:

- First, on a scale of 0 to 100, how sensitive are you to the views of others?
- Second, on a scale of 0 to 100, how critical are others of you?
- Third, do you give equal attention to positive and negative feedback?

If you explore your answers to these questions, you may be able to judge whether you are too vulnerable to other people's opinions, particularly critical comments.

If you are sufficiently clear in your own mind about your strengths and weaknesses and your sensitivity to criticism, you will be better able to evaluate the comments others make about you. Positive feedback will confirm your good points and negative feedback, although painful to hear, should not be too much of a shock. Remember that it is important to keep a balanced and realistic view. Don't overemphasise positive comments; by all means be pleased but keep your feet on the ground. Getting too carried away could simply set you on the path to a high. Likewise, don't catastrophise about negative comments. Even if those comments are presented in a critical way and are difficult to accept, try to work out what that person is trying to tell you. Is there a grain of truth in their comments that you can learn from? Lastly, remember that your reaction to others' comments will be largely dictated by your automatic thoughts. You can manage your feelings by following the classic approaches for modifying such thoughts, starting with an examination of the evidence supporting or refuting the idea.

TEST OUT ALTERNATIVE BELIEFS

If the techniques outlined above do not help you develop a more realistic self-image, it may be that you are overly influenced by a fixed negative belief about yourself. If you are not sure whether this is happening, it might be worth re-reading the section on underlying beliefs and how these can influence your life (see p.74). You may also be able to identify beliefs you hold about yourself by reviewing your automatic thought records. Are there any particular themes to these thoughts that point toward a fixed view of yourself? Can you capture the belief in a few words, by completing the statement 'I am . . . '? If you can identify a core negative belief about yourself, can you rate (on a 0 to 100 scale) how strongly you subscribe to that idea? Next, can you provide all the evidence from throughout your life that supports the accuracy of your negative view? What about evidence that goes against your belief? Reviewing this information, is this a realistic appraisal or have you accepted this belief as true without ever thinking to challenge it?

Most individuals who take themselves through this series of questions find that their beliefs about themselves were based on relatively unreliable evidence. Knowing that your own belief is unhelpful will undoubtedly help you predict situations or events that you will find stressful. However, this information alone will not change how strongly you subscribe to this belief. It takes several months (probably about four to six) to start to change your underlying view of yourself.

The first step is to agree to explore the alternative view of yourself. For example, if you hold the belief that 'I am unlovable', rewrite this belief on a piece of paper as 'I am lovable'. If you hold the belief 'I am incompetent', rewrite the statement as 'I am competent'. Having reframed the statement thus, rate on a 0 to 100 scale how strongly you subscribe to this new belief. The likelihood is that you will give this alternative belief a very low rating. This is understandable, for throughout your whole life so far you have unwillingly collected information to support your *old* view. However, from today, you have to try to collect and record *any* piece of information, no matter how small, that supports the *new* belief. Don't bother with the evidence *against* your new idea; you've been attending to that for years and could fill a textbook with it!

The whole point of this exercise is to raise your awareness of any information in the environment that starts to support your alternative belief. Also, remember you are not aiming for perfection. It is unlikely you will ever believe 100 per cent that 'I am lovable'. However, you may conclude that some individuals find you lovable most of the time. Likewise, being totally competent is unrealistic; try to aim for an acceptable and reasonable level of competency.

Your personal first aid kit: Trauma minimisation

Having worked through the exercises just described, many individuals find that any remaining negative views of themselves are largely dictated by problems in coming to terms with the consequences of severe mood swings or episodes of mood disorder. They feel robbed of their future, are ashamed of some of what they are, and feel stigmatised because of their ill health. The key to coping with these problems is to try to minimise the trauma associated with the changes that you feel have been imposed on your life. Again, it is unhelpful simply to avoid thinking about these issues or to get angry. It is more productive to start self-help and deal with the consequences as best you can.

GRIEF AND LOSS

Some individuals experience severe mood swings or a mood disorder that disrupts their functioning so gravely that they are no longer able to complete college courses or carry on in their employment. These unexpected restrictions not only affect their immediate activities but may also change their career prospects and/or the future course of their lives. Many who have had such an experience feel they have become different people and grieve for their 'lost selves', the people they used to be. This is both common and understandable. These experiences can be compared with bereavement and are compounded by the very real losses that can be associated with having a significant mental health problem, such as loss of income or status. Others find that there are major tensions in their personal lives, sometimes leading to the break-up of important relationships.

If these things happen to you, there is no benefit in trying to underplay the difficulties created by your recurrent mood swings. You will need time to recover from your disappointments, to adjust to your new situation and to move forward. There are a number of key steps that will help you begin this coping process:

- Try to be clear about which problems are genuinely related to mood swings. As with any grief reaction, the real losses will take time to come to terms with. Don't complicate the process by overgeneralising (as described in the section on thinking errors – see p.86) and attributing every negative event in your life to your mood disorder. For one thing, this is unlikely to be 100 per cent true; but more importantly, it is unhelpful and will increase the risk of your giving up on your future.

- Avoid focusing on the 'unfairness' of life. Life certainly is unfair in many ways; but it is unhelpful to spend too much time concentrating on something you can't change. Preoccupation with what has already occurred may simply feed your anger and prevent you implementing strategies that help you move forward.

- Don't pretend it hasn't happened. Avoidance of this kind is likely simply to store up problems for the future. At some point you will have to examine what has happened and what you can do to improve your situation. The problems will not disappear if you ignore them.

- Another way of avoiding the reality is to label yourself as the 'illness'. For example, avoid introducing yourself as 'I'm a manic depressive'. Don't deny the problem but try to remember that there is more to your identity than a mood disorder. Sometimes you will need to remind yourself of this, and it is important to make others aware of it as well.

You will not overcome your grief or sense of loss with these strategies; but they will create the right conditions for you to start the process of adjustment.

One other loss that needs to be mentioned is 'missing highs'. Many individuals report that they are only too glad to be free of depression, but genuinely miss the buzz that they get from a high. As discussed earlier in this chapter, it is important to replace an unrealistic existence with a realistic one. However, like an addiction to a drug, your highs will not be easy to give up simply because it seems a sensible idea.

You might like to try to reduce your dependency on highs by using a step-by-step approach similar to a 'harm reduction' programme, making gradual changes to the degree of upswing in your mood that are acceptable – for example, you might start by only agreeing to take action when your mood rating is + 4, then gradually move toward taking action at + 3 and finally at +2 (or the agreed boundary between your normal and abnormal states). You will also need to look carefully at how to compensate for the loss of this experience from your life. For example, what activities or roles can you take on that give you a similar positive feeling about yourself?

SHAME AND GUILT

A common reason why individuals struggle to move forward is that they feel guilty about the way they used to behave or are ashamed of themselves. Padesky and Greenberger, in their book called *Mind over Mood*, point out that guilt and shame are closely linked emotions. Both are usually associated with a belief that we have violated our own rules about how individuals should behave, that we have failed to live up to our own standards or have been disgraced in the eyes of others. Coping with these thoughts and emotions is difficult; as with other problems we have discussed in this book, the starting point is to acknowledge to yourself what has occurred and then to evaluate the facts of the situation.

First, try to give yourself some positive feedback for choosing to face the problem and not avoiding it. When bad things happen, it is easy to understand why the last thing you want to do is think about them. However, it is equally unhelpful to let any negative thoughts go around and around in your mind. Try to take a problem-solving approach and focus on what you need to do about what happened.

The second step is to record on a piece of paper exactly what occurred – what was the event that makes you feel guilty or ashamed. Padesky and Greenberger suggest that you then list everything and everybody who contributed or *might have* contributed to this outcome. Put yourself at the *bottom* of the list. Next draw a big circle on the paper. Starting at the top of the list, divide the circle up into segments of different sizes according to the degree of responsibility that should be attributed to each circumstance and each person involved. The greater the responsibility, the bigger the piece of the pie.

Having done this exercise, consider how much of the responsibility is yours and yours alone. Do you share responsibility with anyone else and/or did your mood disorder play any part in the event? If you are not totally responsible, does this change how badly you feel about what occurred? Is there anything that you can learn from this experience, or anything that you can do to overcome any difficulties that have occurred?

If the 'responsibility pie' suggests that you shoulder most of the responsibility, examine the details of what happened and try to answer the following questions:

- How serious was the incident? Does my assessment concur with that of other people? (If others think it is less/more serious, can you determine why that is?)

- If someone I cared about had acted this way toward me, how would I view the situation?
- In the longer term (e.g., in six months, in six years), how important will this incident be?
- When I acted in that way, was I aware of the consequences?
- What have I learned and how can I avoid similar incidents in the future?
- What damage has occurred because of what I did?
- What can I do now to start to repair the damage?
- Can I predict (accurately) some of the likely responses of individuals to my attempts to repair the damage? What strategies can I use to help me cope if they are finding it hard to forgive me? What will I do to cope with my own reactions/disappointments?

It is important to try to work through these questions before doing anything. However, don't fall into the trap of becoming more and more negative about yourself. If this starts to happen, you can try to tackle your automatic thoughts; alternatively, try to focus on a 'task-orientating' statement such as 'Doing a bad thing does not prove that I am a bad person' or 'Having done a bad thing in the past does not mean I cannot change how I act in the future.' You may wish to talk through with a trusted confidant any actions you think might repair the damage. Getting feedback at this stage may increase your chances of achieving a successful outcome.

STIGMA

Many individuals feel that their status in society is undermined by the negative views about mental health problems expressed by the public at large. Alas, these prejudices do impact on the lives of many people and will not be removed overnight. But, as you cannot control what others believe or how they view mental health problems, it is unhelpful to target all your energies on them. I am not saying you don't try to play your part in tackling stigma, but the first action that is required is to focus on whether you hold any prejudices against yourself. If you are a perfectionist, do you now see yourself as 'defective'? If you have a desire to be liked or approved of by others (and most of us do), do you fear that you will be rejected? Does this fear of rejection turn from sadness into anger? If these ideas are operating, you may need to review your own beliefs and think about how to tackle the disappointment you feel about yourself. This will probably start with a review of methods of improving your self-esteem. Also, remember that anger often arises as a secondary reaction; you may need to work on the primary emotion, which may be hurt or sadness.

Relationships with others

Clearly it is not possible to deal with all aspects of interpersonal relationships in this short section; the topic has after all been the subject of many books on its own. However, I will briefly comment on three areas that are worth considering:

- communication problems;
- assertion;
- sharing responsibility, including working with pro-fessionals.

Communication

Most of the time, we pay scant attention to the process of our interactions with other people. However, it is important to try to understand this process, particularly if you wish to pre-empt problems in relationships. Here are some guide-lines for tackling inter-personal problems:

- Take your time to think about what you need to say and what issue you are trying to get across.
- Be clear and specific about the problem, but make sure you own it. Avoid placing all the responsibil-ity on the other person. Stating 'You're ruining our relationship' is too general and seems to be blaming them. It may lead to the other person defending themselves against a perceived criticism, or angrily suggesting that you 'sort yourself out'.
- Avoid sweeping statements. 'Always' and 'never' are key words to ban from the conversation. Other unhelpful statements include 'If you loved me you would . . .' or 'If you cared about me you wouldn't have . . .'
- Try to develop a shared view of the problem. If you don't agree on the problem, you will never agree on the solution.

- Be a good listener. Don't interrupt people and don't tell them they're wrong. Remember they are expressing their opinions or feelings.
- Retain your perspective. If the conversation is getting heated, be prepared to negotiate some time out so that both of you can review where the conversation is going and can steer it back on track.
- Try to stay calm. If you get angry, you may begin to use words you regret. Likewise, if you are very distressed, it is hard to come to a shared view of what to do next.
- Try to take a step-by-step approach to any agreed action and set a time when you can both discuss the progress you have made.
- Give to get. Be prepared to play an active role in finding the solution, even if this means giving something up. Don't expect the other person to 'give to get' or to do all the giving.
- Be willing to try a solution suggested by someone else; don't simply push the other person to follow your proposed course of action.

You will not manage to follow these guidelines all the time, but if you bear these ideas in mind you may get nearer to a solution than you have in the past. Lastly, don't be afraid to suggest that you jointly seek help. This is particularly true if you are both struggling to overcome negative or distressing feelings, or if it is not possible to reach a shared view of the problem or the solution. A third party can often help keep a situation calm and help you focus on expressing your views in a constructive way, rather than falling into the trap of attacking the views expressed by someone else.

Assertion

Assertion is one aspect of clear communication. If you have ever been on the receiving end of someone's anger, you will know that anger rarely helps solve a problem. For a start, you may feel unsettled or quite frightened, and second, it's usually difficult to focus on or understand what the person is trying to say. So, expressing yourself through anger is unlikely to help you get your need met. At the other end of the spectrum, it is equally true that you can end up feeling very frustrated or unhappy if you find yourself doing things you did not wish to because you failed to speak up and state what your needs were.

Basically, expressing your views either too forcefully or too meekly leads to problems. To strike the right balance, you have to learn to express your preferences clearly and calmly, and to negotiate with others effectively. The basic rules of assertion are:

- Have respect for yourself and recognise your own needs.
- Be prepared to ask for what you want.
- When expressing your opinions or feelings, always use 'I' statements.
- If you are unsure about a proposal, ask for time to

think it through; avoid being pressured into instant decisions.

- Remember that you can change your mind, but if you do, try to give people clear warning and an explanation.
- Recognise that you are responsible for your own actions, but that you cannot completely control those of other adults.
- Respect that other people have the right to apply the same rules of assertion to their own situations.

Getting this process right takes time. Practice helps, particularly if you have been prone to getting angry in the past or have lacked the confidence to express your own needs.

Sharing responsibility for problems and solutions

We noted earlier that at some point you may wish to repair any damage done to relationships as a consequence of behaviour that occurred during your mood swings. This conversation often begins with you accepting a lot of the responsibility, or for not acting sooner to avert problems. However, this dialogue also allows you to hear other people's opinions on what they may be able to do to help. Rather than instantly rejecting the opportunity to have others involved, take time to think about the advantages and disadvantages. Are there any benefits in their playing a role in helping you overcome your mood swings? Can they help you with any of your other problems? Will it actually improve your relationship if a particular person has a greater understanding of your problems and a clear role in supporting you? No one can make you accept any of these offers, but it is worthwhile considering the pros and cons. There is no rule that says you should always cope on your own.

Working on your problems with professionals

A special case in sharing responsibility relates to how you work with health care professionals. Many individuals with mood disorders report enabling and collaborative relationships; others are disappointed. The frustrations of the latter often relate to thoughts that the doctor or professional they are in contact with does not have a clear understanding of their own situation, problems and needs. If you hit problems, try to remember that this is a clash between two experts. You are an expert on how mood disorders affect you. You have a *depth* of knowledge about your own special circumstances that it would be hard for anyone else to attain. The other person is an expert on mental health in general and will have seen many individuals with similar (but not the same) problems associated with mood disorders. They have a *breadth of* knowledge about mood disorders that you may never develop. Sharing responsibility means that you are both clear about the aims of treatment and are both working toward the same goals. In this relationship, you are entitled to respect, information and choice. In return, you must try to respect the other person's opinion and the advice they offer. Sharing the knowledge you both have and then coming to an informed decision is worthwhile but can be very hard work for both parties. Remember the guidelines for communication also apply to this situation!

Setting goals for the future

You will probably have at least a vague sense of where you would like to be in the future and some views on how you would like your life to be. If you are to turn these aspirations into tangible goals, you have to be able to describe them in more specific terms and also to determine how realistic the goals are. To help begin this process try to complete this statement:

I will know that I am well when I am [insert goal]

This approach is similar to that used to create your symptom profile, but you are now trying to develop a *well-being profile*. Some individuals prefer to divide the list into separate areas, such as: basic day-to-day functioning (e.g., 'I will be in full-time employment'); interpersonal functioning (e.g., 'I will have developed a social network'); view of self (e.g., 'I will be at ease with myself').

Having created this profile, identify which issues you are already working on and which still need to be acted upon. You may wish to list these outstanding issues in order of priority. It is helpful to start with any basic problems, particularly those relating to the aftermath of any recent mood swings. Next, check that each item on the list is written as a goal rather than a problem. For example, financial problems can be defined as a goal to 'reorganise my monthly spending and set money aside so that I can pay off my overdraft by June 2024'. This goal demonstrates two key components: first it is *specific*; and second, it sets a clear *target*. The next questions you must ask are: 'Is my goal realistic; is it achievable?' The final question is: 'How will I measure my progress?' In the example given, you might set sub-goals for how much of your overdraft you will pay off per month, or how much will be paid off during each six-month period.

Once you have identified a specific, realistic and achievable goal and know how you will measure your progress, you next need to establish the steps required to achieve this goal and then to set an appropriate time-frame. To generate the steps, try to use the problem-solving techniques described earlier. If the goal is likely to take some time to achieve, for example returning to full-time employment, you may also wish to set some sub-goals. These sub-goals represent important steps along the way to your target. They also allow you to further divide the task into more manageable units and to detail the steps required between each sub-goal. You can then assess how far you expect to get in the short, medium or long term.

As well as working out a detailed action plan, you will also need to identify any obvious hurdles or barriers to achieving your goal and brainstorm a list of the potential ways to overcome those problems. Finally, set a specific time to start working on the first step toward your goal, and note the cues that will keep you on track and focused.

An example of goal-setting

To help you gauge whether you have understood this approach, you may like to work through the following example:

Joe has recently recovered from a depressive episode. He has been able to use a number of self-management strategies to cope with his problems and is feeling more optimistic about the future. He currently attends a day centre two days a week, but has difficulty filling the rest of his time. He wants to return to full-time employment as a salesman. He realises this will take some time, so he identifies his future goal as: 'To return to full-time employment as a salesman or in a related job, within nine months.'

Can you describe the course of action Joe might take? After you have tried to do this, you may like to compare your approach with the plan I have described in Box 12. Obviously, there is no absolute right or wrong way to tackle the problem, and your version may differ from mine. Whatever your chosen route, try to remember to describe every step you think is required in detail. A good test is whether someone who read your plan could follow it and reach the desired endpoint. If not, which parts have you identified in your mind but not written down?

If you feel comfortable with this approach, you may like to work through your own list of future goals and begin to describe the action plan for each of them. A template for pursuing this idea is provided in the Appendix (see p.390).

BOX 12 JOE'S PLAN FOR RETURNING TO WORK

My goal is: To return to work as a salesman (or similar)
The date I aim to achieve this goal is: Oct. 2022 (9 months from now)

Sub-goal 1: Be able to cope with a full daily routine by the end of February • Start by increasing activities on days when I'm not at the centre • Increase activity scheduling • Work on self-regulation	*Sub-goal 4:* Start reviewing job adverts from May onwards • Order newspapers for Tues and Thurs when travelling salesman jobs are advertised • Send for a few of the application packs to see what they're asking for
Sub-goal 2: Write my CV or resumé, so that I can apply for jobs when they're advertised, by end of March • Get my old CV out and update it	*Sub-goal 5:* Start applying for jobs in June • Make sure I've got an interview suit • Keep working through the things I did with Bob

- Ask Gerald to show me how to use his computer to make CV look professional
- Ask Bob to check it over to see if it reads well
- Get copies made

N.B. Also start to work on my self-esteem a bit more; I need to come across as a bit more confident at interview

Sub-goal 3: Rehearse interviews with Bob during April so that I feel OK about the questions and can start to work on my answers

Also keep working on self-regulation and self-esteem

- Keep working on self-esteem

Have fallback plan – even if I get lots of interviews I can't guarantee I'll get appointed – I need a plan of how to spend my time in a meaningful way; also, I may need to meet with a career adviser or join a job club to start to think of any other options for after September

Sub-goal 6: June–September – apply for posts and attend interviews with view to starting in October

Also – work out who to get personal support from during this time, particularly as I'll probably have to have a few interviews before I get the chance of a job

Being your own cognitive therapist

One of the issues raised in the discussion of future goals above was the need for cues that will help you keep on track. It is only human to show some variability in your commitment to working on a personal target. Like many other people, you may find you are more interested in applying self-help strategies when you have symptoms or problems. Your enthusiasm to write notes, tackle automatic thoughts or work on other issues may recede if you are feeling a bit better and do not see any immediate difficulties on the horizon. However, it is worth thinking about how you can tackle this natural tendency and gain the maximum benefit from the approaches we have discussed. If there were a therapist present, they would probably alert you to three issues:

- doing the basic minimum to maintain your current state;
- dealing with setbacks;
- scheduling therapy sessions regularly.

Minimum maintenance

If your mood is stable and you have no immediate goals you wish to work on, should you give up using self-help? The obvious answer any cognitive therapist would give is no. However, you may be able to tailor the use of the techniques to fit in with your preferences. There are two elements to this strategy.

First, don't stop using all of the techniques. The interventions that got you well will help keep you well. Hence it would be foolish to stop self-regulation or any key approach that has really been of benefit. Try to identify the minimum number of techniques you are prepared to continue using, and then push yourself to keep them going. This is important as you need to feel able to increase the use of these or similar techniques in response to change. Lack of practice may reduce your confidence in using the technique when under stress.

Second, there is a minimum set of commitments that you should try to make in order to maintain your well-being:

A: Awareness of the key features of your mood swings and the associated symptoms and problems.

R: Recognising your relapse signature or when your problems are escalating.

T: Taking *early* action to deal with problems or potential relapses, including seeking help from others.

This approach is described as the ART of well-being.

Dealing with setbacks

It is unlikely that you will go through all the approaches in this book and never hit a problem or setback. Try not to panic or catastrophise; stay as calm as you can and reflect on what has happened. Next try to work through the following steps:

- Using notes you have made or information in this book, try to determine how this setback has arisen and how you might cope with it.
- Write down any techniques that you might use at this moment, e.g., activity scheduling, calming activities, problem-solving.
- What negative automatic thoughts may be contributing to how you are feeling?
- Can you write down any automatic thoughts, and can you challenge the most powerful thoughts?
- What underlying beliefs may have been activated?
- Are there any behavioural or cognitive strategies that you could use to help you cope with this situation?
- Can you list the range of interventions that you could try?
- Can you put these in order of priority and begin with the first approach on the list?
- If none of the above approaches seem to help, who can you talk with to help you deal with this problem and how it has made you feel?

Try to take a problem-solving stance to a setback; giving up is not a helpful approach, no matter how strong your wish to stop trying. Dealing with any negative thoughts and feelings is particularly important, as this may clarify what the real issues are and allow you to work out what steps you need to take next.

Scheduling sessions with yourself

If you were engaged in a course of cognitive therapy you would probably have a regular appointment to see your therapist that you had both agreed in advance. One way to keep focused when working on your own is to schedule appointments with yourself! For example, rather than reviewing progress on self-regulation in an *ad hoc* way, you set time aside every week to monitor your progress and review what to do next. Fixing a time each week is also a way of valuing yourself and looking at your own needs. If self-help approaches are important to you, you owe it to yourself to find a reasonable amount of time to devote to them to increase the likelihood of making them work for you. Merely fitting any review into a spare ten minutes at the end of a tiring day is not giving yourself the best chance of benefiting from the approaches.

If you decide to plan some appointments with yourself, try setting aside about 45 minutes on a regular day each week. Next, try to set an agenda for the session, so that you are clear what aspect of your self-help programme you want to review. A typical schedule is described in Box 13. Obviously, you may not wish to address all the questions listed here; this template can be adapted to your own needs and preferences. It is worth retaining the same items at the beginning and end of the session: that is, start each week with a review of progress since the previous week and end with a clear set of tasks for the next week.

As with any therapy, you may be able to spread out your sessions as you feel that the cognitive and behavioural strategies become second nature. However, if you always find an excuse for not doing your sessions you may also like to explore the thoughts that are linked to your reluctance.

Taking control

I hope that this final chapter has given you some ideas about how to move forward in the future. The cognitive and behavioural strategies that may reduce the risk of further mood swings can also be applied to other aspects of your life. Remember, it is more constructive to regard each attempt to use these techniques as an experiment rather than as a test to be passed or failed. Be kind to yourself if you can't always follow the plan you have set at first. Getting rid of the internal critic and setting the other conditions for improving your self-esteem are important initial steps. This will allow you to address your future goals in a more positive and realistic frame of mind. Finally, remember that the key to overcoming mood swings is being clear what your own responsibilities are in dealing with these problems and then learning to control what you can control.

BOX 13 POSSIBLE AGENDA FOR SESSIONS WITH YOURSELF

Date:

Current mood ratings:

Possible agenda items

1. Review tasks set last week and write a few sentences on what I have learned
2. What symptoms or problems do I have currently?
3. What techniques can I use to deal with them?
4. What goals do I have?
5. Am I making progress?
6. What barriers have I encountered or do I need to be aware of in the coming weeks?
7. What skills do I have to overcome these problems?
8. What areas still keep me vulnerable?
9. What areas do I still need to work on and how am I going to do this?
10. What tasks do I need to address in the coming week?
11. What can I do if I encounter any setbacks?

Write brief notes on the session and ensure time is set aside in diary for next session.

CHAPTER SUMMARY

Looking to the future with confidence requires the following:

- Overcoming low *self-esteem* through:
  - developing a realistic appraisal of your strengths and weaknesses;
  - reducing self-criticism;
  - reducing reliance on the views of others;
  - testing out alternative views of yourself.

- Overcoming poor *self-image* that arises as a consequence of mood swings by trauma minimisation – applying personal first aid to deal with:
  - grief and loss;
  - guilt and shame;
  - stigma.

- Developing *strong relationships* through:
  - clear communication;
  - asserting *yourself*;
  - sharing responsibility if you choose.

- Developing *life goals* that are;
  - specific and realistic;
  - clearly defined in terms of steps or sub-goals;
  - recorded on a time schedule.

- Being your own CBT therapist, which may include the following:
  - ° subscribing to the ART of well-being approach;
  - ° A: awareness of mood swings;
  - ° R: recognising symptoms and problems;
  - ° T: taking early action;
  - ° dealing effectively with setbacks;
  - ° scheduling therapy sessions with yourself.

Useful references

I have tried to restrain myself from offering too many references. I have decided to focus mainly on user guides or self-help manuals that either address CBT, bipolar disorders, or some of the symptoms that are difficult to manage. I have chosen books I have knowledge of personally, so I feel reasonably confident that one or more of these books may be helpful in further developing your understanding of mood disorders and help your CBT skills. Also, I realise that some of these texts have been around for a while (like Aaron T. Beck's book), but I still recommend them to people because they have stood the test of time!

For those who are interested, I have identified clinical books that you may like to browse. Academic textbooks are often written with specific, expert scientific groups in mind, so many of you will not find these books either very exciting or very enlightening. However, I know from talking with individuals with bipolar disorders and with advocacy group members that sometimes people value these. For completeness, I have noted a few standard textbooks that you may like to dip into from time to time.

Self-help books

Aaron T. Beck, *Cognitive Therapy and the Emotional Disorders*, London: Penguin Books, 1991 (first pub. International Universities Press, 1976)

Mary Ellen Copeland, *Living Without Depression and Manic Depression: A Workbook for Maintaining Mood Stability*, California: New Harbinger, 1994

Colin Espie, *Overcoming Insomnia: A Self-help Guide Using Cognitive Behavioural Therapy*, London: Robinson, 2021

Melanie Fennell, *Overcoming Low Self-Esteem: A Self-Help Guide Using Cognitive Behavioural Techniques*, London: Robinson, 2016

Paul Gilbert, *Overcoming Depression: A Self-Help Guide Using Cognitive Behavioural Techniques*, London: Robinson, 2009

Dennis Greenberger and Christine A. Padesky, *Mind Over Mood: Change How You Feel by Changing the Way You Think*, New York: Guilford Press, 2015

Jon Kabat-Zinn, *Full Catastrophe Living: How to Cope with Stress, Pain and Illness Using Mindfulness Meditation*, London: Piatkus, 2013

David Miklowitz, *The Bipolar Disorder Survival Guide: What You and Your Family Need to Know*, New York: Guilford Press, 2019

Stephanie McMurrich Roberts, Louisa Grandin Sylvia and Noreen A. Reilly-Harrington, *The Bipolar II Disorder Workbook: Managing Recurring Depression, Hypomania, and Anxiety*, California: New Harbinger, 2014

Monica Ramirez Basco, *The Bipolar Workbook: Tools for*

Controlling Your Mood Swings, New York: Guilford Press, 2015

Mark Williams and Danny Penman, *Mindfulness: A Practical Guide to Finding Peace in a Frantic World,* London: Piatkus, 2011

Examples of textbooks:

About bipolar disorders

Frederick Goodwin and Kay R. Jamison, *Manic Depressive Illness and Recurrent Depressions*, Oxford: Oxford University Press, 2007

About medications for bipolar disorder

Stephen Stahl, *Essential Psychopharmacology of Depression and Bipolar Disorder, Third edition,* Cambridge: Cambridge University Press, 2008

About cognitive therapy

Aaron T. Beck, A. John Rush, Brian F. Shaw and Gary Emery, *Cognitive Therapy for Depression*, New York: Guilford Press, 1979

Thilo Deckersbach, Britta Hölzel, Lori Eisner, Sarah W. Lazar and Andrew A. Nierenberg, *Mindfulness-Based Cognitive Therapy for Bipolar Disorder*, London: Guilford Press, 2014

Dominic Lam, Steven H. Jones and Peter Hayward, *Cognitive Therapy for Bipolar Disorder: A Therapist's Guide to Concept, Methods and Practice,* Chichester: Wiley-Blackwell, 2010

Monica Ramirez Basco and A. John Rush, *Cognitive Behavior Therapy for Bipolar Disorder,* New York: Guilford Press, 2007

Edward Watkins, *Rumination-Focused Cognitive-Behavioral Therapy for Depression,* London: Guildford, 2016

Useful addresses, websites and apps

There are many organisations that produce written materials, such as leaflets and booklets, or offer conferences or local self-help and support group meetings. In Britain, Bipolar UK has produced some excellent booklets, as has the National Depressive and Manic Depressive Association in the USA. Both organisations are well worth contacting.

Rather than produce an unending list, I have selected organisations on the basis of my own knowledge of their publications, their ability to point people in the right direction with regard to treatment or self-help and my own experiences of working with them. You may wish to contact them to get additional information or to learn about activities they are engaged in, such as face-to-face or online support groups. Finally, I list a couple of websites that display up-to-date health information and I have also selected a few smartphone and digital apps for mood monitoring that I know about. Please note, new apps are being developed all the time and there are many others available. So, I have decided only to mention those that I have observed in use or that I know about in more detail because they have been used by some individuals I have worked with clinically.

UK Organisations

British Association for Behavioural and Cognitive
Psychotherapies (BABCP)
Imperial House
Hornby Street
Bury
Lancashire
BL9 5BN
Email: babcp@babcp.com
Website: www.babcp.com

British Psychological Society
Head Office:
St Andrew's House
48 Princess Road East
Leicester
LE1 7DR
Email: enquiries@bps.org.uk
Website: www.bps.org.uk

Depression Alliance
Depression Alliance merged with Mind in 2016. However, you can access many of their online articles (often dealing with new treatments, etc.) via the website.
Website: www.depressionalliance.org

Bipolar UK
National Office:
11 Belgrave Road
London
SW1V 1RB
Email: info@bipolaruk.org
Website: www.bipolaruk.org

MIND for better Mental Health
Granta House
15–19 Broadway
Stratford
London
E15 4BQ
Email: info@mind.org.uk
Website www.mind.org.uk

Royal College of Psychiatrists
London Office
21 Prescot Street
London
E1 8BB
Email: can be sent via the 'Contact Us' link on the website
Website: www.rcpsych.ac.uk

US Organisations

Beck Institute of Cognitive Therapy
1 Belmont Ave, Suite 700
Bala Cynwyd
PA 19004–1610
Email: info@beckinstitute.org
Website: www.beckinstitute.org

International Society for Bipolar Disorders (ISBD)
PO Box 396
Monroeville
PA 15146
Email: can be sent via the 'Contact Us' link on the website
Website: www.isbd.org

National Alliance on Mental Illness
4301 Wilson Blvd, Suite 300
Arlington
VA 22203
Website: www.nami.org

Depression and Bipolar Support Alliance (DBSA)
55 East Jackson Boulevard
Suite 490
Chicago
IL 60604
Website: www.dbsalliance.org
Email: info@dbsalliance.org

National Institute of Mental Health (NIMH)
6001 Executive Boulevard, Rm 8184
MSC 9663
Bethesda
MD 20892-9663
Email: nimhinfo@nih.org
Website: www.nimh.nih.gov

Websites

National Institute of Clinical Excellence (NICE)
www.nice.org.uk

The Cochrane Collaboration
www.cochrane.org/reviews

Expert Consensus Guidelines
www.psychguides.com

Also: if you type 'Bipolar Disorders Frequently Asked Questions' as free text into a search engine, you will find several useful fact sheets and websites.

Smartphone and online mood apps

Several centres that undertake research in bipolar disorders provide clients and patients with access to apps. However, most of these are only available via the research team.

There are a growing number of apps available for Android and iOS smartphones (or laptops). Here, I have listed a selection of free apps (or apps that include free as well as paid for content) that can be used on android phones or iPhones, or on both. In alphabetical order:

Daylio (Android)
eMoods (iOS)
Mood Log (Android)
Moodnotes (iOS)
T2 Mood Tracker (Android and iOS)

Appendix:
Blank worksheets

My cognitive behavioural cycle (see Figure 4, p.89)

Complete your own cycle, using Figure 4, (p.89) for guidance, as it occurs during depressions and highs using the blank versions that follow. Try to start at the box that represents the first change that you notice, e.g., changes in mood or stress and distress, etc. Then see if you can work your way round the diagrams filling in the blank boxes.

My Cognitive Behavioural Cycle: HIGHS

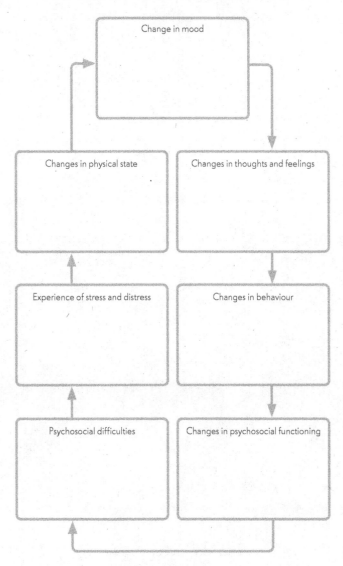

My Cognitive Behavioural Cycle: DEPRESSION

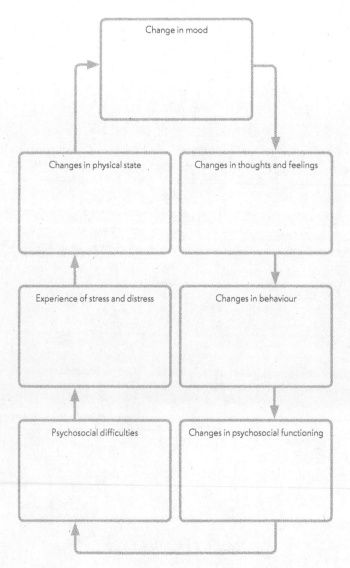

Change in mood

Changes in physical state

Changes in thoughts and feelings

Experience of stress and distress

Changes in behaviour

Psychosocial difficulties

Changes in psychosocial functioning

My life chart (see Figure 5a–c, pp.103–5)

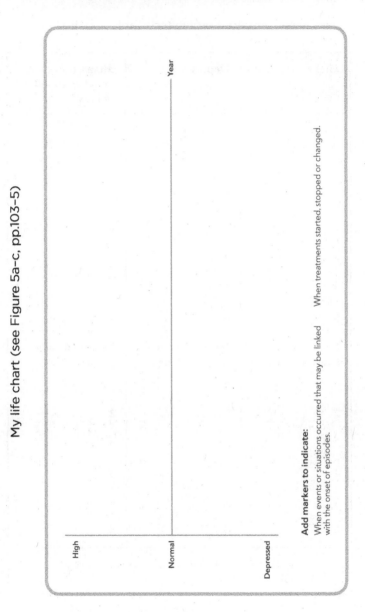

High

Normal

Depressed

Year

Add markers to indicate:

When events or situations occurred that may be linked with the onset of episodes.

When treatments started, stopped or changed.

My symptom profile (see Table 2, p.115)

Highs	Depression	Mixed states or other mood swings
My common symptoms* are: 1 2 3 4 5 6	My common symptoms* are: 1 2 3 4 5 6	My common symptoms* are: 1 2 3 4 5 6
My less common symptoms* are: 1 2 3 4 5 6	My less common symptoms* are: 1 2 3 4 5 6	My less common symptoms* are: 1 2 3 4 5 6

*Put a star next to the symptoms or changes you notice *first*: these are your early warning symptoms

My risk list (as Box 1, p.119)

Risk factors

1   High-risk activities

2   High-risk situations

3   High-risk events

Other important information

e.g. High-risk combinations

e.g. Protective factors

Alternative version of a risk list

	Highs	Depression	Mixed or other states
Risk factors 1 High-risk activities			
2 High-risk situations			
3 High-risk events			
Other important information e.g. High-risk combinations			
e.g. Protective factors			

Outline of a mood chart (see pp.144–53)

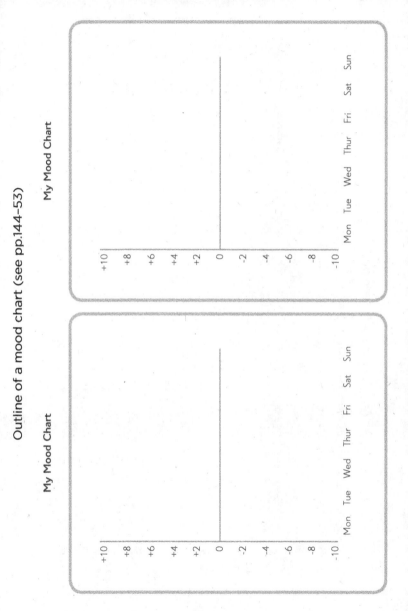

My Mood Chart

My Mood Chart

Activity schedule (see pp.230–42)

Use P ratings to represent *pleasure* (0–10 or 0–100)

Use A ratings to represent a sense of *achievement* (0–10 or 0–100)

TIME	Monday	Tuesday	Wednesday	Thursday	Friday	Saturday	Sunday
12 midnight to 6 a.m.							
6–8 a.m.							
8–10 a.m.							
10 a.m.–midday							
midday–2 p.m.							

						2 –4 p.m.
						4–6 p.m.
						6–8 p.m.
						8–10 p.m.
						10–midnight
						midnight –4 a.m.

You may prefer to redraw your schedule with each box representing one hour of activity during the day and have a single box representing 12 midnight to 7 or 9 a.m. Some individuals find this more useful as it gives them more space to record what they do during daylight hours

Self-regulation chart (see Figure 9, p.165)

Activity*	Time**	Actual time did the activity Mon Tues Wed Thur Fri Sat Sun
Getting up	Preferred	
Going to bed		

*Use the blank boxes to identify your chosen activities

**Put preferred time for undertaking activity opposite the horizontal line in column 2, then choose times about two hours either side of preferred time and record as a graph in column 3 the actual time the activity was undertaken each day

Side-effects of mood stabilisers (see pp.45–8)

Mood stabiliser	Common side effects, particularly early in treatment	Long-term side-effects	Rare, but potentially harmful side-effects
Lithium	Tremor Muscle weakness Thirst Diarrhoea Stomach upset	Weight gain Thyroid problems Kidney problems	Lithium toxicity: vomiting, confusion, unsteadiness, difficulty speaking clearly
Carbamaze-pine	Headaches Dizziness Drowsiness Blurred vision Upset stomach	Reduced white blood cell count Changes in test of liver functioning	Skin rashes Severe drop in white cell count
Sodium valproate	Upset stomach Diarrhoea Drowsiness Tremor	Hair thinning Weight gain Changes in tests of liver functioning	Liver damage

My treatment plan (pp.209–11)

My treatment plan is to:

- Take the following prescribed medication:

  Name of medication   Dose   Frequency

- Have contact with the following professionals

  Name of person   Frequency of contact

The benefits to me of this approach are:

-
-
-
-

The barriers to my sticking to this approach are:

-
-
-
-

The ways I might overcome these barriers are:

-
-
-
-

Template for a cost-benefit analysis (see pp.216–18)

Advantages of taking	Disadvantages of taking
•	•
•	•
•	•
•	•
•	•
•	•
•	•
Advantages of NOT taking	**Disadvantages of NOT taking**
•	•
•	•
•	•
•	•
•	•
•	•
•	•

Activity matrix (see p.233)

Fill the empty boxes along the top of the columns with activities you might try to do, then tick which characteristics (e.g. free to do, can be done alone, helps me relax) apply to the activity.							
Activity							
Do alone							
Do with others							
Early in the day							
Evening							
Night-time							
Free activity							
Costs money							
Uses my mind							
Helps me relax							

Thought record (see pp.249–50)

It is helpful to refer to the questions listed in the text when trying to complete the different columns of the thought record

Situation or event	Emotion (rated 1–100)	Automatic thoughts (belief rated 1–100)	Evidence for and against the thought	Alternative view	Rerate emotion and belief in original automatic thought	Action or outcome

Two-column technique for use when *high*: self versus others (see pp.290–91)

Benefits to me	Risk of harm to others*

*Your goal when high is to concentrate on this column as these thoughts are less accessible to you unless you work hard to think of them

Two-column technique for use when *high*: constructive
and destructive potential (see pp.290–91)

Constructive potential	Destructive (damaging) potential★

★Your goal when high is to concentrate on this column as these
thoughts are less accessible to you unless you work hard to think
of them

Two-column technique for use when *high*: gains and losses (see pp.290–91)

Potential gains	Potential losses★

★Your goal when high is to concentrate on this column as these thoughts are less accessible to you unless you work hard to think of them

Relapse prevention plan (see pp.309–14): Depression

Triggers:

1

2

3

Early warning symptoms:

1

2

3

Frequency of monitoring:

Action plan:

1

2

3

Copies given to:

1

2

3

Relapse prevention plan (see pp.309–14): Highs

Triggers:

1

2

3

Early warning symptoms:

1

2

3

Frequency of monitoring:

Action plan:

1

2

3

Copies given to:

1

2

3

Summary of my strengths and weaknesses
(see pp.323–5)

My strengths	My weaknesses★

Summary statement★

★Write two or three lines that summarise your view of yourself, beginning with comments on your *strengths*.

Planning my future goals (see pp.341–5)

My goal is: The date I aim to achieve this goal is:	
Sub-goal 1:	*Sub-goal 5:*
Sub-goal 2:	*Sub-goal 6:*
Sub-goal 3:	*Sub-goal 7:*
Sub-goal 4:	*Sub-goal 8:*

To use this template, write your goal in the top box, then record each major step as a sub-goal. Use the sub-goal boxes to write notes on what steps you need to complete before moving on to the next sub-goal.

Index

OVERCOMING
Depression
3rd Edition

A self-help guide
using cognitive
behavioural techniques

PAUL GILBERT

OVERCOMING

READING
WELL

Overcoming Depression, 3rd Edition

Break free from the hell of depression

If you suffer from depression you are far from alone. Depression is very common, affecting over 300 million people around the world.

Written by Professor Paul Gilbert, internationally recognised for his work on depression, this highly acclaimed self-help book has been of benefit to thousands of people including sufferers, their friends and families, and those working in the medical profession.

This fully revised third edition has been extensively updated and rewritten to reflect over ten years of new research on understanding and treating depression, particularly the importance of developing compassionate ways of thinking, behaving and feeling. It includes:

- Helpful case studies
- Easy-to-follow, step-by-step suggestions and exercises to help you understand your depression and lift your mood

THE
IMPR⟳VEMENT
ZONE

Looking for life inspiration?

The Improvement Zone has it all, from **expert advice** on how to advance your **career** and boost your **business**, to improving your **relationships**, revitalising your **health** and developing your **mind**.

Whatever your goals, head to our website now.

www.improvementzone.co.uk

INSPIRATION ON THE MOVE

INSPIRATION DIRECT TO YOUR INBOX